A TREASURY OF AMERICAN ANECDOTES

EDITED,
WITH INTRODUCTION AND
COMMENTARY, BY
B. A. Botkin

Galahad Books • New York

A TREASURY OF
AMERICAN
ANECDOTES

Sly, Salty, Shaggy Stories
of Heroes and Hellions, Beguilers
and Buffoons, Spellbinders
and Scapegoats, Gagsters and Gossips,
from the Grassroots and Sidewalks
of America

Published in 1982 by
Galahad Books
95 Madison Avenue
New York, NY 10016

DESIGN: by Betty Crumley

Published by arrangement with Mrs. Gertrude Botkin
Manufactured in the United States of America
10   9   8   7   6   5   4   3   2   1
Library of Congress Catalog Card Number 82–80322
ISBN 0-88365-616-7

*The editor and publisher wish to thank all authors or their respresenta-
tives, publishers and publications for special permission to reprint the
material credited to them, with bibliographical and copyright data, in
Notes. An exhaustive effort has been made to locate all persons having
any rights or interests in material and to clear reprint permissions. If any
required acknowledgments have been omitted or any rights overlooked, it
is by accident and forgiveness is requested.*

Acknowledgments

My thanks are due to the following libraries, among others, which were especially useful and helpful to me in the preparation of this book: The American Antiquarian Society, the Columbia University Library, the Library of the General Society of Mechanics and Tradesmen of the City of New York, the Harvard University Library, the Library of Congress, the New York Public Library, and the University of Illinois Library (Franklin J. Meine American Humor and Folklore Collection).

Among the many friends who have helped me clarify my thinking through discussion and have contributed stories in writing or told me stories to be taken down by dictation or on tape, I should like to thank the following in particular: Cleveland Amory, Josiah H. Combs, Evan Esar, Paul Flowers, Nathan Frankel, Moritz Jagendorf, Oscar and Leah Leonard, Mamie Meredith, George Milburn, Ruth Rubin, and Carl Withers.

In addition, the following have graciously allowed me to use unpublished material: Charles Aguado, Henry Berg, Arthur Boose, Oscar Brand, Verne Bright, Sterling A. Brown, Arthur L. Campa, Richard Del Bourgo, Ryerson Johnson, Lawrence Kalik, Eli Krotman, Raven I. McDavid, Samuel J. Sackett, Tony Schwartz, Fant Thornley, Lawrence Treat, and Frank H. Wardlaw.

For invaluable assistance, I want to thank, once more, my editors, Hiram Haydn and Bertha Krantz, and my wife, Gertrude Botkin.

B. A. B.

Croton-on-Hudson, N. Y.
September 6, 1957

Contents

3 : NEWCOMERS AND DAMN FOOLS

4 : MELTING POT AND PRESSURE COOKER

5 : COOL CUSTOMERS

6 : A PASSEL OF FOOLS

 ## 7 : WHOPPER WIT

8 : "THE GOSPEL ACCORDING TO JOE MILLER"

9 : HEROES WITHOUT HALOES

10 : SPELLBINDERS AND BUREAUCRATS

11 : FABLE AND FOIBLE

14 : WIT'S END

Introduction

Nicholas Murray Butler and Professor Brander
Matthews of Columbia University were having a
conversation and Professor Matthews was giving
his ideas as to plagiarism, from an article of his
own on that subject. "In the case of the first man
to use an anecdote," he said, "there is originality;
in the case of the second, there is plagiarism;
with the third, it is lack of originality; and with
the fourth it is drawing from a common stock."
"Yes," broke in President Butler, "and in the case
of the fifth, it is research."

"MAN IN THE STREET"

There are just three essentials to a good story: humanity, a point, and the storyteller.—J. FRANK DOBIE

This is a book of American storytelling—wise, witty, humorous, fantastic—in anecdote form. The anecdotes (short, pointed, pithy, pungent illustrative or attributed stories) are traveling anecdotes. They travel (and change and are handed down as they travel) by word of mouth and in print. They are swapped or passed along from person to person. They are transmitted through the medium of pulpit, political and lecture platform, stage, screen, radio, and television. They circulate in newspapers, periodicals, joke books, almanacs, books of ana, and almanac collections.

Traveling anecdotes belong to floating literature—literature without known authorship or fixed form. As an illustrative story with a point, easily switched and altered to fit the occasion, the anecdote is folklore in decay or in the making, and may be based on or serve as the basis of a folk tale or proverb. As an attributed ("name" or celebrity) story, referring to a famous person and switched (by change of name) from one person to another, the anecdote is unhistorical history or apocryphal biography.

The humorous anecdote ("funny story") is related to the jest and may be an expanded joke or may be converted into a joke. The anecdote differs from the joke, however, in that it is generally reported as true (whether based on an actual occurrence or not), contains all the elements of narrative—plot, character, setting, and dialogue—and illustrates a trait of an individual or community, or a moral truth. From the point of view of raconteur-collector, Bennett Cerf (an old hand at making anecdotes out of jokes and jokes out of anecdotes), "A joke . . . is a short pointed collection of sentences, usually prefaced by the words, 'Say, have you heard this one?' . . . An anecdote is an overlong story usually told by a portly person who begins by clearing his throat and saying, 'You know, a remarkable thing happened to me the other night.' " In the order of increasing length, complication, and detail, the progression is from wisecrack to gag, gag to joke, joke to anecdote, and anecdote to yarn.

The chief purveyors of anecdotes and jests—the jest book, the almanac, the newspaper and magazine joke column, "exchange," and filler—are forms of subliterature on the printed level. Also entering into the two-way flow between oral and printed humor is the floating material of comparisons, sayings, wisecracks, and jests. While print tends to freeze or fix subliterature, the jest undergoes constant transformation in the prolific, multifarious "Joe Miller" subliterature, beginning with John Mottley's *Joe Miller's Jests* (1739). "Even to this day," writes Evan Esar, in *The Legend of Joe Miller* "joemiller stories may be culled from our best jest books. . . . The more they change, the more they remain the same."

To illustrate the joemiller refurbishing process, Esar cites, first, No. 118 of *Joe Miller's Jests*, which appeared unaltered in *Funny Stories, or The American Jester* (1795).

A melting sermon being preached in a country churchyard, all fell a-weeping but one man who, being asked why he did not weep with the rest, "O," said he, "I belong to another parish."

Then, from Bennett Cerf's *Try and Stop Me* (1944) Esar cites the following modern version:

A ladies' club in New Jersey invited a femme book reviewer to speak at its May meeting. She told the plot of a triple-A tear jerker, and the entire assemblage broke into tears. All but one, that is—a lady who sat dry-eyed and unmoved through the entire recital. After the lecture, the reviewer asked her why she hadn't cried. The lady's answer stopped her cold. "Oh, I'm not a member," she explained.

"The Jest," writes W. Carew Hazlitt, in *Studies in Jocular Literature*, "resembles a tree of many branches" (the apologue, the pun, the quibble, the epigram, the repartee). *Facetiae, Schwänke,* or merry tales, along with the related types of *exemplum* and fable, are themselves branches of folk literature. While these various trees and branches have been studied chiefly for their types, motifs, and parallels (with the result that one often cannot see the woods for the trees), they still remain to be studied, especially in the United States, as social and local history, in relation not only to storytelling situations, functions, motives, and attitudes, but also to settlement history, and regional, ethnic, and occupational groups. As Herbert Halpert, one of the ablest students of the American-English folk tale, points out in an article in the *Journal of American Folklore* for January-March, 1957, the "field needs plowing, or reaping; I am not sure which. . . ."

In America the most popular form of the practical as well as the social anecdote is the funny story. Practically, it packs a maximum of allusiveness, persuasiveness, and applicability into a minimum of space. It is flexible and versatile enough to fit any occasion or storytelling situation, as long as the speaker can find a peg to hang it on. The selfsame story, in fact, may be used to win votes or save souls. And the funny story has a way of suggesting itself when you need it. In the words of Arthur Boose, the street-corner speaker of our final story, "In the Book," when I asked him for examples, "These stories come best to you when you are speaking. You can't always recall them when you're asked to."

Humor has always been the public speaker's ice-breaker and his most effective device for holding an audience without a rope. But anecdotal humor is not merely the sugar coating on the pill; it is also the lemon that one sucks along with the sweet. If "preacher tales" mingle the sacred and the secular, the grave and the ludicrous, without fear of irreverence, they are in good company. John Camden Hotten traces the quaintness of American humor to the Puritans' "sober treatment of comic things and comic treatment of sober matters." But most striking of all is Lincoln's use of jokes to ease a heavy heart as well as to get himself out of a tight spot. "He liked the short farce better than the five-act tragedy," writes John W. Forney.

Lincoln stories afford perhaps the best examples of the varied uses of the funny story for serious purposes. They also exemplify the allusive power of the fable at its best. "There was, perhaps, an outside for each thing as it stood alone," writes Carl Sandburg of the Illinois Aesop, "while inside of it was a fable." Lincoln stripped off the husks and laid bare the association of ideas that lies at the heart of things, so that the anecdote becomes a form of sympathetic magic, by which like attracts or produces like. By using common experience as a frame of reference, Lincoln was able to reduce a complicated situation to its lowest common denominator. And by drawing upon familiar images, symbols, allusions, and incidents, he found the shortest route between himself, his hearers, and his subject. Thus the anecdote brings people as well as things together, in a sympathetic association that binds speaker with audience and the members of the audience with one another. It is a process of collaboration, with everybody meeting everybody else halfway. Provided, of course, that the raconteur follows Lincoln's advice to lawyers: "Don't shoot too high. Aim low, and the common people will understand you."

Anecdotes may be classified by type, theme, motif, application, and motivation; but classification cannot be hard and fast, since the same story may serve more than one purpose and fit more than one situation. The pattern of this book follows roughly the functional pattern of American storytelling situations and story and character types: country store and country wit and humor (*Cracker Barrel*); boasting, boosting, and knocking (*God's Country*); hick versus city slicker (*Newcomers and Fools*); caricature versus folk expression in the humor of minority groups (*Melting Pot and Pressure Cooker*); tricksters and tricksters tricked (*Cool Customers*); wise fools and the foolish wise (*A Passel of Fools*); artistic liars (*Whopper Wit*); preachers and their flocks ("*The Gospel according to Joe Miller*"); hero worship without tears (*Heroes without Haloes*); politics and politicians (*Spellbinders and Bureaucrats*); symbolic and allegorical stories (*Fable and Foible*); bizarre stories (*Spun Yarn*); bedroom and backhouse humor (*Barnyard and Barroom*); and shaggy dog stories (*Wit's End*).

Storytelling—oral, informal, casual, sociable, practical—is one of our few living folk arts. That it is far from vanishing I trust this book will prove. Wherever men and women gather together or are thrown together in the course of daily business and sociability, the storytelling gathering, in city or country, is a genuine folk gathering. There is no sharp distinction between performer and audience: everyone can tell a story. And neither the storyteller nor the hearer is concerned with the ownership of the story. "A good story," says Frank Case, "belongs to the man who tells it last or tells it best."

Storytelling is an oral as well as a folk art. The oral raconteur has at his disposal all the devices of dramatic interpretation, including voice, gesture, facial expression, and mimicry. In print the living voice and presence are supplanted, though never quite replaced, by literary style, which tends to dress up the anecdote and give it a certain amount of polish. But the best anecdotes possess or preserve the ad lib spontaneousness, freedom, and plasticity of the spoken word.

No one can claim an American origin for all the American anecdotes in this book. Traveling anecdotes go back a long way in time and space. And what keeps them traveling is the need for a constant supply of memorable, quotable, handy illustrations, old and new, to keep pace with the constant recurrence of similar traits and situations. If an anecdote "brings out the characteristic of some individual," says J. Frank Dobie, "it will before long find itself attached to another individual, illustrating a similar characteristic in him." Being both versatile and adaptable, the traveling anecdote is never quite the same at any two times, even when told by the same person. The raconteur is under no obligation to tell a story exactly as he heard it. But he is under obligation to his audience to make the story fit the time, place, and occasion. He must also put something of himself into it, give it the stamp of his own personality. "A story you hear," says George Papashvily, "is a letter that comes to you from yesterday. It passes through many hands and each one adds his postscript, 'So it was with me, brother.' And when you tell it you send a letter to tomorrow, 'How is it there with you?'"

Nor does it matter if in the course of traveling and much handling, the "line of veracity has become somewhat undulating." The story's the thing. If it seems true, fine. If not—well, "it makes a good story." The final test of a good anecdote is not so much its truth to experience as its power to sum up and illuminate experience—a power of concentration and crystallization in which the anecdote excels, to a greater degree, perhaps, than any other genre. The anecdote illuminates not only a situation but a human attitude or relationship, including the relationship between the storyteller and his audience. It also illuminates the folkways of a people, as symbols, allusions, bywords, and other forms of popular fantasy are designed to do. Because the fantasies and the folkways constantly reinforce each other, American anecdotes unlock doors to understanding America and open windows on the American past and the American heritage.

According to Bret Harte, who knew what he was talking about, American humor, "of a quality as distinct and original as the country and civilization in which it was developed," gives the American anecdote its peculiar piquancy. Harte also saw the funny story as the "parent of the American 'short story.'" The anecdote has entered into American literature in many other ways. When we examine the sources of our native American writing we find that back of a good many of our professional storytellers and humorists lie generations of reminiscing, wisecracking, and anecdote-swapping Americans. Thomas Wolfe owed much to the "torrential recollectiveness, derived out of [his] mother's stock." Sherwood Anderson's father was a master barroom storyteller. Anderson himself learned a great deal about his art from the vernacular sources. "The best storytellers," he writes in *Hello Towns!*, "are often uneducated men. . . . What a writer has to learn, first of all, is not to have too much respect for the printed word just because it is the printed word. . . . And what stories I occasionally get from people, how beautifully told. People who lead rather isolated lives, like farmers, do it best. Perhaps they have more time to brood."

Because there is nothing sacred about the printed word, or the spoken word, for that matter, the anecdotal imagination at work on the stuff of the American experience flows restlessly back and forth between the bookish and the bookless worlds.

This is my first book of American storytelling. In it—as in my previous collections, containing songs, yarns, legends, and sketches in addition to anecdotes proper—I have tried to give a portrait of the American people through their folk expression, including folklore in the making as well as folklore in decay. In the endeavor to make the book representative of the whole range of the American raconteur's art and repertoire, I have gone to all kinds of sources, oral and printed, old and new, for examples familiar and unfamiliar. Without regard to origins or applications, I have preferred the more readable, fresh, and telling versions. "There seems to be little point," says Robert Graves, "in printing a thousand-times-told tale unless it happens to have a brand-new twist, to be particularly well phrased."

While I have often been attracted to a story for its content, as representing some important phase of American life, I have tried to subordinate my documentary to my literary interests. I have also avoided the contrived and the cute, the quaint for quaintness' sake, the mere witticism, pun, practical joke, or smart retort, and the simply local and topical.

If this book proves anything about American storytelling, it is that "Old stories never die." The reason is, of course, that there are always new storytellers to put old wine into new bottles. Moreover, through long, hard, rough usage, traveling anecdotes have acquired a briar-patch-bred toughness and resilience that enables them to endure and, in enduring, to outlast more ambitious works. They have been around for a long, long while, and are here to stay.

———

All sources, including authors, titles, and publishers, informants, contributors of unpublished material, and other bibliographical and provenience data, are listed in the *Notes*, where they may be located, first under the section title and then by story title. Since this is a book for the general reader, all scholarly notes on motifs and parallels have been omitted. The notes, however, serve not only to identify sources but also to locate the story in time, place, and medium of diffusion, and so have a historical value. Taken together, the notes also constitute a selective bibliography of American anecdote literature.

Within sections the arrangement of material is roughly geographical, from North to South and from East to West.

☞ **1** ☜

Cracker Barrel

Perhaps, Dear Reader, you would like to join the
Sit, Whittle, and Spit Club, official organization
for all adult males who know and practice these
three rules: 1. Don't sit in the sun. 2. Don't
whittle toward yourself. 3. Don't spit
against the wind.

CLYDE W. WILKINSON

Introduction

Beginning with cracker-barrel Yankeedotes and ending in the shaggy-doghouse, this book more or less follows the course of anecdotal humor from the grassroots to the sidewalks of America.

Cracker-barrel humor, naturally enough, begins in the country store with the comic contest of wits between the sharp or close merchant and his snug or cool customer. Around the cracker barrel, where talk is cheap and speech is free, everything that goes on in the store, the neighborhood, and the countryside furnishes material for the store habitués, deliberating in a kind of anecdotal court of human relations. How did the overshy swain finally pop the question to the beautiful maiden? How do you cure sore eyes or the heaves? Which will last longest—white oak or chestnut fence posts? To what does the spry nonagenarian attribute his good health and longevity?

Originally New England Yankee, "cracker barrel" is now American Yankee, with perhaps more of the hillbilly drawl than the down-East twang in its speech. With the diffusion of cracker-barrel humor via the jokelore of stage, press, radio, and television, it has become increasingly difficult to separate the home-grown from the store-bought product. Still, there was a certain authenticity even in the vaudeville rube comedy of the Weaver Brothers and Elviry and the radio country-store humor of Lum and Abner.

As part of the journalistic and literary exploitation of rural humor, the cracker-barrel comedian became the cracker-box philosopher. For a hundred years, from Seba Smith's Jack Downing to Will Rogers, the uneducated, native wit and sage has served as the mouthpiece of the social and political critic.

Cracker-barrel wit and humor, according to Walter Blair, have always been close to cracker-barrel wisdom, whimsy, and fantasy in native American humor. Just as horse sense sobers horseplay, so both are touched with "queer notions." In fact, there is a bit of the crackpot or crank in every cracker-barrel wiseacre, as in the following adaptation of Earl A. Collins' story from the Missouri Ozarks.

A salesman was making his way far back into the hills to a country store, along a road that led down the bed of a dry creek. On his way back, although there had been no sign of rain, the creek was full. "Yep," said a hillman, in response to the salesman's query, "it's the same crick. It's fed by a spring up yander that flows a half-day and then rests a half-day." "That's very peculiar. What do you suppose causes it to do that?" "Waal, yer see, they tells me the worl' turns over ever' twenty-four hours, er sech a matter. When it's right side up the water can't run out an' when it's upside down the water jest spills out."

In the Country Store

In one of the country stores, where they sell everything from a silk dress and a tub of butter to a hot drink and a cold meal, a lot of farmers were sitting around the stove one cold winter day, when in came Farmer Evans, who was greeted with, "How d' do, Ezry?"

"How d' do, boys?" After a while he continued, "Wa-al, I've killed my hog."

"That so? How much did he weigh?"

Farmer Evans stroked his chin whiskers meditatively and replied, "Wa-al, guess."

" 'Bout three hundred," said one farmer.

"No."

"Two seventy-five?" ventured another.

"No."

"I guess about three twenty-five," said a third.

"No."

Then all together demanded, "Well, how much did he weigh?"

"Dunno. Hain't weighed him yet."

Other men kept dropping in and hugging the stove, for the day was cold and snowy outside. In came Cy Hopkins, wrapped in a big overcoat, yet almost frozen to death; but there wasn't room enough around that stove to warm his little finger.

But he didn't get mad about it; he just said to Bill Stebbins, who kept the store, "Bill, got any raw oysters?"

"Yes, Cy."

"Well, just open a dozen and feed 'em to my hoss."

Well, Stebbins never was scared by an order from a man whose credit was good, as Cy's was, so he opened the oysters an' took them out, an' the whole crowd followed to see a horse eat oysters. Then Cy picked out the best seat near the stove and dropped into it as if he had come to stay, as he had.

Pretty soon the crowd came back, and the storekeeper said, "Why, Cy, your hoss won't eat them oysters."

"Won't he? Well, then, bring 'em here an' I'll eat 'em myself."

"He Don't Say"

A Vermonter seldom hurries and he never wastes a motion. Vermont humor is like that—it ambles along, takes its time, and never wastes a word.

Vermonters have little patience with even an accepted area of word wasting. Some years back a politician was addressing a small audience in a meeting house. He had been speaking for fifteen minutes when an elderly man in the front row took his cupped hand away from his ear and turned to the people behind him.

"What's he talking about?" he asked in the piercing tones of the partially deaf.

The group behind him considered the question for some time. Finally a spokesman leaned forward and said, "He don't say."

"He Ain't Home"

A theme of clannishness and rejection of the outsider runs through a lot of Vermont stories.

One couple bought an old house and started down the road to find a man named Olin Warren, who, they had been told, not only lived in the neighborhood but would be willing to make some basic repairs on the house. After walking about a half mile, they saw a man cutting the roadside brush with a scythe.

"Do you know where Olin Warren lives?" asked the wife.

Without looking up, the man said, "Yup."

They waited for information. None came.

"Will you tell us where he lives?" the husband asked.

The man put down his scythe and pointed to a small house a mile up on the mountain.

"It's quite a walk," the husband continued. "You don't happen to know if he's home or not, do you?"

"Nope," said the man. "He ain't home." Then he looked at the couple for the first time. "What did you want with him?"

"Well," said the wife, "we bought the old Gokey place down the road, and somebody told us Olin Warren might be willing to do some repairing for us."

The man rested his scythe for a moment. "I be he," he said.

A Pair of New Boots

"Makes me think [said Uncle Lisha] o' the feller 'at went tu a neighbor's a-visitin' wi' a pair o' bran'-new boots on, which for all he spread 'em aout on the stove ha'th, an' stuck 'em top o' chairs, the' wouldn't nob'dy notice 'em, an' so when he see they wan't a-goin' tu say nothin' abaout 'em, he up an' says, says he, 'Ye needn't think strange if ye smell new luther.'"

A Shovel for "Uncle Ed"

"Uncle Ed" is on relief, employed on the Middlebury highways. He is complaining to the foreman, "It ain't fair, an' you know it. I want a shovel."

"Never you mind, Uncle Ed, about a shovel; you're on the payroll all right; you'll get your pay."

"Yes, I will mind, too. It's my rights to have a shovel, and I mean to have a shovel ef I have to write t' Congress about it. Kin I have a shovel or can't I?"

"Now, Uncle Ed, go easy. You're goin' t' get y'r money all right, don't you worry."

"It ain't fair. I want a shovel. Ev'ybody but me's got sunthin' t' lean on."

Why He Talked to Himself

Back some years ago there was a storekeeper in Stoddard, New Hampshire, who had a habit of talking to himself when alone and at other times when he thought he was alone. He was asked one day what motive he could have in talking to himself. Jacob replied that he had two very good and very substantial reasons: in the first place, he liked to talk to a sensible man; and in the second place, he liked to hear a sensible man talk.

Rock Farm

[A] Maine farmer . . . was asked by a summer visitor how there happened to be so many rocks on his farm. "Glacier brought 'em," he said. What was he going to do about it? the summer visitor asked. "Wait for another glacier to take 'em away again," he said.

Building Wall

One of our [Maine] country men was building a stone wall, as everybody did when I was a boy. This particular wall was four feet wide and three feet high. A neighbor came by and asked the old farmer why he was building such an odd-shaped wall—wider than it was high. Without looking up from his work, the farmer said, "So 'f it ever blows over it'll be higher than it was before."

The Proposal

The [Maine] man was overshy; the maiden was beautiful and seemed to him too wonderful to be asked for. He went on loving her in silence for ten years. He built a fine house, with garden and rockery, barn and outbuildings, though he hadn't yet dared to propose.

When everything was finished he invited the maiden and her family to come over and see his estate. They all went through the house together and visited the garden and rockery. Finally he jockeyed so as to get Anna separated from the family, and they went together to see the outbuildings. They stood silently looking into the pigpen. He looked up sweetly and said, "Anna, shall *we* keep a pig?" And Anna said, "Yes."

Grandma's Coffin

An old [Monhegan] lady died one early spring. There seemed to be no wood on hand suitable for a coffin. Not even an old dory. But in the fishhouse was a good topsail, a little too large, but useful enough once the reefs were tied.

At the funeral one little granddaughter marred the solemnity of the occasion by a sudden shout of laughter as Grandmother's body was lowered into the grave. Nothing was said at the time, but when the family were home again her mother turned to her. "What did you mean, Almira, laughing like that when your grandmother was being buried?"

The little girl twisted her toe about on the rag rug. "I know," she said, "it was awful. But I just couldn't help laughing when I thought of Grandma scudding through hell in a close-reefed topsail!"

Fanny Kemble and the Yankee Farmer

When Boston was Fanny Kemble's home, and her summers were spent here and there in rural Massachusetts, she engaged a worthy neighbor to be her charioteer during the season of one of her country sojournings. With kind-hearted loquacity he was beginning to expatiate on the country, the crops and the history of the people roundabout, when Fanny remarked, in her imperious dogmatic fashion, "Sir, I have engaged you to drive for me, not to talk to me." The farmer ceased, pursed up his lips, and ever after kept his peace.

When the vacation weeks were over, and Miss Kemble was about to return to town, she sent for her Jehu and his bill. Running her eyes down its awkward columns, she paused. "What is this item, sir?"

said she. "I cannot understand it." And with equal gravity he rejoined, "Sass, five dollars. I don't often take it, but when I do I charge."

A Cure for Sore Eyes

"Good morning, landlord," said a man the other day, as he stepped into a tavern to get something to drink. "Good morning," replied mine host. "How do you do?" "Oh, I don't know," said the man, raising his goggles and wiping away the rheum. "I'm plagued most to death with these here pesky sore eyes. I wish you'd tell me how to cure 'em." "Willingly," said the merry host, "wear your goggles over your mouth, wash your eyes in brandy—and I will warrant a cure."

A Cure for the Heaves

Colonel Thomas was once defending a man who was sued for the price of a horse, and the defense was that the horse had the heaves. He put on a well-known stablekeeper, and after a few introductory questions asked, "Mr.—, do you know this horse described here?" "Yes sir, I know him." "How long have you kept a stable in Boston?" "Forty years successfully." "What was the matter with this horse?" "Why, Colonel, I can't give you the botanical name of the disease, but we stablemen call it the heaves." "Is there any cure for it?" asked Colonel Thomas. "Yes, sir," said the witness. Colonel Thomas was somewhat staggered, knowing that there was not; but after such an answer he found he had put his foot in it and must go on. He said, "What is it?" "Take a big knife, Colonel, and [suiting the action to the word] begin back of his ear, and cut till you reach his throat."

The Glanders

An Irishman . . . bought a horse, and when a man owns property he thinks it is the best thing in the world. He let out his horse and showed it to his neighbors. One neighbor, wishing to worry him, asked him whether his horse had the glanders. "What is it you call the glanders?" asked the Irishman. "It is not for me to tell you, but

I want to know whether your horse has the glanders?" "Well," said he, "if he is better for the glanders he has the glanders enough, but if he is worse for the glanders he has not the glanders at all."

The Fence-Post Controversy

Men used to gather in Uncle Jeb's store on winter evenings to discuss. When their arguments seemed beyond agreement, they referred decision to the aged storekeeper.

Jeb was old, all right. He had been tending the counter now long before most of the men were born. Their most blatant disputation failed to excite him.

Tonight the men were equally divided over the matter of fence posts. Half of the men believed white oak fence posts would last longer than chestnut posts. The other half believed just the opposite. Finally, the men thought they'd like to settle the matter once for all and consult Uncle Jeb.

"Now, Unc," says Ben, "what we want to know is, which'll last the longest, white oak fence posts or chestnut fence posts?"

By and by, Jeb's rocker came to a standstill. Slowly his pipe came from his lips and he said, "Oak."

The chestnut men were silent.

At last Will spoke up. "Well, Uncle Jeb, if you say oak lasts longer, how much longer?"

Again everyone was quiet while Uncle Jeb stopped rocking. "About twenty minutes."

Uncle Jed

"Uncle Jed," said Ezra one day, "ben't you gittin' a leetle hard of hearin'?"

"Yes," said Uncle Jed, "I'm afraid I'm gittin' a mite deef."

Whereupon Ezra made Uncle Jed go down to Boston to see an ear doctor.

Uncle Jed came back. And Ezra asked what happened. "Well," said Uncle Jed, "that doctor asked me if I had been drinkin' any. And I said, 'Yes, I been drinkin' a mite.'

"And then the doctor said, 'Well, Jed, I might just as well tell you now that if you don't want to lose your hearin', you've got to give up drinkin'.'

"Well," said Uncle Jed, "I thought it over; and then I said, 'Doc, I like what I've been drinkin' so much better than what I've been a-hearin' [lately] that I reckon I'll jest keep on gittin' deef!' "

Advice to a Young Lawyer

The [following] advice [was] given by an old [North Carolina] lawyer to a young one.

The old lawyer said, "If the evidence is against you, talk about the law. If the law is against you, talk about the evidence."

The young lawyer asked, "But what do you do when both the law and the evidence are against you?"

"In that case," replied the old lawyer, "give somebody hell. That'll distract the judge and the jury from the weakness of your case."

Georgia Justice

Among Attorney Theo. Titus' first efforts was a case in a Country Justice Court. Mr. Titus was closing for the plaintiff, and was making an eloquent but long-drawn-out argument. The court became very impatient. Finally a cloud came up, and a clap of thunder almost shook the house.

"Look here, Colonel Titus," said the court. "When you git through with your speech you'll find my judgment right under this book. The court is got to set out some taters before the rain."

How They Raise Men in Georgia

Not many years ago I had occasion to make a saddle journey through the pine barrens of Georgia, where almost everybody is a "cracker" and mighty shiftless. One day, however, I rode into a little community that showed such signs of thrift as to be quite out of keeping with the general character of the barrens. I rode up to a cabin where a gaunt old woman stood in the doorway, and asked her who owned these little farms that were so well kept. "That farm on the left belongs to my son Jabez," said she, "and the next one to my boy Zalim, and the next to my lad Jason, and the next is my boy Potiphar's place, and—" "Hold on, sister," said I. "How did you manage to raise such a fine lot of boys way off here in the woods?" "Waal, stranger," she answered, "I am a widdy woman, and all I had to raise 'em on was prayer an' hickory, but I raised 'em powerful frequent."

Gum Starter

Soon after I. B. Tigrett became president of the railroad which now is known as the G. M. & O., he made a trip over the route and emphasized the necessity for politeness on the part of personnel.

One veteran conductor told him, "Look here, Mr. Tigrett, how far do you want us to go with this courtesy business? One day last week an old lady and a child got on my train, and when I went around to take up the tickets the child was bawling. Remembering your suggestion about making friends with the public, I gave the child a piece of chewing gum, and I offered a piece to the lady. 'Don't care if I do,' she told me, 'but I don't have any teeth, so you'll have to start it for me.' "

War and Peace

A [Kentucky] mountaineer fighting overseas in the First World War kept getting nagging letters from his wife back home. He was too busy fighting to write letters, even to his wife. At last, stung to action by his wife's scolding missives, he sat down and wrote her:

Dear Nancy: I been a-gittin yore naggin letters all along. Now I want to tell ye, I'm dam tired of them. For the first time in my life I'm a-fightin in a big war, and I want to enjoy it in peace as long as it lasts.
Yours, etc.

The Indispensable Man

A certain tradesman in a small Kentucky town . . . bought a quantity of goods from a Paducah wholesaler and did not pay up in time.

After six months had gone by, and innumerable dunning letters had been ignored, the wholesaler sat down and wrote a final demand for payment. At the same time he addressed several other inquiries to the town where the tradesman operated. He wrote the railroad station agent, asking if the goods had been delivered. He wrote the local bank president, inquiring about the man's credit. Finally he wrote the mayor of the town, asking the name of a good lawyer in case he had to bring suit.

In a few days he received from the debtor himself the following reply:

Dear Sir: As station agent of this town, I am glad to advise you that the goods were delivered. As president of the local bank, it gives me pleasure to inform you that my credit is good. As mayor of the town, I am compelled to advise you that I am the only lawyer here. And if it were not for the fact that I am also pastor of the Baptist church, I would tell you to go to hell!

Longevity

Every time I get to thinking about longevity . . . I am reminded of an old neighbor I have in Kentucky, who is ninety-nine years old and going strong. Some years ago, when he was a young man of only ninety-two, he was vigorous, physically and mentally, worked regularly, and walked straight as an Indian. One day a neighbor asked him, "To what do you attribute your good health and longevity?"

"Well," my old friend answered, "before my wife and I were married, we entered into an agreement. Any time I railed at her, nagged at her, or picked a fuss with her, she would take her knitting, go out into the kitchen, and knit until it was all over. On the other hand, any time she would pick a fuss with me, I would put on my hat, go outdoors, and stay there until the atmosphere was once again serene."

"But what's that got to do with your health and longevity?" the neighbor inquired.

"Why," said the nonagenarian, "I've spent most of my life in the open air."

"Make Me Take It"

[An] old fellow in Mississippi . . . thought he was dying. As the sun sank slowly in the west, casting its benign rays over the horizon, he motioned to his wife to come over to his bedside.

"Mary!" he whispered. "You remember the old trunk in the basement?"

"Yes, John," she answered tearfully, "I believe there is an old trunk down there."

"Well, Mary," he whispered, "there's a quart of bourbon—fine, old bourbon—in it. Go down and get it."

"Yes, John," she said. "What then?"

Well, John gave her specific instructions. He told her to fill a glass with finely crushed ice, to bruise some mint and stir it up in the glass, with just a pinch of sugar. Then he told her to pour the bourbon liberally over the concoction, and to decorate it with sprigs of mint and set it aside until a frost formed on the outside.

"And then, Mary," gasped the old man, his voice now all but extinct, "bring it up here—bring it in here to me. And when you bring it in here, Mary, no matter what I do or say—make me take it!"

The Path to the Grave

An old couple once lived in a section of Bourbon County, [Kentucky], known as "The Pocket." Time passed, the old woman was seized with a mighty illness, and she fell into a sleep of death. The day of her funeral arrived. The coffin was loaded on a wagon, friends and acquaintances fell in behind it on foot and horseback, and the procession wound slowly and solemnly to the graveyard gate.

The coffin was unloaded from the wagon at the gate. As the pallbearers started up the rough, steep path to the grave, one of them slipped and the coffin fell to the ground. The old woman rolled out, came to life, was taken home, and lived seven more years.

The next time she died, the funeral procession wended its way to the same graveyard, over the same rough road. But when the gate was reached, and the pallbearers lifted the coffin out of the wagon to carry it up the steep path to the grave, the bereaved husband quickly stepped to the head of the procession. Then he turned and admonished the pallbearers. "Steady, men, steady."

Two Chances

A hillbilly walked down the street near the draft board. A neighbor said, "You had better stay away—you are liable to get drafted." The boy, who actually had not even heard of the war, was unable to understand. The neighbor explained the situation. The hillbilly said, "Well, I always figure I have got two chances: I might get drafted and I might not. And even if I'm drafted, I still have two chances: I might pass and I might not. And if I pass, I still have two chances: I might go across and I might not. And even if I go across, I still have two chances: I might get shot and I might not. And even if I get shot, I still have two chances: I might die, and I might not. And even if I die, I still have got two chances!"

Breaking the News

In the Texas of older days, courts of law and law-enforcement officials were few and far between. As a result, people sometimes took the law in their own hands and set up what were called "Jack Rabbit" courts. In one of these "courts" a man was hastily tried for cattle rustling, found guilty, and strung up. Before his body quit swinging in the breeze, the real culprit was dragged up, and it was evident that the "court" had erred grievously. One of the cowboys noted for his tact and diplomacy was sent out to break the news as gently and tactfully as he could to the wife of the man who had been hanged. The cowboy reined in his pony in front of Mrs. Stebbins' house, and the following matter-of-fact dialogue took place:

Cowboy: Hello in there! Does Mr. Stebbins live here?

Mrs. Stebbins: Yeah, he does.

Cowboy: No, he don't. Are you his wife?

Mrs. S.: Yeah, I am.

Cowboy: No, y' ain't, you're his widder. I jist stopped to tell ye about a hour ago we strung yer husband up fer cattle-rustlin', and then found out we had the wrong man, so the joke's on us. So long, Mrs. Stebbins. [Riding away.] Git up, Gopher!

☞ **2** ☜

God's Country

[A] Beacon Hill lady . . . , chided for her lack of travel, asked simply, "Why should I travel when I'm already here?"

CLEVELAND AMORY

Introduction

The proper Bostonian's smugness with regard to travel and geography is raised to infinity in the story of the Bostonian (sometimes the Texan) who dies and goes to heaven, only to be greeted by St. Peter with a weary, "You may come in, but I know you won't like it."

For the provincial American the particular part of the country where he was born and raised and prefers to live and die is "God's country," the place from which all blessings flow, and under God's special care. By invidious comparison, any other part of the country is likely to be "poor country," God-forsaken, the place that God forgot. Since one man's heaven may be another man's hell, the same place may be viewed nostalgically through rose-colored glasses, or critically, through dark glasses.

Praise for "God's country" and blame for "poor country" have produced the anecdotal humor of local cracks and slams. Such vaunts and taunts are related to the American's traditional habit of boasting, boosting, and knocking. They are also interwoven with regional, state, and local stereotypes, bearing complimentary or libelous labels, such as sharp Yankee, proper Bostonian, first-family Virginian, bragging Texan. These myths may be based on mutually antagonistic folkways, but more often they are the product of ignorance and indifference as to how the other half of the country lives.

When provincialism crosses the line into sectionalism, it results in the searing anecdotes of the War between the States and of the standing feud between North and South. The playful antagonism that often exists between neighboring states is seen in the friendly exchange of insults between Missourians and Arkansawyers.

Stories of loyal natives who cling to their local heaven on earth are matched by gibes at "hell on earth," inspired by the disappointment of the migrant "going in search of God's country" or the disgruntlement of the temporary exile.

When General Philip H. Sheridan was in command of the Military Division of the Gulf, with headquarters at San Antonio, Texas, he was asked by a reporter what he thought of Texas as a country to live in. "If I owned two plantations," said General Sheridan, "and one was located in Texas and the other one was in hell, I'd rent out the one in Texas and live on the other one." The editor of a Waco newspaper printed the remark with a single line of editorial comment. "Well, damn a man that won't stand up for his own country."

Passionate Pilgrims

A Boston woman . . . was planning her first trip to the West. The travel agent asked, "How would you like to go? By Buffalo?" "Why, really," replied the lady, "I planned to go by train."

Two women from Boston . . . were riding across the prairie and came upon a lone tombstone with the simple inscription: "John Jones—he came from Boston." They looked at it reverently, and finally one said, "How brief, but how sufficient."

Two Boston women . . . went to the San Francisco Fair and ran into a hot spell. As they were stewing on Treasure Island, one said to the other, "My dear, I *never* expected to be so hot in San Francisco." "But, my dear," replied her companion, "you must remember that we are three thousand miles from the ocean."

A colleague from Leland Stanford . . . insisted that once, when he was having tea in a Boston home, the lady of the house inquired, "How long did it take you to come from Leland Stanford to Boston?" "About four days," replied my friend, "at least I was four nights on the train." "Why, really," said his hostess, "I never was on a train so long in my life. But then, of course, I'm here already."

"Proper Bostonians"

There is a story in Boston that in the palmy days of the twenties a Chicago banking house asked the Boston investment firm of Lee, Higginson & Co. for a letter of recommendation about a young Bostonian they were considering employing. Lee, Higginson could not say enough for the young man. His father, they wrote, was a Cabot, his mother a Lowell; farther back his background was a happy blend of Saltonstalls, Appletons, Peabodys, and others of Boston's First Families. The recommendation was given without hesitation.

Several days later came a curt acknowledgment from Chicago. Lee, Higginson was thanked for its trouble. Unfortunately, however, the material supplied on the young man was not exactly of the type the Chicago firm was seeking. "We were not," their letter declared, "contemplating using Mr. —— for breeding purposes."

[A] Boston woman . . . , reluctantly transplanted to another part of the country, returned to be asked how she liked being home again. Having been well taught in the Proper Boston school, she was taken aback. "Like it?" she said. "Why, I never thought of it that way. Liking Boston is like saluting the flag."

A visitor to Harvard sought to see the late Lawrence Lowell, then president of the university. Having been called to the nation's capital on a matter of business, Lowell could not be seen. The visitor was stopped by a secretary in the outer office. "The President is in Washington," she said, "seeing Mr. Taft."

At the age of eighty-eight "Aunt Sarah" [Palfrey] went to Europe all alone, shortly before World War I, for what she declared was her "last look around." She came back to this country to take up during her final illness the study of Hebrew. When a friend remonstrated with her for the effort this involved, she said that she had always intended to take up the language and had put it off far too long as it was. "I wish to be able," she said with some finality, "to greet my Creator in his native tongue."

Ex-Ambassador [Joseph P.] Kennedy has no illusions about being a Proper Bostonian. He would settle for the privilege of not being referred to in the Boston press as an Irishman. "I was born here," he says. "My children were born here. What the hell do I have to do to be an American?"

The Hallowell Boy's Prayer

In Boston . . . a small Hallowell boy . . . went to the Saltonstall house for his first overnight visit. That evening the Saltonstalls, fearing homesickness, left their young visitor's door open and were surprised to overhear him start his prayers: "Our Father who art in Heaven, Saltonstall be Thy name." Thinking the boy was upset, the Saltonstalls did nothing about it until the next morning. Then, apologetically, they admitted they had overheard his prayer and asked him if he always said it like that.

"Oh, no," he answered politely, "in our house we always say 'Hallowell be Thy name,' but in your house I thought I should say 'Saltonstall.'"

New England, There She Stands!

I was deeply impressed with manufacturers and the ingenuity of New England people from whom we were getting so many finished products, and I decided to make a trip to Boston to see what these New England people looked like. I went to Baltimore by train and thence by the Merchants and Miners Line to Boston, and stopped at the old Adams House, where I ate a good New England dinner.

In the lobby after dinner, I made the acquaintance of a very gracious New England gentleman who was willing to talk and give me some information. I asked him if he could tell me some of the fundamental reasons why the New England people were so select, so ingenious, and so successful in manufacturing. With a twinkle in his eye, he spoke as follows: "Did you come in this morning against a heavy east wind?" I answered, "Yes." "Did you have baked beans for your dinner?" I admitted that there were baked beans on the table. "In these two things you have the answer to your question as to why the people of New England are so select. It is this: Persons of weak lungs are soon cut off by east winds and those of weak stomachs are early killed by baked beans! We have here a survival of the fittest."

Kansas versus Maine

Some years ago, when the annual encampment of the G.A.R. was held at Portland, Maine, a few delegates from the "wild and woolly," of that class who are eternally cramming the advantages of what they term "God's country" down everybody's throat, took a jaunt up that way to see the country and sneer at "primitive methods," etc.

In a particularly rocky and uninviting section of the state they alighted at a station for exercise, and ran across an aged farmer sitting on a baggage truck and chewing tobacco. "Well, ye don't look as though ye'd had a boom here lately," said the Kansas man, addressing the aged agriculturist; "you fellers are foolish to stay in this country, where ye have to do yer spring plowin' with a pickaxe and yer plantin' with a shotgun. I sh'd think ye'd starve to death. Why don't ye come out to Kansas? Not a stump nor a stun in sight; soil ten feet deep; crops o' one year make ye rich."

The Maine man listened with a face full of interest, and finally took a fresh chew of tobacco. He rose from the baggage truck and faced the crowd of Kansans. "So ye're all doin' well, are ye? I'm mighty glad to hear it. I'm holdin' six mortgages on Kansas farms today, an' if you fellers will just keep it up an' pay your int'rest, I'll try an' pull along here."

Prospects of a Northern Lawyer in the South

A young lawyer from Pennsylvania sought to locate in the South. He wrote to a friend in Alabama, asking him what the prospects seemed to be for "an honest young lawyer and Republican." The friend replied, "If you are an honest lawyer you will have absolutely no competition. If you are a Republican, don't be uneasy. The game laws will protect you."

Southern Virtues

An aged woman, born and nurtured in the South, . . . was endeavoring to impress upon her nephews and nieces the beauties of the South and its people, when one of the young men spoke up. "Auntie," he asked, "do you think that all the virtues originated in and have been preserved by the Southern people?" "No, not all, but most of them," she replied. "Do you think that Jesus Christ was a Southerner?" The old lady hesitated a moment and said, "He was good enough to be a Southerner."

Blue Blood

Colonel Watson was bedridden during the latter portion of his life. He had a Negro named Mose, who waited on him hand and foot, and carried him up and down stairs, and was a very excellent man. Now Mose took unto himself a wife very suddenly. Colonel Watson had never met the woman whom he married, and asked Mose to bring her in so he could meet her and give her a wedding present. Mose brought her in to see him, and Colonel Watson looked at her and turned to Mose and said, without thinking, "Why, Mose, your wife is almost white."

She bristled up immediately. "No, sir, boss, that ain't so. I ain't got a drop of white blood in me. My ma was a Cherokee Indian and my daddy was a Yankee."

Private John Allen and the Union Soldier

One of [Private John] Allen's closest friends after the war was George R. Peck, who had served in the Union Army as a colonel. The two men were like two boys who refused to grow up. Their witty darts were aimed at each other continually. A dinner was to be given in honor of Private John Allen, C.S.A., in Chicago by Mr. Peck and a number of officers of his old regiment. Peck wrote Private John that he would meet him in the lobby of the Palmer House. Allen arrived on time but breathless.

Rushing up to Peck he said, "George, lend me five dollars so that I can pay for my cab. I have just given away my last cent."

Without questioning him Mr. Peck handed him the bill. Private John disappeared through the hotel entrance and quickly returned.

Turning to Peck, who was surrounded by his comrades, Allen said, "When I got off the train at the I.C. Station and walked through the waiting room I saw an old fellow in a G.A.R. uniform with his hat held out for contributions. He had one eye missing, one arm gone and one leg off. I had only a twenty-dollar bill, so I walked over to him and put it in his hat, saying, 'You're a Yank and I'm a Johnny Reb and I fit against you, but I'm going to give you the last twenty dollars I've got.' He asked, 'Why do you, a Johnny Reb, give me, a Yank, your last twenty dollars, when we fit against each other?' I told him the truth: 'Because you're the only Yank I ever saw who was trimmed up exactly according to my notion.'"

Arkansas and the Civil War

[During the Civil War] the soldiers at Helena, in Arkansas, used to amuse the inhabitants of that place, on their first arrival, by telling them yarns, of which the following is a sample:

Some time ago Jeff Davis got tired of the war, and invited President Lincoln to meet him on neutral ground to discuss terms of peace. They met accordingly, and after a talk concluded to settle the war by dividing the territory and stopping the fighting. The North took the Northern states, and the South the Gulf and seaboard Southern states. Lincoln took Texas and Missouri, and Davis [took] Kentucky and Tennessee; so that all were parceled off excepting Arkansas. Lincoln didn't want it—Jeff wouldn't have it. Neither would consent to take it, and on that they split; and the war has been going on ever since.

Nothing Wrong in Heaven

On one occasion a great revival was being held in Greene County, [Tennessee]. Two old Methodist soldiers of the cross were warming the hearts of multitudes. These two preachers were warm personal friends but belonged to the two rival branches which have since united to form the Methodist Church. One was a Rebel preacher who had served in the Confederate Army and the other was a Northern Methodist preacher who had soldiered in the Union Army and had lost his eye in battle. They were holding their meeting jointly. John R. Hughes was the Unionist, the name of the Southern Methodist minister is now unknown.

The Southern Methodist preacher in the course of his exhortation to sinners to hit the trail said, "All will be right in heaven—there'll be nothing wrong in heaven," and then turning to Reverend Hughes, he said, "Brother Hughes, there won't be any one-eyed men in heaven."

Although the words were from a loving heart, they must have caused a momentary lapse into an old hate. Reverend Hughes shot back in a flare to his brother preacher, "No, there won't be any Rebels up there to shoot 'em out."

Candidates for Heaven

THE TENNESSEAN

Grandpa, who was about ninety-seven and a half on the record books, had never gone what he called "an overnight piece" from his birthplace in the Appalachian Valley, never, not even once. So, after church one Sunday, he waited to talk to the mountain preacher, and he got the Reverend to one side, and, stroking his beard thoughtfully, he said, "Parson, I don't reckon I'll ever get to do no traveling till I'm a spirit. But," he said, "I've allus had a hankering to see a big town, and I wish you'd just mention casually to the Lord that, while I'm on my way to heaven, I'd like it powerful well if I could make a little detour down around Knoxville."

THE HOOSIER

On an occasion when St. Peter was examining candidates for the land of bliss, a fellow was handed to him in [a] halter. Upon his reception he was tied to a post to await his turn for inspection. He soon gave signs of restlessness and occasionally surged back on his halter-strap in an effort to break loose. A bystander inquired what was wrong with him. St. Peter promptly replied, "Oh, that fellow is a Hoosier and the fool wants to go back to Indiana."

THE ARKANSAWYER

A minister called on all of the congregation who wanted to go to heaven to stand up. Everyone stood up except one man, and when the Reverend asked him why he did not stand up, he said, "Well, I was thinking of going back to Arkansas, but if I am unable to do that, I will consider your proposition."

The Wise and the Foolish Virginians

[A] colored Baptist preacher from Richmond . . . was attending a Baptist convention in Mississippi. A Mississippi preacher, reading the Scripture lesson for a morning session, read: "Now the Kingdom of Heaven was likened unto ten Virginians which took their lamps and went forth to meet the bridegroom. And five of them were wise and five were foolish." Thereupon the Richmond preacher said, "Brother, would you be so good as to recapitulate that Scripture lesson for me?" When the Mississippi preacher read it again in the same way, the Richmond preacher replied, "Now that Scripture lesson do sound familiar and I don't want you to think that I question what the Good Book says, but it did seem to me that the percentage of foolish Virginians was too high."

Missourians versus Arkansawyers

Some stories featuring the supposed antagonism between Missouri and Arkansas are still heard in certain quarters.

Once in a Missouri village I sat with a bunch of loafers, and there was one man from Arkansas in the crowd, so several of the boys began to make dirty cracks about Arkansas. Finally one fellow remarked that he had once spent seven weeks near Harrisonville, Arkansas, and didn't have anything to eat but hemlock bark. Then the Arkansas man said, positively, that he had lived in Harrison for twenty years, and that there wasn't a hemlock tree within three hundred miles of the place. The Missouri boy said, "Of course not. There ain't no trees down there, because the soil's too thin. Parties which goes to Arkansas has to pack in their own hemlock bark. We trucked our'n all the way from St. Louis!"

An Arkansas boy . . . got his first pair of shoes at the age of twenty. "He started walkin' backward, so he could see what fine tracks he was a-makin'," runs the Missouri version of the tale. "Seein' them tracks tickled him so much that he walked clear up into Missouri afore the folks could stop him." An Arkansas man in the audience replies, "Yeah, that's all true. I knowed that feller well. He never did get back to Arkansas. When the folks in Missouri found out he could count up to twenty, *without takin' off his boots*, they made a schoolteacher out of him!"

North Dakota Baby

A Dakota farmer was waiting at the hospital for his first baby. The nurse announced an eight-pound baby to the man waiting with him and to the Dakota farmer she announced a three-pound one and to the surprise of the other he seemed very happy. "Man," said the father, "three pounds is a smidgen of a baby. Don't look to me that baby's got a chance. Why are you so happy?" "I'm a farmer from North Dakota." "What's that got to do with it?" "Why, everything. In North Dakota we're darn glad to get our seed back!"

Bird of Paradise in West Texas

The Easterner . . . was being driven by a rancher over a blistering and almost barren stretch of West Texas when a gaudy bird, new to him, scurried in front of them. The Easterner asked what it was.

"That is a bird of paradise," said the rancher.

The stranger rode on in silence for a time and then said, "Pretty long way from home, isn't he?"

☞ **3** ☜

Newcomers and Damn Fools

"Is the river fordable?" inquired the Traveler. "I guess so," replied the native, "my ducks been a-fordin' it ever'day." "Old man, what makes your corn so yellow?" asked the Traveler with thinly veiled scorn. "You fool, you, I *planted* yaller corn," retorted the native. "Where does this road go?" queried the Traveler. " 'Tain't never gone nowhar yit—it stays right thar all the time."

THE ARKANSAW TRAVELER

Introduction

"Divided we stand" in America, not only as boosters of "God's country" and knockers of "poor country," but also as hick versus city slicker. The lessening of the distance between city and country may have relaxed the rural-urban tensions and antagonisms in American life. But they are still strong in American anecdotal humor and jokelore, where hick and city slicker still regard each other as fools and, to prove it, are constantly trying to make fools out of each other. The feud between the two is the comic feud between the inquiring traveler and the quizzical native, in which the Country Mouse and the City Mouse keep exchanging roles with each other.

The humor of the "green 'un" in the city or the country takes on the aspect of both the practical joke of the "fool's-errand" variety and the "ingenu satire" of the naïve traveler. It is partly the humor of contrast—the contrast between the raw countryman's apparent innocence and his actual toughness and agility; between the tenderfoot's or tourist's vaunted city slickness and his fish-out-of-water helplessness and embarrassment when not in his element. Here the newcomer is always a fool, until proved otherwise, whether the country bumpkin, boorishly ignorant and distrustful of city manners and contraptions, or the "furriner," bumptiously ignorant and distrustful of nature in the raw. As the practical joker is quick to take advantage of the stranger's ignorance, so the latter may be clever enough to turn the tables.

One evening, relates A. W. Eddins, a fresh young city feller, in derby hat and store-bought clothes, walked into a Texas saloon and ordered a drink. As he wiped his mouth with a bright silk handkerchief, he remarked to the disapproving onlookers, "Well, I believe it's going to rain." "My friend," said the local wag, "did you know that there were only two kinds of people who prophesy about Texas weather?" "Two kinds of people who prophesy about Texas weather? That's very queer. Who are they?" "Newcomers and damn fools!" In response to the chorus of, "The drinks are on you, stranger!" the latter stood treat. Then he said quietly to his tormentor, "You say there are only two kinds of people who prophesy about Texas weather—newcomers and damn fools. You are right. Those are the only two kinds of people in Texas."

Country Fools versus Town Fools

A hillbilly came into Tulsa, Oklahoma, and started walking down the street. His coonskin cap attracted a lot of attention, and young folk gathered about him, gaping and giggling. He paid no attention until some smart aleck said, "Tell me, do they have many damn fools in Arkansas?" The visitor shifted his quid. "Well," said he, "we come acrost one every once in a while. But they don't run round in droves, like they do here."

Country Boy in Chicago

A country boy . . . went to Chicago. When he was on the train the porter came to him and said, "Boss, does you want me to brush you off?" The boy said, "No, I'll just get off the usual way." When he arrived at the station in Chicago he caught a hack—there were no taxis then. He went to a hotel and told the clerk that he wanted a room, and the clerk told him to register, handed him the pen and shoved the book to him, and the boy looked at the clerk and then at the book and said, "No, sir, I ain't a-goin' ter sign no documents."

Then the clerk told the bell boy to take him to a room on the third floor.

In telling about this when he got back home [the country boy] said, "I got in a big box with some ropes tied to the top of it and we went up like a sky rocket. We stepped out into the room. I set around awhile and decided to go to bed. I looked around for the lamp to blow out and I couldn't find one. Then I saw a glass bottle hanging down from the ceiling by two strings—it was full of red hot hairpins. I tried to blow them out and I be dern if the thing would go out, so I just took out my knife and cut the strings, and I be blamed if I ever seen so much hell come out of two little old strings. Well, I went to bed and after a while somebody hollered fire. I jumped outer bed and made a dive fer that elevator thing and do you know what?—it warn't there—but I didn't know it till I got down to the bottom."

Uncle Monroe's First Visit to the City

Uncle Monroe, a white-haired country Negro, visited a city for the first time. Walking through the park, he found $2.85, which enabled him to take his first ride on the streetcar. To the old Negro, the stopping and calling of the names of streets indicated miraculous power.

"Lawdy," mused Monroe to himself, "dat man is sho' smaht. He calls Washington, an' Mistah Washington git off. Den he calls Adams, an' Mistah Adams git off. Den he calls Jefferson, an' Mistah Jefferson git off. But he doan know mah name an' he cain't put me off." Just then the conductor called, "Monroe!"

"Yas, suh, Ah's Monroe. Heah Ah comes." And as he stepped off the car, he marveled at the knowledge of the conductor. Then a big touring car drove up, and the driver inquired, "Is this Monroe?"

"Yas, suh, dis am Monroe," answered the Negro.

"Good," said the driver, "I'm looking for two eighty-five."

"Mah Lawd!" exclaimed the old Negro, reaching for the purse. "Dese sho' is awful smaht white folks!"

The Kentuckian and the Cuspidor

A Kentuckian visited a merchant of New York, with whom, after dinner, he drank wine and smoked cigars, spitting on the carpet, much to the annoyance of his host, who desired a spittoon to be brought for his troublesome visitor; he, however, pushed it away with his foot, and when it was replaced he kicked it away again, quite unaware of its use. When it had been thrice replaced, the Kentuckian drawled out to the servant who had brought it, "I tell you what; you've been pretty considerable troublesome with that ere thing, I guess; if you put it there again, I'm hung if I don't spit in it."

Their First Automobile

When the first automobile [was] seen in the hills, an old man and his son were in the corn patch. They heard it coming up the road. "Gee whilakers, Paw, what is it?" "Don't know, son," said the father, "but I better git my gun." He ran into the cabin and came out with a shot gun. When he saw "the thing" was still moving toward him, he fired at it. The driver stopped the car and ran down the hill. "Did you kill the varmint?" the son called from the field. "Nope," said the old man, "but I made him turn loose the man he had."

"Come and Eat"

There was a dry old fellow out in Jefferson County, in this state [of Virginia] who called one day on the member of Congress-elect. The family were at breakfast, and the old man was not in a decent trim to be invited to sit by; but he was hungry, and determined to get an invitation.

"What's the news?" inquired the congressman.

"Nothing much, but one of my neighbors gave his child such a queer name."

"Ah! And what was that?"

"Why, Come and Eat."

The name was so peculiar that it was repeated.

"*Come and Eat?*"

"Yes, thank you," said the old man, "I don't care if I do," and drew up to the table.

Good Enough

Uncle Simon was invited [to a marriage feast in North Iredell, North Carolina], not because he belonged to the four hundred, for he did not, but because he was a member of the family. When they were properly seated, Uncle Si noticed a pound cake near him and was just about to ruin it. One of the family, noticing his activity and fearing a scarcity like that at the Galilean feast, said, "Uncle Si, won't you have some of these nice biscuits?"

"No, this punkin bread is good enough for me."

Toothpick Shortage

Some years ago, when I was on vacation one summer down at Uncle Lon's in the rock and cedar country of Middle Tennessee, the Reverend Vesta Cawthon, Mount Juliet, Tennessee, was holding a revival nearby, and Aunt Emma invited him home to dinner one day.

Brother Cawthon related that he once held a revival in Georgia and, during the course of it, was invited home for dinner by one of the leading elders of the church. At the close of a bountiful and delicious meal, the good woman picked up the toothpick holder to pass around. It turned out to be empty, and there were no toothpicks in the pantry, either.

The head of the house broke the embarrassed silence by turning to his children at the table and exclaiming sternly, "Now see what's happened! No toothpicks! How many more times must I tell you young 'uns to put toothpicks back after using 'em?"

The Hillbilly Enlistee

A boy from the hills section of Arkansas arrived at a G.I. camp for training. His first day there he spent in wandering around, looking at the sights, when a general came along. The boy, being a friendly sort, said, "Howdy." The general stopped and proceeded to lecture the recruit at some length on how to address his superior officers.

The boy heard him through in silence, then spat into the dust and said, "Effen I had a knowed you was agoin' to take on thataway, I wouldn't of spoke to you atall!"

What Maine People Do in the Winter

There was a local character who was fond of stringing along people from the city. When asked what the Maine people did in the winter, he always would say, "Chase rabbits." "Do you shoot them?" they would ask. "Oh no," he would answer, "just wind them."

Vermonters versus Summer Visitors

A New Yorker . . . , in the course of a motoring trip in Vermont, became completely lost. Finally, he saw a farmer chopping wood in his barnyard, and with some difficulty attracted his attention. . . . The farmer responded with very explicit instructions. After he had covered some ten miles, the stranger found himself in front of the same house, and inquired with some heat what the farmer meant. "Oh," said he, "I just wanted to make sure you could follow directions."

A party [of summer visitors] were hurrying home to St. Johnsbury after a long afternoon of motoring. As they rounded a curve on a downgrade, they found the road completely blocked by two wagons, the drivers of which had stopped to gossip. The chauffeur applied his brakes and by good luck managed to stop less than a yard from the wagons. When he recovered his breath, he shouted out, "Hey, what do you fellers think you're doing, blocking the whole road?"

Only then did one of the farmers turn around and, carefully removing his pipe, reply, "Visitin'; and we got a right ter."

The Silent Vermonter

A tourist spending the night in a small Vermont town joined a group of men sitting on the porch of the general store. After several vain attempts to start a conversation, he finally asked, "Is there a law against talking in this town?"

"No law against it," answered one Vermonter, "but there's an understanding that no one's to speak unless he's sure he can improve on silence."

The Dude from Memphis

[There was] an Arkansas bear-hunter named Jack Smith. Some sportsmen from Memphis, Tennessee, asked him how it was that he killed so much more game than anybody else. Jack told 'em that the secret was in his dress. Whenever he went hunting, he said, he always dressed up like a dude from Memphis. The bear and deer, seeing him thus attired, figured that he couldn't hit a barn at ten paces, and was probably too drunk to do any shooting anyhow. Thus Jack was able to approach very close to his quarry, and killed nearly all his game at point-blank range.

Crossed Tracks

A city sportsman lost in a snow storm [in the Ozarks] . . . circled until he crossed his own trail. "I guess I'd better follow this fellow's track," he said, figuring that this would surely lead him to a settlement or at least to a hunting camp. Following his own trail, naturally he circled again, and finally returned to the place where two tracks joined. "Well," he reflected, "two of these fellows have met now— we must be getting pretty close to the camp." Completing another circle, the tracker noted that a third man had joined the party he was trailing. Running at top speed now, expecting to overtake three hunters at any moment, the city feller was well-nigh exhausted when the tracks of a fourth traveler appeared in the well-defined trail! At this point a local woodsman appeared and led the weary sportsman back to his camp. This man read the trail at a glance, but never told the city feller that he was alone in the woods that day, and had been following his own tracks all the time.

Deceiving Distances

Owing to the altitude, the [South Dakota] air is so light that hills which are miles away stand out against the sky with knifelike clearness. People who come here from the East are invariably fooled as to distances. They have always associated clearness with nearness, and sometimes they learn the difference to their sorrow. An old-timer told me how, when he first came here, he tried out a new rifle on the slopes of Bear Butte and was much disappointed at not seeing the dust fly from it. He learned later that the butte was many miles away.

They tell a story of a stranger who set out one morning to walk to a certain butte before breakfast. He walked a mile or two and then met a native who told him that the butte was still several miles away, so he decided to return. They traveled by a slightly different route and came to a small stream, a mere trickle across the sand. As the native stopped to water his horse, he was amazed to see the stranger busily stripping off his clothes. "What are you going to do?" he asked. "I'm going to swim this river," was the dogged response. "Swim it!" ejaculated the native. "Why, you can step across it!" "Well, I don't know," was the cautious answer. "Distances are deceiving in this country, and I'm not taking any chances."

Liver Regulator

[On the XIT round-up] an unhappy tenderfoot [from Colorado] . . . was attached to Ruck Tanner's wagon. A chronic grumbler, especially about the chuck wagon, he never liked the camping place the cook had picked and he never liked the food. One day, however, Tanner, having decided that he had had enough of this, told the man he needed liver medicine.

"A chuck-wagon dough-roller always carries the best liver regulator in the world." Tanner's voice was sympathetic. "You ought to mention it to him. He may decide you need it an' give it to you good and proper."

Others, taking up the suggestion, also urged the man to ask for some of the cook's regulator. So one evening, after complaining through a meal, he walked to the cook and said, "Say, they tell me you've got some liver regulator. Is it any better than your lousy sourdough?"

The cook surveyed him calmly. "They're right," he said. "I got the best liver regulator in the world. Right here in the chuck box."

The cook reached into a compartment and pulled out his .44-caliber six-shooter. Slowly he pulled back the hammer until it clicked. "This is the best liver regulator I know anything about," he said, "an' I'm a good mind to give it to you right now. If you grumble another damn' word, you'll get it."

It was potent medicine. Thereafter the outside man's tongue behaved much better.

☞ **4** ☜

Melting Pot and Pressure Cooker

[An] Indian . . . went to New York from the
reservation. While strolling along one of those
mad thoroughfares he was approached by a home-
towner, who inquired, "And how do you like our
city?"

"Fine," replied the redskin, taking it on the fly,
"and how do you like our country?"

PAUL FLOWERS

Introduction

"Once there were two Ethiopians, Sambo and Rastus." "Once there were two Irishmen named Pat and Mike."

Perhaps more than any other phase of anecdotal humor in America, intercultural stories reflect the changes in fashion, taste, and social acceptability with reference to what is funny. With each new wave of immigration another foreign group took its place in the succession of comic stereotypes as it did in the progression of occupations. As newcomer-fool and the butt of jokes, in dialect songs, stories, readings, and recitations that seem sadly unfunny to us now, the stage Irishman, German, Italian, Jew, and other greenhorns were added to the Yankee, backwoods, and Negro or blackface clowns. These were the scapegoats of the melting pot, which was as quick to ridicule difference as it was slow to produce uniformity. "Greenhorn" humor was strictly "made in America" from the outside looking in, in quizzical condescension.

In each nationality group, however, there is an authentic folk humor which comes from the inside looking out. As the melting pot illusion was dispelled by the pressure-cooker dynamics of cultural conflict, interchange, and diversity, each minority began to find in its own cultural history, idiom, and situation the key to self-understanding and self-respect— and thus to understanding and respect on the part of others. An important part of this heritage is folk laughter.

Turning this laughter upon itself as well as upon other groups, each group feels free to tell jokes on itself which, if told by others, might be considered chauvinistic, and which, in fact, may sometimes seem chauvinistic toward other groups. At its best, such esoteric humor satisfies the need of both identification and acceptance. In contrast to the synthetic flavor of stereotype and scapegoat humor, ethnic folk humor has the racy tang and geniality of genuine cracker-barrel wit, wisdom, and fantasy.

A few years back, Sam Levenson told John Crosby in an interview: "I don't think humor has to have a victim . . . Take my story about Mama and the pushcart peddler. Mama had to bargain. Eight kids? With eight kids you got to bargain or nobody eats. And the peddler—he's poor, too. So one day on his cart there's a rusty old spoon. 'How much?' says Mama. 'A penny,' says the peddler. 'Too much,' says Mama. 'So?' says the peddler. 'Make me an offer.' " "A story like that," concludes Crosby, "tells volumes about the life on Orchard Street, about Mama and also about the peddler."

The Receipt

A [North Country] "Canuck" bought a horse from a sharp trader named Melt, demanding from him a receipt. Melt pretended to be surprised at the request. "Well," said the Frenchie, "I die, you die. Saint Pierre say to me, 'You have any deals with Melt? Got reeceep?' Suppose I hunt all over hell to find you?"

The Celestial Automobiles

Due to circumstances beyond his control, the Reverend Whiteman departed this world and came up to the portals of heaven. He is accosted by St. Peter, who opens the gate. And St. Peter says, "Hello, Tom, how are you?"

And Reverend Whiteman looks at him in great surprise and says, "I take it you're St. Peter, the celestial custodian."

He says, "That's right. I'm glad to know you, Reverend. You've been a pretty good feller. Come right in and I'll sign you up."

Reverend Whiteman walks in. "Reverend," says St. Peter, "you're going to have this celestial Chevrolet," he says. "And you're going to have a celestial ranch home, because you've been a good man," he says, "you've been a fine man!"

And Reverend Whiteman looks at him and says, "St. Peter," he says, "it's just wonderful," he says. "I don't know how to thank you," he says. "Just give me directions and I'll be on my way. I know you're busy."

Upon which he went into his celestial Chevrolet and took a turn and was going on his way to Sunrise Boulevard to his celestial home. Upon which he sees the priest, Father Murphy, whom he never particularly cared for—the Catholic priest—and he's driving a Buick. Reverend Whiteman makes a U-turn on Sunrise Boulevard, comes back to St. Peter, and he says to St. Peter, he says, "St. Peter," he says, "I'm not one to complain. But I'd like to know *why* Father Murphy rates a Buick and I a Chevrolet," he says, "if you don't mind my asking."

"Oh," says St. Peter, "not at all," he says. "I just want you to know," he says, "that you had a fine wife—"

"Yes."

"Two daughters."

"Yes."

He says, "The poor priest was never married. He never had any of the joys you had. He suffered a good deal. He was celibate."

"St. Peter," says Reverend Whiteman, "I just can't begin to tell you how bad I feel," he says. "I just never learned how to be nice about these things," he says. "Excuse me and I'm going right on my way."

Upon which he left, merrily pondering upon the inscrutable ways of the Lord. He continued for quite a while, going along, and he passed out of Sunrise Boulevard and got into Sunset Drive. He got past there and was getting close to his home when he sees a tre-men-dous Cadillac, about a block long, with a chauffeur, and a two-way radio, and there is Rabbi Ginsberg—Rabbi Ginsberg!

"Well," he thinks, "there's a reason for his." And he kept right on. He couldn't stand it any longer. Another U-turn, back to St. Peter, and he says to St. Peter, "St. Peter," he says, "I've pondered this. You told me about the priest," he says. "But I saw Rabbi Ginsberg in a Cadillac with a chauffeur!" he says. "And he had two beautiful daughters! And he had a son! He was happy. Now," he says, "I'd like to know why *he* rates a Cadillac!"

Upon which St. Peter looks around, closes the door, peers over his glasses, and whispers, "He's a relative of the boss."

Al Smith's Morning After

It seems that one day in Albany, in the midst of an important political convention, but not forgetful of high jinks, Herbert Lehman, Al Smith, Jimmy Walker, and many others of the old timers, had a big night of it. The next day was a Catholic holy day. Al Smith and Walker and the other Catholic members of the group decided that they had to make the early mass. They all occupied the same suite of rooms. As they tiptoed, groggy-eyed, through the rooms and looked at Lehman and others of the Jewish faith sleeping so quietly and beautifully, Al Smith turned to Walker and said, "Gee, I hope we're right!"

The Prayer Shawl

A smartly dressed gentleman, wearing a black frock coat, walked into the religious articles section of a large New York department store and, in a dignified, resonant voice, inquired of the clerk whether she might not have a fine-quality *talles* (prayer shawl).

The young lady disappeared into the back room and emerged with a black, sealed box. When the box was opened the gentleman's eyes lit up. Here was a *talles* unique amongst *tallesim*. Not the run-of-the-mill, skimpy-type, with blue stripes and flimsy tassels, but an immense, heavy shawl, with *gedichteh* (thick) black stripes and tassels weighted with heavy knots—a *talles* to be treasured. And when the young lady added that it had been made in the Holy Land . . . Well. . . . That settled it. Yes! He would take it, and money was no object.

"Just one detail, though," he concluded. "Please wrap it in colorful paper. I'm giving it as a Christmas present!"

Jewish Quakers

Several families of Philadelphia Jews have, in the last decade especially, been attracted to Quakerism. A man asked a rabbi whether he realized that some of his people were becoming Quakers. The rabbi replied, "Oh, yes, some of my best Jews are Friends."

Wonders of America

Malke, an elderly Yiddish-speaking woman, was on a train going from Chicago to New York. After stopping off at Pittsburgh, she got on the wrong train, which was going in the opposite direction. Before the conductor discovered the error, Malke noticed another Yiddish-speaking woman, Rivke, sitting on the other side of the car. A social chat ensued.

"Where are you going?" asked Malke.

"To Chicago."

"Is it not marvelous?" said Malke. "I sit on this side of the car and go to New York and you sit on the other side of the car and you go to Chicago. These railroads are truly wonderful."

The Compromise

Groucho Marx applied for membership in a [California] athletic club since he wished his children to enjoy the privileges of its swimming pool. He was turned down because the club did not admit Jews. Upon receiving the rejection slip Groucho wrote to the president:

> Sir, it is not my wish to have you change the rules of your organization. However, since my children are only half Jewish, I request that you grant them a special permit to enable them to go into the pool up to their navels.

The Last Straw

On a New York subway train a Jewish fellow noticed a Negro sitting opposite him reading a Yiddish newspaper. After puzzling over this for a while, he approached the other and tapped him on the shoulder. "Excuse me, mister, are you Jewish?" The Negro looked up, shrugged, and said, "That's all I need?"

Wendell Phillips and the Waiter

Before Wendell Phillips, the great Abolitionist, was very well known, he had occasion to visit Charleston, South Carolina, and put up at a hotel. In the morning he ordered his breakfast served in his room, and was waited upon by a slave.

Mr. Phillips seized upon the opportunity to impress upon the Negro, in a sentimental way, that he regarded him as a man and brother, and more than that, he himself was for the abolition of slavery.

The Negro, however, seemed more anxious about his patron's breakfast than he was about his own position in the social scale or the conditions of his soul, until finally Mr. Phillips became discouraged and told the servant to go away, saying that he could not bear to be waited on by a slave.

"You must excuse me," said the Negro, "I am obliged to stay here 'cause I'm responsible for the silverware."

Frederick Douglass and the Ship's Officer

There was a story many years going the round of our papers about a black man who was traveling on one of the Sound steamers from New York to Boston, and found there was no room for him in a stateroom, upstairs or down, and no such chance of his getting comfortably through the night as there would have been for a decent yellow dog.

It was a wild night, and was getting dark, when one of the officers on the steamer discovered this man trying to make the best of it in as snug a corner as he could find, pitied his forlorn condition, and thought he would try to help him. He noticed he was not so very black, so he hit on a plan for giving him a stateroom. There would be no sort of trouble about an Indian if he should come and look as well, generally, as this Negro did. And so he said to himself, "I will run him in as an Indian." He went up to the man, looked him in the eyes, and said, "You are an Indian, ain't you?"

Well, Douglass, for it was Fred, saw in an instant what the man was after. I don't know how he felt, but I know exactly how I should have felt if I had been in his place. I should have felt like giving a little nod, and saying, "Well, yes, I guess I'm an Indian." But what this black man did was to look right back into the eyes of the officer, and say, "No, I'm a nigger," to curl himself up as the officer turned and left him, and get what comfort he could in his gusty nest.

Horse Stay Out

["Marse" Henry] Watterson, who always maintained that the anti-slavery Republicans like Sumner, Greeley and old Ben Wade only loved the colored man just to get his vote and use, delights to quote this speech which Watterson says was delivered by old Abram Jasper at the colored picnic at Louisville during the last presidential campaign:

"Feller freemen," says he, "you all know me. I am Abram Jasper, a Republican from way back. When there has been any work to do, I has done it. When there has been any votin' to do, I has voted early and often. When there has been any fightin' to do, I has been in the thick of it. I are 'bove proof, old line and tax paid. And I has seed many changes, too. I has seed the Republicans up. I has seed the Democrats up. But I is yit to see a colored man up. T'other night I had a dream. I dreampt that I died and went to heaven.

"When I got to de pearly gates old Salt Peter he says, 'Who's dar?' says he.

" 'Abram Jasper,' says I.

" 'Is you mounted or is you afoot?' says he.

" 'I is afoot,' says I.

" 'Well, you can't get in here,' says he. 'Nobody 'lowed in here 'cept them as come mounted,' says he.

" 'Dat's hard on me,' says I, 'arter comin' all dat distance.' But he never says nothin' mo', and so I starts back an' about halfway down de hill who does I meet but dat good ol' Horace Greeley. 'Whar's you gwine, Mr. Greeley?' says I.

" 'I is gwine to heaven wid Mr. Sumner,' says he.

" 'Why, Horace,' says I, 'tain't no use. I's just been up dar an' nobody's 'lowed to get in 'cept dey comes mounted, an' you's afoot."

" 'Is dat so?' says he.

"Mr. Greeley sorter scratched his head, an' arter a while he says,

says he, 'Abram, I tell what let's do. You is a likely lad. Suppose you git down on all fours and Sumner and I'll mount an' ride you in, an' dat way we kin all git in.'

" 'Gen'lemen,' says I, 'do you think you could work it?'

" 'I know I kin,' says bof of 'em.

"So down I gits on all fours, and Greeley and Sumner gets astraddle, an' we ambles up de hill agin, an' prances up to de gate, an' old Salt Peter says, 'Who's dar?'

" 'We is, Charles Sumner and Horace Greeley,' shouted Horace.

" 'Is you bof mounted or is you afoot?' says Peter.

" 'We is bof mounted,' says Greeley.

" 'All right,' says Peter, 'all right,' says he; 'jest hitch your hoss outside, gen'lemen, and come right in.' "

Givin'-Away Liquor

In the South the word "drinkin' liquor" is always used. They always ask you, "Cap'n, got any good drinkin' liquor?" You see, there's a distinction made between drinkin' liquor and givin'-away liquor. That's liquor you give to your neighbor or give to your butler but you won't drink it yourself.

This old gentleman, Christmas morning, called in his colored retainer and gave him a quart of liquor. And about New Year's Day he happened to think about it and said, "George, how'd you like that liquor?"

"Well, Cap'n, I reckon it was just about right."

"What do you mean, 'just about right'?"

"Well, Cap'n, I figures it kinda this way. If it were any wuss, I figure I couldn't have drunk it, and if it were any better I figure you'd have drunk it yourself."

Jackleg

It seems that an old Negro was being cross-examined by a young white lawyer who was trying to shake his credibility as a witness. The young lawyer, who was just out of law school, was trying to show that he knew all the tricks of cross-examination. The old Negro was bearing it with great dignity and you could see he was a little provoked at the way he was being treated, but under the mores of the situation he couldn't very well do anything about it. Finally the young lawyer said, "Now, what do you do for a living?"

He says, "Well, Cap'n, I farms a little and I cuts wood a little and I fishes a little and I works a little for Colonel Frank up the plantation, and on Sundays I reckon I's a kind of a jackleg preacher."

"A jackleg preacher! What do you mean by a jackleg preacher, anyhow?"

"Well, Cap'n—now excuse me, Cap'n, I ain't mean to hurt nobody's feelings, but since you done ax me I reckon a jackleg preacher like me is to a real preacher like what you is to a good lawyer."

Point of View

A student of sociology visited an old woman's cabin in the Black Belt. The cabin was ramshackly; boards were off the sides and at night the stars could be seen through the openings in the roof. The student asked the old woman, "Does it leak in here?" The old woman looked long at the questioner, took her pipe out of her mouth and spat. "No, honey, it doan leak in here. When it rain, it rain in here, and it leak outside."

Burying the Gasoline

[A] patriotic Louisiana sharecropper read in the town newspaper about gas rationing.

The next night the plantation owner, who was hoarding gasoline, summoned the sharecropper to his house and gave him a gallon can of gasoline with instructions to take it out back of the barn and bury it.

An hour later, the cropper returned. "I buried that gasoline like you told me," he reported. "What do you want me to do with the empty can?"

The Troublesome Tenant Farmer

There was a [Negro tenant farmer] here [on Alligator Lake plantation] a while back named Blue that thought he was smart. . . . He didn't gin all his cotton. He kept one bale hid in his cotton-house. Then when settlin' time come, he shows up here at the commissary and goes on back into Mr. Wootan's office. Mr. Wootan puts on his specs and picks up that there book where he keeps your 'counts and looks into it. "Well, Blue," he says, "you made fourteen bales this year, and you jest 'bout broke even." Blue looked pleased as the cat that et the canary. "That's fine, Mr. Wootan," he says, "but I still got a bale I ain't ginned yit. That ought to make me clear somethin', oughten hit?" Mr. Wootan put down his book and looked at Blue over his specs, like he do when he mad. "Damn hit!" he says. "What you mean by holdin' out cotton on me? Now I got to figger hit all over agin to make hit come out even."

Six-Seeded Cotton

I useta live on a place . . . where we raised six-seeded cotton. We seed hit when we planted hit. We seed hit when we hoed hit. We seed hit when we plowed hit. We seed hit when we picked hit. We seed hit when we hauled hit to the gin. We seed hit ginned. But we ain't never seed hit no more, nor no money neither.

Working on Halves

"Yassuh, boss," the old Negro answered cheerfully, "I'se workin' twenty acres of land for Mister Johnny, on de halves. Half an' half, suh; half an' half."

"Did you make a big crop?"

"Tol'able, suh, tol'able. De most I could do was jest to make Mister Johnny's half."

Too Many "Ups"

One time there was a Negro farmer by the name of George Davis, who left the farm he was working on and went into Aiken to work. One Saturday while he was downtown at a grocery store he met his former farm boss.

"George," said the farmer, "how about gittin' you to farm for me again this year?"

"Naw, suh, Cap," replies George, "Ah wouldn't mind it, but dere's too many 'ups' in dat thing."

"What do you mean by too many 'ups'?" inquired the farmer.

"Oh, well," replied George, "when Ah goes to bed at night, de first thing in de mawnin' Ah got to wake UP; then Ah got to git UP; then Ah got to dress UP—go to the lot an' feed UP. When Ah git back to de house Ah got to eat UP sumpin; time as Ah finish Ah got to go gear UP—then hitch UP. Ah can't let de mule stan' dere so Ah haf to say git UP; time Ah done work all de summer an' gather UP mah crop an' sell it here Ah come to you to settle UP; you gits yo' pencil out an' figger UP an' say to me, 'Ah'm sorry but you done eat it UP.' Naw, suh, Ah don't think Ah'll try it."

Efficiency

A Negro, recently from Georgia, came North with the exodusters. In Waycross he had always been bent on pleasing his boss. He was hired at one of Ford's plants. His job was to thrust a strip of metal into a punching machine with his right hand. Thrust, withdraw, thrust, withdraw for eight hours a day with one hour for lunch and ten minutes out for the can. His foreman noticed that he was dissatisfied. "What's the matter, Booker?" he asked. Booker said, "I was jes' thinkin' that my left hand ain't doin' nothing. Maybe I could punch with my left hand."

So they fixed a contraption so that his left hand could thrust a second strip a little bit above the first. Booker was still dissatisfied. His feet were idle. So Ford got his engineers together and they fixed up a treadle for his right foot to work. Booker pointed to his left foot, just standing there. So they fixed a treadle for that foot. Then Booker was happy, pedaling with both feet, punching with both hands.

A week later, Booker was moping again. He thought if they put a metal collar around his neck and attached it to the machinery he could get more work done by bobbing his head back and forth. Henry Ford and his son worked on such an invention, got it patented and put it on Booker's neck. Booker beamed.

Nevertheless, two weeks later, he was nearly crying. The foreman asked him what was the matter. Booker told him that he thought he wasn't doing enough work. The foreman was amazed. After all, he was a benevolent friend of labor. "You got both hands punching, both feet pedaling, and your head bobbing. Why ain't you satisfied?" Booker brightened up. "I done figured it out. You see, Mister Bossman, I believe dat if you stuck a broom up my a—, I could sweep de floor."

Seeing Things

Some colored people . . . , particularly *Northern* ones, were quite sensitive about being considered poor. They had a habit, sometimes, of pretending to be wealthy to persons who did not know their true circumstances.

"You see 'at big mansion yon'ah?" asked one of Muskegon's colored barbers of a strange Negro who was visiting the town. "'At's my residence," he explained.

"Good Lawdy, bruddah, I sees two suns!" declared the amazed new arrival.

"'At big hotel's mine," said the Muskegonite.

"Lawdy, bruddah, I sees de stahs!" cried the bewildered visitor.

"'At sawmill's mine," continued the barber, "an' yon steamboat. 'N' I owns dis streetcar line, 'n' sev'ul o' dese big sto'es. 'N' I got money in *all* de banks!"

"Lawdy, bruddah!" exclaimed the awed newcomer, "I's a-seein' *diamonds!*"

"See 'at li'l', no-count bahber shop, yon'ah—all propped up wid bo'ds; look lak it g'ine t' fall down? I means 'at hole on de co'ner 'at's disgracin' de town. Well, I owns 'at, too. But I'm 'shame uv it!" (And *this* was all he *did* own!)

"Lawdy, ma bruddah!" exclaimed his new friend. "Now I's a-seein' *straight!*"

Black, White, and Blue

Two men [were] standing on the corner. One was a white man, the other wasn't. The first said, "I've got nothing but trouble. My house just burned down and I had no insurance. My wife just ran away with my best friend in my automobile and there are still ten payments due on it. My doctor just told me that I have to go to the hospital and have a serious operation. I sure have tough luck."

The second just looked at him and said, "What you kickin' 'bout? You white, ain' yuh?"

Farthest South

[A Cajun from the bayous of Louisiana] met up with [a] Virginia lady and mystified her with his speech and manner. At last she observed that he was like no other Southerner whom she had ever met. To this the bayou man replied, "Ma'am, if I'd be born any further to the south, I'd be a sof'-shell crab right now."

Cheese for the Swede

A greenhorn fresh from Sweden was sent to the Commercial Union, a grocery at Main and Seminary, [Galesburg, Illinois], run by Swedes. By mistake he went to a grocery where they didn't speak Swedish. He called for *ost*, meaning "cheese." They couldn't make out what he wanted. As he began repeating "*Ost! Ost!*" (pronounced "oost") they thought him a queer fish and a comic. After more of his howling "*Ost!*" they shooed him toward a door. There with his hand on a doorknob he gave them one final insulting blast, an ancient Swedish phrase, "*Kyss mej i röva*," meaning "Kiss my behind," the word *kyss* pronounced "shees." The Americans sprang to it, showed him just the cheese he wanted, and he brought home what he was sent for and said he had to fight for it.

The Letter

Once a German family emigrated to America and settled in Milwaukee. The oldest son, in his teens, concluded he would start out for himself. He "fetched up" in New York, and without any money, so he wrote home: "Dear Father, I am sick and lonely and without a single cent. Send me some money quick. Your son John." The old man couldn't read, so he took the letter to a friend—a great strapping butcher with a loud gruff voice and an arrogant manner of reading. When the letter was read to him the father was furious and declared he would not send his son a cent—not even to keep him from starving. But on his way home he kept thinking about the letter and wanting to hear it again, so he took it to another friend—a consumptive undertaker who had a gentle voice with an appealing inflection in it. When this man read the letter the father burst into tears and exclaimed, "My poor boy! I shall send him all the money he wants."

The Three Dreams

Once upon a time there were three hobos, an Italian, a Mexican, and an American. Upon arriving at a small town, they jumped off the train and began looking for something to eat. They walked and walked but could not find anything.

"Listen, my companions, we'll stay here tonight in this town," said the Mexican, "and when it begins to get dark, we'll go to a house that I'm acquainted with and where I know there are many chickens. We'll take one and bring it here for breakfast."

So at dusk they started out to get the chicken. Soon they returned with a nice fat hen and immediately began to cook it in their campfire. The three were so hungry that each one could have eaten the entire chicken alone. The Italian suggested that they lie down and go to sleep, and the one that had the nicest dream should have the entire chicken for his breakfast. They agreed to this and lay down to their dreams.

When the Mexican saw that his two companions were sound asleep, he got up very quietly and ate the hen, [then went back to sleep]. The American was the first to wake up, and he awoke the other two.

The Mexican told the Italian to tell his dream first, and this is what he said he dreamed. "I had the most wonderful dream that I've ever had. I dreamed that I was marrying a beautiful princess, and I was marrying in Heaven. The largest band in the city of New York was there to play for us."

Then the American said, "Yes, and I dreamt that you had come to invite me to be your best man, so I asked the bride's sister to be the maid of honor."

The Mexican joined in, "When I saw you going heavenward, I thought, 'I don't know when they'll return, and the chicken might spoil in the meantime,' and so I got up and ate it."

The Tourist and the Indian

A tourist bought a buckskin and bead trinket at the [Albuquerque] station, paying the Indian his asking price of $1.00. Later, in Los Angeles, he saw the same article in a curio store for fifty cents.

Again in Albuquerque he happened to see the very same Indian offering the same beaded work for $1.00.

"Look here," said the tourist, "I bought one of those from you the last time I was here. Then in Los Angeles I saw the very same thing for fifty cents. How come?"

The Indian was unperturbed. "Oh," he sighed, "you never can trust a white man."

Foreigners

Mr. and Mrs. Mandelbaum were on a train passing through Albuquerque, New Mexico. At the station Mandelbaum got off and an Indian offered to sell him a rug. The two argued and haggled but no purchase was made.

When Mandelbaum returned to the train, his wife remarked, "That was a beautiful rug. Sorry you didn't buy it."

"We couldn't get together," explained Mandelbaum. "I couldn't understand his language and he couldn't understand my language."

"Well," said Mrs. Mandelbaum, "I suppose he hasn't been long in the country."

☞ **5** ☜

Cool Customers

"How much are herrings this morning?" "Three cents apiece." "Ah, I'll take one.—Keep beer?" "Yes." "How much a glass?" "Three cents." "Oh, ah, well, I won't take the herring—I'll take beer; herring's three cents; beer's three cents; give me the beer—there's the herring." "See here, you haven't paid for the beer." "Paid for it; of course I haven't; I gave you the herring for it; both the same price, you said." "Y-e-s—I know, but you didn't pay for the herring." "Pay for it! Of course I didn't. Why should I? I didn't take it, did I?"

MARSHALL BROWN

Introduction

"Down South," writes O. Henry, "whenever any one perpetrates some particularly monumental piece of foolishness, everybody says: 'Send for Jesse Holmes.'" Although this club-wielding imaginary Fool Killer, or hoaxer and mauler of fools, took knaves for his favorite victims, the greatest fool baiter in anecdotal humor is the knave himself, who replaced a club with "sharp practice spiced with good humor."

On coming to America, the cheerful rogue, one of the oldest and most universal of comic types, found that he had more than a few new tricks to learn, especially tricks of the trade. Some of these required new words, Americanisms associated with the predatory and cheating practices of pursuit and capture, humbug and confidence games: badger game, ballyhoo, buncombe, bunco-steerer, four-flusher, gimmick, gold brick, guyascutus, poker face, spellbinder; to bulldoze, to call one's bluff or throw a bluff, to get one's goat, to play possum, to play someone for a sucker, to put someone up a stump or tree, to raise the wind, to settle one's hash, to skin, to skunk, to swallow hook, line and sinker.

In borrowing the vocabulary and the technique of deception and imposition, the practical, artistic trickster inevitably became something of a showman, spellbinder, and humbug himself. At the same time, as illustrated elsewhere in this book, others have been quick to learn the use of stratagem, ruse, and hoax. This was especially true in backwoods America, where "irrepressible cussedness" had to be met with irrepressible cussedness.

In the wide regional, occupational, and social diversity of America the trickster displays considerable variation, from the sharp Yorker tricks of horse-trading David Hannum to the cruel Western hoaxes of Roy Bean, from the roguish mischief of the Delaware River raftsman hero, "Boney" Quillan, to the Wall Street operations of Jay Gould.

For refreshing relief from the exploitations of the cool, tough, hard customers, we turn to the strategy of the queer customers, who succeed in giving their tormentors or oppressors their come-uppance. These are the "originals" and "rugged individualists," like the "Fighting Farmer" and the Young Kentuckian, who insist on their rights, including the right to be themselves. In the democracy of our picaresque anecdotal humor there is room for both the predatory slyness of Brer Fox and the retaliatory resilience of Brer Rabbit.

Fighting Farmer

A farmer in Vermont, who was a plain, pious man, regular in the discharge of his duty, both to God and his neighbor, was for a long time plagued by an overgrown bear, which had learned its cue so thoroughly as only to commit its depredations on the Sabbath, when he knew by experience the coast was clear. Wearied out with his repeated trespasses, the good man resolved to take his gun and conceal himself in the fields on the following Sunday. The bear came, according to custom; he fired, and shot it dead. This explosion, during the hours of worship, put the pious people in consternation.

As soon as the minister and deacons ascertained the cause, they ordered him to attend a special church meeting, and show cause, if he had any, why he should not be excommunicated for his daring impiety. He did attend; but not satisfied to be so publicly scandalized for an action he believed to be his duty, he went to the appointment with a loaded gun.

Scarcely had the holy parson pronounced the words "offending brother," when the honest veteran leveled his deadly weapon and cried out, "Proceed, if you dare—proceed, and you are a dead man." After a pause, the terrified parson gave the paper to the eldest deacon, and desired him to read it. The deacon, with stammering accents and startling eyes, began as he was ordered; but again the devoted victim aimed his gun, and exclaimed, "Desist and march. I will not live in shame. March, I say, or you are all dead men." The parson leaped from the desk, the deacons followed in great trepidation; and the women, with shrieks, sought their homes. The victor, thus left to himself, locked the church, sent the keys to the pastor, with his best respects, and lived thirteen years after, a brother in full communion.

Rotten Eggs

We bought eggs in unlimited quantities. From July on we had to be careful. Farmers were busy with haying, and the hens weren't watched so closely. One would steal away a nest and set on the eggs a week or so. Of course, the eggs would go in the crate just the same, and once a lot got by the clerk and caused trouble. The next time the farmer came in, the clerk said, "Mr. Crymble, those last eggs you brought in were rotten." The old farmer struck an attitude of surprise and said, "Well—damn a hen that will lay rotten eggs!"

Juggling the Expense Account

In White River Junction one might be driven to do anything, but usually there were two or three of us stranded together, so we found some way of entertaining ourselves even if we were reduced to exchanging stories about the ways we managed to get ahead of the home office. Personally, I never did pad my expense account unless I was driven to it; but however scrupulous I was, the treasurer always found some item of expense to complain about. Once I was goaded into telling him that if it was his idea that my job was to save money for the firm, the best way he could do it was to take me off the road. That kept him quiet for a while.

One traveler I met told how he had charged an item for taking a customer to a show, and the treasurer made a great howl about it. The next week when the drummer was given his money, the treasurer said, "I didn't see any item this week for entertainment." As the drummer put his money in his pocket, he answered, "No, you didn't see it, but it was there just the same."

Our favorite story at that time was about the new man that a company sent to Maine to make one trip for their old salesman, who was sick. When he came back to the office, the treasurer said the young fellow had forgotten to charge for a team to Vinalhaven and he should have included it, as the old man always did. The salesman was on the spot. He didn't like to point out that Vinalhaven is an island about ten miles offshore.

Rabbit Sandwiches

Clem was quite a feller. He was deacon in the church, assistant treasurer of the lodge, sergeant in the fire department, truant officer, on the committee for Bigger and Better and More Profitable Business, and lots of other things. Clem had more titles than a porcupine has quills.

How Clem got the idea, the Lord only knows, but somehow he got the notion he could make quite a bit of change by selling rabbit sandwiches. Anyhow, he put a stock out in front the house and started selling them like hot cakes to the autos what come through with out-of-state folks in them.

He went along pretty good for a couple of months cutting bread and spreading on rabbit meat, and then one day the pure-food officer come down from Bangor and dropped in on him. He says to Clem, "How in Sam Hill do you git enough rabbit meat to put in all them sandwiches?"

"Oh, I git it," says Clem.

"Is it all rabbit meat you use?" says the feller.

"Every bit of it's rabbit meat," says Clem, "that is all but just a mite."

"Then you do use a little other meat?"

"Just a mite now and then," says Clem.

"What other kind of meat do you use?"

"Sometimes I just put in a pinch of horse meat to give it foundation."

"I don't see how you have enough rabbit meat even then," says the feller. "What proportion do you use?"

"Fifty-fifty," says Clem.

"Fifty-fifty, eh? Seems to me that's quite a 'pinch.' How do you measure to be sure it's fifty-fifty?"

"There ain't no trouble to that." says Clem. "I take one rabbit and one horse."

Bringing in the Log

A rather tyrannical *paterfamilias* . . . , one cold night, noting that the fire needed replenishing, sent his young son out to the barnyard with orders to bring in a certain big log which had been lying there for some time. The boy returned in a few minutes to say that, though he had tried his best, he couldn't lift the log. "What's that?" cried the tyrant. "Now you git out there, and don't you come back into this house without that log!" The boy, who had stood about all he could of such treatment, and whose patience was about exhausted, went out, walked down to the docks, and stowed away on a whaler which he knew was sailing at dawn.

Something more than three years later he returned to the old home port and walked up town to see the folks. Passing through the yard, he noticed the same old log still lying there. Having grown in stature and strength, he shouldered it with ease, opened the door, and stalked into the kitchen, where the old man, who had long mourned him as lost, sat smoking his pipe before the fire. Throwing his burden down on the hearth, the boy greeted his dad with: "There, Pa. There's your d—d old log!"

Dreaming-Match

Sir William Jones, who was superintendent of Indian affairs in America previous to the Revolution, received several suits of clothes from England richly laced, when Hendrick, king of one of the five nations of Mohawks, was present. The chief admired them much, but said nothing at the time. In a few days Hendrick called on Sir William, and told him he had had a particular dream. When Sir William inquired what it was, he told him that he had dreamed that he gave him one of those fine suits which he had received from over the water.

Sir William took the hint, and presented him with one of the richest dresses; and Hendrick, much pleased with his generosity, retired. A short time after, Sir William, happening to be in company with the Indian chief, told him that he also had had a dream. Hendrick, being very solicitous to know what it was, Sir William informed him that he dreamed he had made him a present of a particular tract of land of about 5,000 acres. The land was the most valuable on the Mohawk River; however, Hendrick immediately presented it, with this shrewd remark, "Now, Sir William, I will never dream with you again. You dream too hard for me." The tract thus obtained is still called Sir William's Dreaming Land.

Stolen Flour

Long before America was settled there were stories about millers who got the better of their customers. In Chenango County, [New York], they tell how a farmer tried to turn the tables. At Chenango Forks he went to the grist mill to get a sack of flour; and while the miller's back was turned, he dipped a few scoops from an open bag into his own. Next day the farmer returned.

"Say," he said, "that flour you sold me was no good: my wife tried to make some bread with it, and the dum stuff wouldn't rise."

"I'm not surprised," said the miller mildly. "I didn't think the bread would rise when I saw you putting in that lime."

David Hannum and the Kicker

Cortland County, [New York], is full of horse-dealers . . . but . . . all acknowledged that David Hannum [the original of "David Harum"] was the greatest horse-swapper ever known in that part of the country. . . . He was never known to get the worst of a horse-trade, [except in] one instance. . . .

Hannum had a horse known to be a kicker in all the country, and for this reason the animal was only worth twenty or thirty dollars, when it looked worth five hundred dollars. David tried to trade him off in half a dozen trades, but the kicker always came back. Dave finally worked the beast off on an unsuspecting citizen of Cortland. The horse was practically useless to anyone. Whenever he was hitched up he proceeded at once to kick the dashboard and everything else in reach to flinders.

One day a man named Miller, who had long had it in for Hannum, conceived an idea to get even, so he bought the horse for a song and had him clipped. In those days clipping horses was a new thing, and clipping this horse made a great difference in his appearance. Miller hitched the horse to an old streetcar that ran from Cortland to Homer, and started out. The horse began to kick, but the iron dashboard of the car was as hard as his heels, so it did not do him any good. The horse was game, however, and kicked steadily all the way, but by the time he got to Homer he was a pretty limp and used-up animal. His spirit was all gone, for the time at least. This was just as Miller wanted him to be, and without losing any time he set out to find David Hannum. As usual Hannum was in Zimmer's barbershop telling stories.

"I have got a fine horse I want to sell you," said Miller.

There was not a more welcome word that came to Hannum's ears. He set out at once to look at the animal. With his hair clipped off and with broken-down spirits and a look of meekness in his eyes, Hannum failed to recognize the kicker that he had sold a few days before, and he bought the horse back again for two or three hundred dollars, thinking he was getting a great bargain. He did get more than he anticipated, for next morning when he started to take the horse out to test its gait the beast had recovered all its old-time spirit, and in the short trip from the stable to the street, managed to kick the buggy into little pieces and to throw Hannum and a friend out of the buggy into the dirt. David got to his feet as quickly as he could and said "damn" a few times. That was the extent of his profanity but he never again spoke to Miller as long as he lived.

Les Hathaway and the Game Warden

[A] young [game] warden kept after [Les Hathaway] . . . and finally caught him ten miles back in the woods, sitting beside a pack basket filled with fresh meat. "This time I got you with the evidence," the warden said. "Off we go to the judge."

"Yep," Les agreed, "but you got to carry the evidence. The law can hang a man but it don't say he has to tote his own gallows."

The warden picked up the pack basket, which weighed about fifty pounds, and lugged it out of the woods. Les followed behind like a carefree beagle. They got to the judge. The warden was about to present his case when Les said, "Judge, is there any law about letting a man buy a calf, skin it out, and take the meat into the woods, just to have it handy in case he gets hungry?" At that, Les opened the basket and took out the meat. "You can see for yourself, Judge," Les said. "That's veal, not venison. Sorry it was so heavy, Warden."

The Umbrella Dog

When I was about fourteen years old, my father lived on the old farm up at Poughkeepsie. One day after I had finished a five-acre field of corn my father let me go to town to see a circus. When in town I saw for the first time a spotted coach dog. It took my fancy and I bought it and took it home. When father saw it his good old Puritan face fell.

"Why, Chauncey," he said sadly, "we don't want any spotted dog on the farm. It would drive the cattle crazy."

"No, he won't, Father," I said, "he's a blooded dog."

The next day it was raining and I took the dog out in the woods to try him on a coon, but the rain was too much for him. It washed the spots off. That night I took the dog back to the dog dealer with a long face. Said I, "Look at that dog, sir. The spots have all washed off."

"Great guns, boy!" exclaimed the dog dealer. "There was an umbrella went with that dog. Didn't you get an umbrella?"

Why He Was a Democrat

The teacher of the district school up at Peekskill called up the three brightest boys in his class one day and said, "Tom, you are a Republican?"

"Yes, sir."

"And, Jim, you are a Prohibitionist?"

"Yes, sir."

"And, Sam, you are a Democrat?"

"Yes, sir."

"Well, now, the one of you that can give me the best reason why he belongs to his party can have this woodchuck I caught on my way to school this morning. Now, Tom, why are you a Republican?"

"I am a Republican," said the boy, "because the Republican party saved the country in this war, abolished slavery, and brought about the resumption of specie payments, and has done everything for the good of the country."

"That's very good," said the teacher.

"I am a Prohibitionist," said the Prohibitionist boy glibly, "because rum is filling the jail and filling the poorhouse, and ultimately it will ruin the country, and if we could have prohibition we would not need any prison or poorhouse. Everybody would be well off."

"That is a good reason," said the teacher. "Now what is the reason you are a Democrat, Sam?"

"Well, sir," was the reply, "I am a Democrat because I want the woodchuck."

Jay Gould and the Rector

The rector of the church which was attended by Jay Gould, the great Wall Street tycoon . . . , was getting ready to retire and fortunately had accumulated about thirty thousand dollars during his lifetime by scrimping and saving. He asked for advice.

"I'm going to tell you something with the understanding the information is for your ears only," said Mr. Gould. The preacher agreed.

"Take your money and buy Missouri Pacific."

He did and for some months the stock went up, and each day the minister was richer on paper. Then suddenly bad times came, and he was wiped out. Sadly he went to see Mr. Gould.

"I took your advice and have lost all my savings," he reported.

"I am sorry," replied the great man. "You say the amount was thirty thousand dollars. To restore your faith, I am going to give you a check for forty thousand dollars."

He wrote it out and handed it to him. The minister looked at it reluctantly.

"I must confess something," he began as he fumbled with the piece of paper. "I didn't keep my word to you, I told several members of the congregation."

"Oh, I know that," replied Mr. Gould cheerfully. "They were the ones I was after."

A Deal in Manure

As Commodore [Vanderbilt] controlled the old horse-car stables on Fourth Avenue, William [H. Vanderbilt] suggested buying there the manure with which to enrich his fields at New Dorp. He told his father that he would pay him at the rate of $4.00 per load for the treasure. The price being princely and the deal having been consummated, the Commodore, a week or two later, asked his son how many loads had been ferried to Staten Island.

The answer being, "One," the Commodore seemed a little surprised.

"Why, son, they tell me that your men put as high as twenty loads on that big scow of yours."

"No, Father, I never let them put more than one load on, at a time: one scow-load, I mean."

The Commodore, realizing suddenly that he had, all unaware, brought a Machiavelli into the world, thereupon persuaded him to desert the thin soil of Staten Island for richer fields of finance.

A Switch in Tactics

The devices by which publications solicit advertising are often masterpieces of statistical strategy; sometimes, however, the charts and graphs fail, and a switch in tactics is indicated.

There was the time, for example, that a magazine which specializes in gaudy and slightly risqué cartoons, as well as slick paintings of more-or-less naked young ladies, was hell-bent on persuading a famous piano manufacturer to advertise in its pages. The piano company executive in charge of advertising was an exceedingly strait-laced and primly proper pillar of society, and he wanted no part of this lush and lavish magazine. In fact, after the magazine's chief salesman had made several impassioned presentations of circulation figures and relevant statistics, the executive gave orders that the man was not to be admitted to his office again.

In desperation, the salesman one day fought his way past several secretaries and burst breathlessly into the executive's sanctum.

"Mr. Smith," he gasped, accosting the startled gentleman at his desk, "is it true that yesterday at lunch with my friend Brown you told him you thought the circulation of my magazine was chiefly in bawdy houses?"

"Well—ah," said the executive, "I may have made such an observation."

"And a mighty keen observation it was," screamed the salesman. "And now, let me ask you just one question: *Have you ever been in a bawdy house that didn't have a piano?*"

The Quaker and the Dashing Buck

A venerable Friend and a dashing buck, driving their respective vehicles, met in a narrow road, where neither could pass without the consent of the other. After some dispute, as to which should first turn out, the buck drew a newspaper from his pocket and set about perusing it very diligently; upon which the Friend, with characteristic composure, asked, "Friend, has thee another paper in thy pocket?" "No!" "Then when thee has done reading the one in thy hand, I would thank thee to loan it to me!"

The Chalk Line

"Once upon a time" there came to this city [of Richmond] a young Kentuckian, for the purpose of learning the sciences of medicine and surgery. He was tall and athletic, shrewd, apt, and intelligent, with a "little sprinkling" of waggishness. He was inducted into the Charity Hospital, and a room in the third story given him as a study. On entering into his new quarters, he was introduced to a young French gentleman, occupying the room also as a student.

The young Frenchman, it seems, was very frank in his manners, courteous, yet cold, and he thus addressed his new companion:

"Sir, I am indeed pleased to see you, and hope that we may prove mutually agreeable; but in order that this may be the case, I will inform you that I have had several former roommates, with none of whom I could ever agree—we could never pursue our studies together. This room contains two beds; as the oldest occupant, I claim that nearest the window."

The Kentuckian assented.

"Now," says the Frenchman, "I'll draw the boundary line between our territories, and we shall agree not to encroach upon the other's rights," and taking a piece of chalk from his pocket, he made the mark of division, midway, from one side of the room to the other. "Sir," he added, "I hope you have no objection to the treaty."

"None in the world, sir," answered the stranger, "I am perfectly satisfied with it." He then sent down for his baggage and both students sat down with their books.

The Frenchman was soon deeply engaged, while "Old Kentuck" was watching him, and thinking what a singular genius he must be, and how he might "fix" him.

Thus things went on until dinner time came. The bell was rung; the Frenchman popped up, adjusted his cravat, brushed up his whiskers and mustachios, and essayed to depart.

"Stand, sir!" said the stranger, suddenly placing himself with toe to the mark, directly before the French student. "If you cross that line, you are a dead man."

The Frenchman stood pale with astonishment. The Kentuckian moved not a muscle of his face. Both remained in silence for some moments, when the Frenchman exclaimed, "Is it possible that I did not reserve the right of passage?"

"No, sir, indeed you did not; and you pass this line at your peril."

"But how shall I get out of the room?"

"There is the window which you *reserved* to yourself—you may use that; but you pass not that door—my door, which you generously left me."

The poor Frenchman was fairly caught. He was in a quandary, and made all sorts of explanations and entreaties. The Kentuckian took compassion on him, and thinking that going out of a third-story window was not "what it's cracked up to be," said to his new friend, "Sir, in order that we may be mutually agreeable, I'll rub out that hateful chalk line and let you pass."

The Frenchman politely thanked him, and since the settlement of that "boundary question" they have been the very best friends.

Non-Transferable

The use of passes by senators and representatives was an open secret. . . . All newspaper editors and correspondents were known to have annual railroad passes, and into this category fell Colonel Henry Watterson, editor of the Louisville *Courier-Journal*, as did one of the *Courier-Journal's* correspondents, a certain Mr. Smith. Of course the passes were stamped "Not transferable," and it was the duty of the conductors to seize any railroad pass in the possession of a passenger not entitled to it.

One day on the Louisville and Nashville Railway a passenger presented the pass that had been issued to Mr. Smith, correspondent of the *Courier-Journal*. The conductor scrutinized him suspiciously. "You may be Mr. Smith," he declared, "but I don't recognize you." "But I'm Smith," the passenger protested. "And I work for Colonel Henry Watterson." "In that case," the dubious conductor replied, "we'll soon find out. Colonel Watterson happens to be in the car ahead. Suppose you come up and be identified."

There was nothing for the impostor to do but comply with the request. He could not escape from the moving train. The conductor, perhaps with a vision of triumph, led him forward. He stopped at the seat occupied by a most distinguished-looking passenger. "Colonel Watterson," he said, "this man tells me he works for you, that his name is Mr. Smith." "Yes," was the reply. "Sit down, Smith."

The impostor was bewildered at his luck, but he sat down as requested, and the conductor, apologizing, left the two. The two men talked briefly, but after a time the conversation began to lag. The impostor, who had borrowed the pass from the real Smith, had had such a pleasant and unexpected reception he became conscience-stricken. Finally, he decided to apologize, now feeling sure that Colonel Watterson was testing him and biding his time. "It was magnanimous of you, Colonel Watterson, to save me from embarrassment. You knew all the time I wasn't Smith." A smile circled the lips of the other. "Compose yourself, young man," he said, "I don't happen to be Colonel Watterson, but I am riding on his railroad pass."

"Old Bell-Ringer"

On one of the Western rivers flourished, once, a steamboat captain, . . . known under the *sobriquet* of Captain Windy, as well as "The Bell-Ringer." . . . 'Tis said—and 'tis very likely, for the captain was very pompous, and much given to "showing his authority"—that upon one occasion, having engaged a second clerk who was supposed to be rather unsophisticated in relation to river matters, our windy friend thought he had a subject, and convened a congregation of the pilots, the clerks, the mates, the barkeepers, etc., in the "Social Hall," under the pretext of "liquoring all round." While expectancy was at its height, he arose in his majesty, and addressed his new subordinate, in a "top-lofty" strain, to the following effect:

"My friend, you have entered upon the responsible office of second clerk of the steamer *Gas Blower*, and it is of the utmost importance that you should understand and attend to the bell signals in vogue upon this institution. I wish you to give close attention to my words while I explain them, so that you may understand, and I may not be under the necessity of explaining them again for your benefit. Young man, do you hear?"

"Yes, sir," meekly responded the victim of eloquence.

"Very well," resumed the orator. "One stroke means, 'Sound on the starboard'; two means, 'Sound on the larboard'—with these you have nothing to do; three strokes of the bell means, 'Come aboard all, for the boat is about to start.' When you are attending to anything ashore you need not come aboard until you hear *the three strokes*, then you must hurry over the stages. Young man, do you understand?"

"I think I do," was the response.

"Repeat the signals."

The clerk did as required; and the captain, having achieved this oratorical effort entirely to his satisfaction, ordered on the liquor.

Matters went on smooth enough for a day or two, while the new clerk had time to "learn the ropes"; but one fine morning, as the steamer was lying at ————, and the young man was comfortably seated upon a pile of lumber on the levee, where he had been checking freight, the captain made ready to start, and was about to order the stages to be drawn in when, casting his eye ashore, he espied his clerk in the position described.

"Come aboard," said he.

"Ring your bell," said the clerk, making no movement to come aboard.

The captain, provoked, seized the bell-rope, and gave three furious pulls, but no voice from the bell; and he pulled again, more furiously than before, but to no avail—the bell was mute.

"Come aboard!" thundered he to his clerk.

"Ring your bell!"

The captain again tried, but could not win the slightest tinkle from the "brazen throat of the bell."

"Come aboard, or we will leave you!" cried the captain, amidst renewed efforts to ring the bell, and the whole boat's crew laughing at him. Again the captain tried, with curses loud and deep, but to no avail.

"Pilot!" yelled he. "Shove off—"

"Ring your bell," pealed in from the shore before he could finish the order.

The captain seized an ax, rushed to the hurricane deck and struck three sounding blows upon the obstinate bell.

The clerk then coolly picked himself from the pile of boards, and walked aboard, while the wrathful commander tore from the clapper a quantity of old carpeting, with which the bell had been muffled. And since that day the captain of the *Gas Blower* has been known as "Old Bell-Ringer."

Putting a Yankee in His Place

Colonel Carrington was a fair specimen of an Arkansas gentleman; if not fully up to all the ways of genteel society, he was courteous and affable, extremely sensitive to insult, and of a hasty temper. During the fall of 1844 he was a passenger on board of a steamboat ascending the Arkansas River. One day, at dinner, he was seated opposite a Yankee who was full of talk, and ambitious of playing the agreeable to those around him. The colonel, with the freedom of Western manners, had helped himself to the butter with his own knife. Then he took a dish of preserves, and with the same knife raked off upon his plate what he wished. This was too much for the Yankee's ideas of good manners, and in his opinion it required reproof. Raising a butter knife that was lying by the butter plate, he held it up, and then, in a tone of voice loud enough to be heard by all at the table, he addressed the colonel: "Will you inform me what this is, sir?"

"A butter knife," replied the colonel.

"Good!" said the Yankee, and raising a spoon, he continued, "*Now* tell me what this is?"

"A spoon," said the colonel.

"Good, you answer very correctly," added the impertinent questioner, and resumed his dinner.

Those who knew Colonel Carrington looked to see him leap over the table to cut the fellow in two. But not so; he preferred to cut him up more leisurely. Drawing a bowie knife from the back of his neck, with a blade at least eighteen inches long, he held it up, and, imitating the Yankee's manner, said, "Do you know what *that* is?"

The man hesitated a moment. "Speak out!" roared the colonel fiercely.

"A bo-owie knife!" stammered the other.

"Good!" said the colonel, placing it upon the butter knife. Then pulling a pistol from his pocket, he went on in the same tremendous tone, "Now, sir, tell me what *that* is," pointing the muzzle right at the fellow's head.

"For mercy's sake," cried he, "don't shoot me! I meant no harm; indeed I did not!" gasped the frightened man.

"Then speak out," thundered the colonel, "or I will!"

"A p-p-pistol!" groaned the man, now ready to wilt in his seat.

"Good, you answer very correctly indeed," and the colonel placed the pistol across the spoon, and resumed his dinner, as if nothing had occurred. In a moment afterward the Yankee rose to steal away from the table. The colonel insisted on his keeping his seat, and a glance at the toothpick and shooting iron kept him there for a few minutes, but he soon evaporated, and was seen no more on that trip.

Yankee Pilot

My friend the captain was formerly in command of one of the Mississippi River steamers, and one morning, while his boat was lying at her moorings at New Orleans, waiting for the tardy pilot—who, it appears, was a rather uncertain sort of a fellow—a tall, gaunt Yankee made his appearance before the captain's office, and sung out, "Hello, Cap'n! You don't want a pilot nor nothin' about this 'ere craft, do ye?"

"How do you know I don't?" responded the captain.

"Oh, you don't understand; I axed you s'posin' you *did*?"

"Then, supposing I do, what of it?"

"Well," said the Yankee, "I reckon I know suthin' about that ere sort o' business, provided you wanted a feller of jest about my size."

The captain gave him a scrutinizing glance, and with an expression of countenance which seemed to say, "I should pity the snags!" asked, "Are you acquainted with the river, and do you know where the snags are?"

"Well, ye-as," responded the Yankee, rather hesitatingly, "I'm pretty well acquainted with the river; but—the snags—I don't know exactly so much about."

"Don't know about the snags!" exclaimed the captain contemptuously. "Don't know about the snags! You'd make a pretty pilot!"

At this the Yankee's countenance assumed anything but an angelic expression, and with a darkened brow and a fiercely flashing eye, he drew himself up to his full height, and indignantly roared back in a voice of thunder, "What do I want to know where the snags are for, old sea-hoss? I know *where they ain't*; and there's where I do my sailing!"

It is sufficient to know that the Yankee was promptly engaged, and that the captain takes pleasure in saying that he proved himself one of the best pilots on the river.

Calling Dalton's Bluff

During the early Kansas days, when the notorious Dalton gang was terrorizing the state, trainmen on railroads were always terrified when any of the Dalton boys boarded their train, fearing they contemplated a holdup.

One of the Dalton boys, the recognized leader of the gang, had a habit, when traveling from one point to another, of bluffing the conductors into carrying him free.

One day the Dalton gang leader boarded a train, and when the conductor came around and demanded his fare, Dalton whipped out his gun and snarled, "There's my fare," as he shoved his gun into the conductor's ribs.

"All right, you ride, Dalton," coolly answered the conductor, walking on through the car.

The conductor proceeded into the baggage car and procured a sawed-off shotgun. When he returned, Dalton was leaning out of the car window, so taking him unaware, the conductor calmly walked up to him, shoved the gun into his ribs and said, "Say, Dalton, I'm ready to punch your ticket now." And Dalton came across.

How Roy Bean Collected for the Beer

The passenger trains always stopped at Langtry for the engines to take on water. One hot day when the train stopped, a passenger alighted and hurried over to the Jersey Lily, the sign on which was very visible from the railroad, for a bottle of beer. He found the proprietor sleeping peacefully on a billiard table.

Raising himself lazily on his elbow, Roy Bean said, "You'll find a cold bottle behind the bar. Help yourself." Then he relapsed to the reclining posture. He heard his customer run out of the room, but he did not hear the tinkle of coin on the bar. He sat up and looked. There was no money on the bar. He was filled with wrath.

Grabbing from the pool table on which he lay his cartridge belt, with the ever reliable Colt's attached to it, he began buckling it on and making tracks for the train. As he ran up, the conductor was about to signal the engineer to go ahead. "Hold that train," the judge yelled. The conductor saw the judge still fooling with his belt and obeyed. "I got business on this train," old Roy hastily explained. "Hold it till I get back."

As he entered the smoking car, his gun was in a working position. He had no trouble locating his customer. He demanded four-bits for the bottle of beer. The startled customer took one look at the gun and quickly held out a ten-dollar bill. The judge jammed it into his pocket.

"Fifty cents for the beer and nine dollars and fifty for collecting," he announced. "This squares your account. You can keep the bottle." As he stepped off the car, he thanked the conductor, adding, "You can go ahead now as soon as you damn please."

The Corn Thief

When I was a boy my daddy had a log barn. He noticed that somebody was regular swiping corn through a chink in the logs. So one evening he sets a steel trap jest inside the chink.

Well, early next morning when he goes down to the crib to feed and milk, he notices a neighbor standing on his tiptoes right beside the chink and his hand inside. But he don't pay him any particular mind. Jest says, "Mawnin', neighbor," and goes on doing the milking. The neighbor sorter shifts toes and mumbles something and keeps on standing there. After a while, though, he can't stand it any longer, or makes up his mind, or something, and begins to beg for mercy.

Well, Dad goes inside and opens up the trap and the neighbor goes away. And, by gosh, do you know, we never did miss nary 'nuther ear of corn.

 **6**

A Passel of Fools

When I was a boy . . . I attended a circus down here in the hills of old Kentucky. As I stood looking at the first monkey I ever saw, an old man stepped up behind me and took a good look at the monkey. He turned to me and said: "I've always heard these things look like a human being. But they don't look any more like a human than I do."

JOHN O. REID

Introduction

The typical American fool is a "character." A character, as any American knows, is a damn fool who insists on being himself instead of being like everybody else, or a crazy fool who runs around the country poking his nose into every corner and into everybody else's business.

The relativity of characters is the point of the story about the spinster who had enjoyed her summer on Cape Cod so much that she could not refrain from confiding in the native who was driving her to the station with her luggage. "The thing I like about Provincetown," she said, "is that it is so full of quaint people." "Yes," the driver agreed, "but they all leave after Labor Day."

The local character is either a stubborn old fool, "sot" in his ways, or a callow young fool, still wet behind the ears, who doesn't know, care, or say beans about anything. But the favorite American fool is the newcomer who rushes in where natives fear to tread, like the tough kid from Brooklyn who, according to Jack Paar, was spending his vacation on a dude ranch out west. One morning after a hike, he returned with two rattles off a rattlesnake. Asked where he got them, the tough kid replied, "Off a woim!"

While America has no proverbial fool towns, comparable to Gotham and Chelm, the backwoods, as the place where "rusticity reigns supreme," is the natural habitat of fools, with the illiterate hillbilly (the comic version of the poor white) as the modern counterpart of the uncouth backwoodsman and the foil of the educated fool.

Since the stranger and ignoramus invariably give themselves away by asking foolish questions, the inquiring traveler, from the inquisitive Yankee to the Arkansaw Traveler, is a subtype of the newcomer fool. According to Hoffman Birney, the Grand Canyon rangers' favorite story is that of the lady who told her guide that "the only thing I can't understand is how the river got 'way down there at the bottom.'" "Lady," he told her solemnly, "that's one of th' funniest things about this here place. Th' river used to be up here on th' rim, but one day it just slipped off."

Thus, linking the fool, the trickster, and the liar, the tenderfoot tall tale developed out of the need to teach the "young and tender . . . the great verities by generous untruths."

Blundering upon Wealth

[Lord Timothy Dexter, a native of Newburyport, Massachusetts],
"more famed for his money than his wit," very anxiously inquired of
some merchants, whom he knew, how he should dispose of a few
hundred dollars. Willing to hoax him, they answered, "Why, buy a
cargo of warming-pans, and send them to the West Indies, to be
sure." Not suspecting the trick, he bought all the warming-pans he
could find, and sent them to a climate where there was every reason
to suppose that ice would be far more acceptable. But "Providence
sometimes shows his contempt of wealth by giving it to fools." The
warming-pans met with a rapid sale; the tops being used for strain-
ers and the lower part for dippers, in the manufacture of molasses.

With the proceeds of this profitable cargo, he built a vessel; and
being informed by the carpenter that wales were wanting, he called
on an acquaintance, and said, "My head workman sends me word
that he wants wales for the vessel. What does he mean?" "Why,
whale bones, to be sure," answered the man, who, like everybody
else, was willing to impose on his stupidity. Whale bones were accordingly bought; but finding that Boston could not furnish enough,
he emptied New York and Philadelphia. The ship carpenters,

of course, had a hearty laugh at his expense; but, by a singular turn of fortune, this blunder also was the means of increasing his wealth. It soon after became fashionable for ladies to wear stays completely lined with whale bone; and as none was to be found in the country, it brought an immense price. Thus his coffers were a second time filled by his odd speculations.

Great-Coats and Children

Judge Lightfoot, of Rhode Island, used to relate that when at the bar and going to Connecticut on circuit, he traveled from Newport to Pomfret, when he was overtaken by a snowstorm. He had no great-coat, and took refuge in a public-house and called for some refreshment. The landlady was very inquisitive, and according to her custom put several searching interrogatories, to which he gave his answers, though famishing. Where had he come from? From Newport. Where was he going to? To visit the Six Nations. Had he no great-coat? No, he never wore one. How many children had he? Nine. At this point her amazement could not be contained, and she shouted out, "Husband, husband! Come here. Here is a man with nine children, and he says he never wore a great-coat; and yet I have made you a dozen, and child never a one have we had—never a one!"

The Limits of Telegraphy

When it was first reported that Professor Morse had succeeded in conveying intelligence between Baltimore and Washington, through the wires of the magnetic telegraph, one old *savant*, who had been a schoolmaster, and a member of the Legislature, gave it as *his* opinion, that the report was "a humbug." In fact, from his knowledge of "astronomy," he said he *knew* the thing could not be done!

Shortly after, [line] men were seen setting the poles directly by the old man's dwelling. One day he joined the crowd who were witnessing the operation of stretching the wire. Upon being asked what he thought of the matter *then*, he hesitated a moment—assuming an air of importance—and then replied, "Well, gentlemen, while in the Legislature I gave the subject considerable attention, and after much investigation and reflection, I have come to the conclusion that it may answer very well for small packages, but it will never do for large bundles—never!"

Straining the Milk

In New York State [a health] inspector following the trail of disease in a small city traced it to impure milk supplied by a certain farm. In the absence of the man he insisted on inspecting the dairy arrangements, being followed from room to room by the farmer's indignant wife. Finally he said, "Show me the strainer which you use in the milk," and she brought an old shirt, very much soiled. Looking at it in dismay the inspector said, "Could you not, at least, use a clean shirt?" At this the woman's patience gave way and she declared, "Well, you needn't expect me to use a clean shirt to strain dirty milk!"

The Rescue

Two friends, Chaim and Moishe, were rowing on a lake when their boat capsized.

"Help! Help!" shouted Chaim, who could not swim. "I'm drowning!"

Moishe paid no attention to his comrade and swam rapidly toward the shore. But no sooner had he landed than he plunged right in again and saved Chaim, who had been struggling desperately all this time.

When both were safely ashore, Chaim said, "Moishe, why did you swim first ashore and then return for me, when you could have saved me right after the boat capsized?"

"*Goylem!*" retorted Moishe. "Didn't I have to save myself first?"

Ob Hoag

On a Saturday night, filled with hard cider, Ob Hoag fell into bed beside his spouse. Soon his dreams were interrupted by a natural consequence of much drinking.

Obeying long custom, he staggered out the back door to the corner of the house. A slight rain was falling and the drain pipe near which Ob took his stance gave out a gentle, sibilant sizzling sound which, in his befuddled state, he associated with the result of his own efforts.

Thus he stood, one hand braced against the side of the house, waiting for the sound to cease. Minute after minute went by without interruption, and a feeling approaching awe swept over him. He was a phenomenon! Realization of the fact was not to be coped with alone, and so finally in a great voice that aroused the slumbering neighbors, he bellowed, "Matilda! Matilda! Wake ye! I've sprung the eternal and everlasting leak!"

"T.M."

A Pennsylvania German farmer's wife, . . . having baked a large number of very fine pies, some mince and some apple, marked the crust of each with two letters—"T.M." Being asked by a neighbor what these letters stood for, she said, "Vy, 'T.M.' on this pie means ' 'Tis mince,' and on that pie it means ' 'Tain't mince.' "

The Fertile Gondolas

When the Chicago World's Fair of 1893 was planned it was built around a Venice motif: with lagoons, Italian folk songs, and, even, gondolas. The issue of gondolas arose before the Board of Aldermen, and it was suggested that twelve be purchased. At this stage a rather sleepy alderman, concerned for the budget, objected: "Why buy twelve? We have plenty of time. Why not buy a male and female and let nature take its course?"

Old Jake and President Cleveland

Cleveland being the first Democratic President since the Civil War, there was great clamor throughout the South for him to visit various cities there. He eventually consented, taking his twenty-two-year-old bride . . .

Cleveland's Southern tour was a veritable procession of triumphs. He was acclaimed with frenzied enthusiasm by record-breaking crowds. Nowhere was his reception more lavish and enthusiastic than in Montgomery, Alabama, the state's capital. The Governor of Alabama fairly outdid himself in preparation for the event. He ordered a new phaeton to be drawn by four magnificent horses, and the horses were equipped with silver-mounted harness imported from New York. A strapping mulatto driver, who had been especially trained for the occasion, was outfitted in a suit with four rows of brass buttons up and down his breast, a sort of drum major's hat with a smart plume, and other ornaments.

The Governor had for years had a special Negro bodyguard. Old Jake, now quite along in years, approached the Governor during the preparations. "Guv'nah," he said, "I ain't never seen a President. I allus wanted to see one befoh I died. Ain't they some way you can fix it so's old Jake can git to see this here President that's comin' to Montgomery?"

The ground from the station to the capitol at Montgomery is a gradual incline. This was the route by which the parade would ascend to the capitol. Accordingly, the Governor, sympathizing with the wish of his old bodyguard, had a platform erected for Jake's sole use.

The great day arrived and passed with all the pomp and splendor which the Governor had planned. That night, when the festivities were over, he thought of Jake and wondered what his trusted servant's impression of the President had been. He, therefore, sent for Jake, whose beaming, black countenance was soon at the threshold. "Well, Jake," he asked, "did you see the President?" "Yassuh, boss," Jake replied. "I seed him good." "How did you like him, Jake?" "He sho' looked fine! I ain't never seen a man in my whole life that looked so fine! My, how he did sit up there drivin' them hosses! And them brass buttons and that fine hat! But say, Guv'nah, there's one thing I wants to know?" "What's that, Jake?" The old Negro frowned strangely. "Who in the world was that funny-looking ole fat man sittin' in the back seat with you?"

Callahan Makes Up His Mind

Probably the strangest of [the] strange breed [of preliminary boxers] was a tough-looking boy named Callahan, who appeared out of nowhere one afternoon [at "Diamond Lew" Bailey's "Bucket of Blood" in Miami]. A preliminary boxer had been taken suddenly ill, and Lew needed someone to take his place. He offered the newcomer five dollars.

"I don't know," the boy hesitated. "I'll be back by six o'clock and let you know."

The ex-barber was in no hurry. Callahan departed. Promptly at six he thrust a battered nose through the door, and accepted the afternoon's offer.

"What in hell took you so long to make up your mind?" asked "Diamond Lew."

The boy shrugged. "Well," he said, "I ain't never been in the ring, and wasn't sure how I'd do. So, I went around to diff'rent saloons and picked fights with the toughest guys I could find. I licked 'em all, so I guess I'll do okay."

The Lawyer and the Poodle

Lawyer Stowers, of Pikeville, [Kentucky], was a suave gentleman and a born diplomat. One day a lady accompanied by a poodle dog met him on the street, and they began to chat. Pretty soon the dog sneaked over, began to sniff at Stowers' legs, then started to raise a hind paw to perform a very common canine function. Stowers jumped back out of the way. The lady hurried to say, "Oh, Mr. Stowers, I'm so sorry!" "Oh, never mind, madam," said Stowers, "I thought he was going to kick me."

Barnstorming

[A] barnstorming aviator at a county fair in Kentucky . . . was hauling sight-seers at ten dollars per head. One persistent fellow began nagging him to take up both his wife and himself for half price.

Finally the pilot agreed, on condition that the pest would have to pay double if he so much as opened his mouth once during the flight. Loading the couple into the rear cockpit, he took off and practically shook his plane to pieces. . . . However, they landed without the passenger uttering a single word or sound.

When they touched the ground, the pilot called back, "How in tarnation did you manage not to call out?"

"Well," the fellow said, "to tell you the truth, I almost spoke once."

"When was that?" asked the pilot.

The man answered, "When my wife fell out."

The Helpful Woodpeckers

I once had a red-headed nephew by name of Stuart Conrad. He married a red-headed girl, and, in the natural course of events, their marriage was blessed with five red-headed children. Stuart was a tenant farmer in Hardin County, [Kentucky].

One day I drove down to his place. "How are you getting along, Stuart?" I asked.

"Oh, good 'nuf, I guess," he drawled. "Leastwise, me an' Elvira, we kinda manage." He paused, and then went on: "But effen it warn't for the woodpeckers, feedin' the young 'uns mought be a problem."

I looked my astonishment, but before I could question him, Stuart continued: "Ye see, them danged woodpeckers think everything that's got a red head is another woodpecker. So we jest set the young 'uns out on the rail fence afore me an' Elvira go to the field . . . 'n' when we get back, them danged woodpeckers have fed 'em all day!"

The Traveling Man's Acquaintance

[A] . . . traveling man [in Tennessee] was sitting on a counter talking to a merchant about selling him some goods. He and the merchant got into a general conversation, and among other things he said to the merchant, "I used to sell goods in Kaufman County, Texas." At this, a seedy, ragged, hard-looking fellow who was sitting on the counter said, "My friend, did you say you had lived in Kaufman County, Texas?" "Yes, sir," said the salesman. "Did you ever know a man out there by the name of John F. Williams?" "Oh, yes, I used to sell John goods," he said. "Well, sir, he is my brother." "Oh, I'm glad to meet you." "Yes, sir, John Williams is my brother. How was John when you saw him?" "Oh, John was doing very well, he had a good farm with plenty of stock on it, he was out of debt and he was doing well." The man said, "Well, if you should go back to Kaufman County at any time, and see anything of John I wish you would tell him that I am mighty hard up, that my farm is mortgaged and I do not believe I am ever going to be able to raise and educate my children. Times are mighty hard with me, and I do not see any chance of ever getting out of debt. If he is ever going to help me, now is the time."

After a while the traveling man felt like taking a drink and he invited John's brother out to take a drink with him. When the drink began to have its effects the man said, "So you know my brother John in Texas?" "Yes," said the salesman. "Well, when you go out there say that I'm getting along tolerably well."

They sauntered around a while and the traveling man asked his acquaintance to take another drink. Then the fellow began to warm up. He said, "So you know my brother John out in Kaufman County, Texas?" "Yes," he said. "Well, if you are out there anytime, just tell him I am making a good living and am getting along first rate."

Late in the evening my friend met the fellow again; he had meanwhile had two or three more drinks and was pretty mellow, so he said, "You are the gentleman that knowed my brother John out in Kaufman County." "Yes," said the salesman. "Well, if you should go back to Kaufman and see anything of John, tell him if he needs anything, just to draw on me."

The Judge and the Hog

Less than a generation ago, there lived in Mississippi a most profound lawyer and an able one, Judge——, who was not free from the eccentricities of genius, in that he too often imbibed from the flowing bowl. His brilliancy was dazzling and his moral lapses were freely forgiven by his friends, who forgot all else but his captivating personality when sober. . . .

On [one] occasion, the judge became hopelessly intoxicated. He staggered on bravely for some distance though the odds were against him, then fell ingloriously into a puddle of water, where the hogs were accustomed to wallow. No one saw him fall and he lay undisturbed for the best part of the afternoon. Finally he was aroused by the grunting and splashing of a companionable and gentle hog. The judge and the hog had lain down together. The judge rolled over and patted his companion on the back, saying, "Partner, do you know the difference, the only difference, between you and me?"

The porker grunted in the negative.

"Well, it's this," said the judge, "tomorrow, I'll be Judge———, but you'll be a damned old hog still."

Big Flood

A bunch of hillmen . . . died and went to Hell. Every night they sat around the fire like a bunch of fox-hunters, talking mostly about what great things they had done on earth, and what noble deaths they died. One loud-mouthed bore named Taylor had been drowned in the big flood at Pine Bluff, Arkansas, and he talked about this disaster at great length. One evening, as Taylor began his interminable tale, an old sailor got up and walked away from the fire in disgust. "Who's that ole bastard?" asked Taylor. Everybody roared with laughter. The old sailor's name was Noah.

Wishes and Horses

There was this poor family living in a shack near the edge of town. They had a big passel of younguns and they were all just about starving to death. The only furniture they had to sit on was a bunch of wooden boxes. One night, just as the last bit of coal oil was being used up in the smoky lamp, the old father sat on the most comfortable box and began ruminating. All the children clustered around him while he talked. " 'Y God," he said, "I wish we had us a settin' hen and a clutch of eggs. We'd set 'em and raise us a flock of chickens. You know if we was to get us a flock of chickens, I wouldn't be surprised but what we could trade 'em for a heifer calf and if we took care of that there heifer calf right it would grow up to be a milk cow. And if we was to have us a milk cow and I managed things just right, wouldn't surprise me at all if we couldn't trade it off and get us a horse."

About this time little Bobbie, who was sitting astride an orange crate, began jouncing up and down, yelling, "Goody, goody! We got us a horse. Git up! Git up!" Whereupon the old man gave him a back-handed blow, knocking him off the orange crate, and shouted, "Git off that there horse!"

Mule Egg

There was a weak-minded boy in our town by the name of DeWitt Clinton Forebrusher and the village sports who hung around the barber shop, the pool hall, and Danziger's drug store were always playing jokes on him. They would send him off on errands for left-handed monkey wrenches, envelope stretchers, meat augers, and the like.

Well, on one of his trips to Muskogee, Pearl Day, the owner of the Palace Barbershop, brought back a big hairy cocoanut. After he had shown it around, instead of breaking it and eating it, he called De-Witt in and solemnly assured him that it was a mule egg. DeWitt listened wide-eyed while Pearl held it just out of his reach and gave him instructions on what to do with it.

"Now, DeWitt," Pearl said, "you take this here mule egg home and you take it out to the henhouse and you sit on it for six weeks and you will hatch yourself out a nice mule colt. I'm giving it to you if you promise to do just like I say."

"Yes, sir. I shore will do that, Mr. Pearly," DeWitt said.

"All right, then. Now you know what you have got to do. If you get up off this here mule egg and let it get cold, it never will hatch out, and if it does, you'll prollerrie [probably] have a dead mule colt on your hands."

So DeWitt took the cocoanut home and began sitting on it in the henhouse. The first night his mother couldn't even get him to come into the house to eat supper or to go to bed. A few honest people tried to persuade DeWitt that it was all just a joke, but he wouldn't believe a word they said. He just kept sitting on his mule egg.

After a few days of having to carry food to him out to the henhouse, his mother finally did get him to go to sleep in the house, but only after she had agreed that he could take the cocoanut to bed with him.

Six weeks passed before DeWitt began to have his doubts about whether the mule egg was ever going to hatch. Finally, he carried it into the Palace Barbershop and said, "Look here, Mr. Pearly, I don't believe that this here mule is ever going to hatch out."

"Well, did you sit on it just like I told you to?"

"Yes, sir. I shore been keeping it warm."

So Pearl said, "You prollerrie ain't given it much time. A mule egg ain't like a hen egg. You got to give 'em time. You take that there mule egg back home and keep it warm another month and then if you ain't got no mule colt, then something is prollerrie gone wrong."

DeWitt took the cocoanut home and sat on it for another month before he got disgusted with the whole project. So he got up and took the cocoanut and went out to a vacant lot which was all grown up in weeds and threw it just as hard as he could into the center of the weed patch. Just as the cocoanut landed, a great big, floppy-eared jackrabbit came running out of the weed patch. DeWitt stared after it, astonished, before he thought to yell, "Come back here, you fool mule. Don't you know I'm your pappy?"

The Bet

After being on the ranch for several months working hard with not a day off or a vacation of any kind, the boss told these two cowboys they might go into town and bring back a load of chuck. As soon as they arrived in the city they went to the hotel, registered, got 'em a room and went up to it. They were hot and dry and immediately ordered something to quench their thirst and cool them off. They were on the third floor in a big room that would accommodate all their friends. They didn't close the door opening out into the hall and welcomed everybody that came by. Finally, a drummer came along, and he joined them. They ordered more drinks and did really put on a party till after midnight.

Next morning when they woke up, one of them had a leg broke, one arm in a sling, his head bandaged and one eye blacked. He said to his partner, "What in the world happened last night?" His partner told him, "You bet that drummer you could jump out of that window and fly plumb around this hotel and come back in at the same window." The crippled man said, "You didn't let me, did you?" "Let you—hell! I lost ten dollars on you myself."

Sobering Up

A cowboy from the L.F.D. Ranch went into Roswell, [New Mexico], in a four-mule wagon to load up with chuck for the fall roundup. He got on a big spree and stayed drunk for four days, but finally got out of town. Along about three o'clock that afternoon the sun was scorching hot, and this old boy hadn't had a drop of water since he left Roswell early that morning. He came to a creek about forty feet wide and three feet deep. He drove his wagon right out in the middle of it and climbed down off the wagon seat and waded in on his all fours, just like a horse. The wagon wheels were muddy. Naturally, the water below the wagon was muddy and above it was nice and clear. Prager Miller happened to ride up just at this time, and he said to him, "Why don't you get up above your wagon where the water is clear?" The cowboy quit drinking long enough to raise his head, and replied to Prager, "I'm gonna drink it all anyway, just as well commence on this muddy."

How Two Santa Fe Brothers Sold a Keg of Whisky

Many years ago Pablo and his brother José had tried their hands at many things, without success. Discovering that they had between them enough money to purchase a keg of whisky, they bought one from a Santa Fe merchant who, knowing the brothers, exacted a solemn promise that they would not give each other a single drink but sell the entire contents of the keg. The brothers started out along the road to Taos, with the keg of whisky loaded on a cart.

After a short distance, the men had begun to regret their promise when José put his hand in his pocket and, much to his surprise, discovered a coin piece. "Pablo," he said, "we made a promise not to give each other a drink, but we could sell it to each other, could we not?" "That is true," answered Pablo, adding with a sigh, "if we had any money." "I have, so sell me a drink," cried José happily. Pablo complied, and continued the journey frowning thoughtfully while José smiled and licked his lips. Pablo then said, "I now have money, José, so you must sell me a drink."

Thus the coin continued to change hands, while the level in the keg steadily descended. After a time, the cart struck a rock and a wheel broke. The brothers waited philosophically for help, meanwhile buying one drink after another until the key was empty. Then they lay down to sleep.

A traveler, passing that way, dismounted to investigate the broken cart and, attracted by a sound, discovered the brothers under a tree, snoring lustily, a coin lying in Pablo's hand. He laughingly removed the money and went on his way.

When the men came back to Santa Fe, the merchant asked them if they had kept their promise. "Yes," said José piously. "We sold every drop, and gave each other none." "But," Pablo added, "while we slept a thief stole every centavo we had, so we come back poorer than when we started."

The Promoter and the Banker

[In] the Gay Nineties, when mining promoters were still active in San Francisco, memories of skyrocketing Comstock days were not entirely forgotten in banking circles. Promoters still talked glibly of rich veins of gold, a thousand per cent return, the advantages of a "ground floor" investment and a huge profit. Financial backing was sought wherever they thought they could find it.

A promoter, well known among bankers as a gatherer of funds who seldom returned them, approached Wellington Gregg, then cashier of the old Crocker-Woolworth Bank, for a loan. The promoter opened the subject by picking imaginary threads and flicking imaginary dust off Gregg's shoulders—a friendly gesture which he thought would inspire confidence. Naturally, he was asked for security. He had none. But he continued to press the subject of getting ten thousand dollars merely by signing a note for that amount. After several polite refusals, Gregg's patience was exhausted and he said, "No! You can't have it, and furthermore, put that dust back."

 **7**

Whopper Wit

The very Tails of the American Sheep are so laden with Wooll, that each has a little Car or Waggon on four little Wheels, to support & keep it from trailing on the Ground . . . Cod, like other Fish when attack'd by their Enemies, fly into any Waters where they can be safest; . . . Whales, when they have a mind to eat Cod, pursue them wherever they fly; and . . . the grand Leap of the Whale in that Chase up the Fall of Niagara is esteemed, by all who have seen it, as one of the finest Spectacles in Nature.

BENJAMIN FRANKLIN

Introduction

The exaggerations of trickster and fool tales lead from the cracker barrel to the Liars' Bench. The first American tall tales were travelers' tales and booster tales full of the wonders of a new country and of people seeking them. In frontier days, when the hoaxing tall tale served to "load" and string along the stranger, the narrator had reason and leisure to pile detail upon detail and to string the story out into a yarn. But with our modern preference for shorter, snappier forms of storytelling, the long-winded tall tale is becoming out of date and out of fashion. Even the Liars' Clubs have gone in for the abbreviated tall tale. In fact, the lying anecdote may well have been the parent form and the yarn a later literary development, as in the case of the Paul Bunyan tale, which seems to have originated in independent jokes. Certainly, before the tall story there was comic exaggeration or overstatement in the form of a hyperbolic comparison or witticism.

Understatement, however, is sometimes the more effective form of whopper wit. "Had a big windstorm here yesterday," said the forlorn native of Western Kansas to the solicitous traveler, "that blew away my house, my wife, and my three children." "That's terrible! But why aren't you out looking for them?" "No use to look for them. Wind'll change next week and they'll come back."

Here is the unhumorous economy of speech and detail generally associated with Yankee "reluctant eloquence," plus the Westerner's casualness or "slow blitheness" that Struthers Burt sees as the product of Western "patience and stoic laughter."

Save for the addition of new contraptions like the Tin Lizzie, the subjects of whopper wit continue to be pretty much the same as they have always been: hunting and fishing brags; smart hogs and coon dogs in the South and smart burros and pack rats in the West; freaks and extremes of climate and weather; superlatives like the laziest or stingiest man. We hear less about giant vegetables and fearsome critters. In general, the modern trend is away from the bragging tale and toward the mock or ironic tall tale, the cynical shaggy-dog deflation of "F-ant-astic" and "The Quail Boy."

Just as tall tales tend to form cycles built around a hero like Paul Bunyan, so the liar himself may become a hero in his own right. One of the most charming of these liar heroes was Johnny Caesar Cicero Darling of Sullivan County, New York, of whom it was said, "Darlin' was the biggest liar ever lived. But he'd tell whoppers so good you'd most believe 'm."

Joe Ma Frau, Strong Man

Joe Ma Frau one time took a trip cross de ocean, and one big storm come up. Every one was vera much fraid. De storm last for two day and two night. Dan de captain and de sailor men say dere was a Jonah on de ship. So de captain say, "Every one must draw straws, and de one dat get de short straw is de Jonah." It was a ole lady wot draw de short straw, and de captain say dey must trow de ole lady overboard. Just at dese tam dere came a big shark side of de ship, and Jo Ma Frau say to "wait a little while." So de captain say, "All right."

Joe was settin' on a camp chair on de front part of de ship. Dere was a box of oranges by Joe's side. So he trowed de box of oranges overboard to de shark, and de shark swallow de whole box of oranges —box an' all, but de shark still follow de ship. Den Joe he trowed de camp chair to de shark. Den de captain he got mad and say to de sailor men to trow de ole lady over in ocean. So dey grab de ole lady and over dey trow her. Den Joe Ma Frau pull out a knife, so long as hee's arm, and he jump overboard, after de shark. Dese shark weigh five hunder' pound. When Joe reach de ocean he grab de shark by de tail and trow de shark way up on de deck of de ship, and den he clim' up vera quick on de ship, took his big knife and cut de shark open from hee's mout to hee's tail, and dere sat de ole lady on de camp chair, and holler out, "Oranges, two for a nickel!" Oh, Joe Ma Frau ees strong man!

The Laziest Man in Vermont

Lazy? Yes, Nathan is it, one hundred and thirty-three per cent. When he was young his pa got him a job working to New York. He worked with the cleaners in them sky scrapings. Yes, he was one of the brass polishers. No, he didn't wipe none. He was the one what walked ahead and went "Huh-Huh" on the doorknobs.

When me and him got married he used to snore pretty vocal. I got used to it and couldn't sleep without it. But his snoring died out on him. It was then he hired the hired man to snore for him.

His prize? Yes, the committee come up from the Center to give him the ten dollars for being the laziest man north of the Massachusetts line. Nathan was in the orchard when they come watching nature.

"Boys," Nathan said, "are y' bent on givin' this t' me? Y're makin' me a lotta trouble. How be it, ef y're set on it, d' y' mind rollin' me over an' puttin' it in my backside pocket?"

The sheriff's funeral? Yes, that was a grand sight. Nathan was real interested. He was restin' in the Cape Cod hammick when it passed our gate. I come out and told him who all was in the carriages and autamobiles, his kinfolk and his nephews and nieces wavin' to him.

Nathan was kinda peeved.

"Just my luck," he said. "T' be facin' th' other way."

Wolf Dog

A gentleman in Maine, who wanted a hunting dog, heard that a farmer living in a neighboring county had one for sale, which he recommended very highly. He called upon the farmer, saw the dog and took a schedule of his merits, which were as numerous as the hairs on his body. The purchaser was particularly anxious to have a good wolf dog, and, upon that point, the assurances of the farmer were full and satisfactory. It was the best wolf dog in the State. Satisfied with his trade, the gentleman paid the price, which was by no means moderate, and took the dog home. Not long after, a light fall of snow furnished an opportunity to test the merits of his purchase. A wolf was started and the probationer was put on his track. Both animals were soon out of sight, and the owner or proprietor followed on as fast as he could. Presently he came up to a farmhouse, where he saw a man chopping wood. He asked him if he had seen a dog and a wolf passing that way. "Yes," was the prompt reply. "Well, how was it with them?" was the next question. "Well, it was nip and tuck, but I think the dog was a leetle ahead."

The Bent Gun and the Thieving Fox

[The gunsmith] told about a neighbor who was after a thieving fox. "Maltiah, he saw the fox leavin' his hen-house at daylight," explained the gunsmith. "The fox took out across the medder, right in plain sight, and Maltiah right after him." The fox got a haystack between himself and his pursuer, and ran around it at the approach of the hunter, always keeping the stack between. Finally the exasperated hunter stuck his gun barrel in a fence post, and bent it into a curve. Then, holding the muzzle low, he fired around the stack.

"Oh, sartin, he got the fox," related the gunsmith with a chuckle, "but the shot kept right on a-goin' and filled his starn chock-full!"

Les Hathaway and the Buck

[Les Hathaway] had gone out into the woods alone. . . . He got up some time about dawn, climbed in his little boat, and paddled up the river. He hiked six miles to his hut in the backwoods. In no time he spotted a fine eight-point buck, four hundred yards off, so he said, much too far for any kind of shot. He fired anyway. The deer went plunging down the hill.

Les . . . didn't follow as other hunters might have done. He went up the hill and just over to the other side. In a half hour along came an eight-point buck. Les shot and killed him. "It takes a smart man to outthink a deer," Les said. "That deer figured most hunters would chase downhill after that first shot, so he went a short ways, hid, then came back up the hill and I shot him. How do I know it was the same buck? Mister, he had the point of one antler chipped right off when I clipped him with that first shot. I remember seeing it fly. How could I see at that distance? Mister, I saw well enough to hit the point of the antler at four hundred yards, didn't I?"

F-ant-astic

A man was sent up for a thirty-year stretch. One day he noticed an ant crawling across his cell floor. He put his finger out to stop it and the ant jumped over his finger. "Now," he figured, "this ant must be very smart, because ordinary ants would just walk around my finger." So he picked the ant up and decided to teach it tricks.

First he taught it how to jump over his finger. Then he taught it to jump over a stick. For five years he taught the ant to jump over sticks, and finally he made small hoops for the ant to jump through. So he got this ant to be real strong. Still he figured that wasn't too good. But he had about twenty-five more years left, so he had time.

For five more years he got the ant to build up its muscles real strong, so it could jump over a wall about one foot high, which no ant had ever done before. Still he figured that wasn't good enough for him, though. So for five years, every spare minute he had, he taught the ant how to read. But after five years he figured that nobody would believe it. So for five more years he labored to get the ant to write. He put a small piece of lead in the ant's mouth and then the ant would write out what it just read.

He figured that this ant was fantastic. So he decided he'd teach it some more things. For about five years he worked to get the ant to talk. Every morning he'd get up at six o'clock and he'd be splitting rocks all day. After he was finished, every second of his spare time he'd spend with the ant.

Finally, after five years, he got the ant to have a vocabulary of about two hundred words. He'd have to hold a microphone next to it because the ant couldn't talk too loud. And then for the last five years of his stretch he expanded the ant's vocabulary until it was fantastic. The ant could say anything. And it could read, write, and jump over a wall a foot high, and everything like that.

So finally after he got out he went down to a bar and he took the ant out of its little box and he put it on the bar. And he called over the bartender and says to him, "I'd like you to look at this ant." And the bartender said, "Oh, that one!" And he crushed it with his thumb.

The Safest Safe

Two safe-agents were presenting their relative claims to an admiring crowd. One was a Yankee, and the other wasn't. He that wasn't told his story. A rooster had been shut up in one of his safes, and then it was exposed for three days to an intense degree of heat. When the door was opened, the rooster stalked out as if nothing had happened. It was now the Yankee's turn. A rooster had also been shut up in his safe, and it was submitted to the trial of a tremendous heat for more than a week. Parts of the safe had been melted away, and the door itself had been so welded as to require the use of cold chisels to get it open. When at last it was opened, the rooster was found frozen to death.

The Biggest Tobacco Chewer on Ocracoke Island

Old Marty . . . was the biggest tobacco chewer on [Ocracoke] Island. Marty's wife got mad at him and said she'd never talk to him again. Marty thought a while how he'd make her talk, and then he took out the false teeth he was wearing, and tied a long string to 'em, and went out in front of his house and began dragging 'em all around the grass, just like he was walking a dog. His old woman waited for a long time without saying anything, and then she couldn't hold in any longer. "You stop that foolishness right away," she burst out. "Look at them people standing in the street, come from all over town just to watch you. What you dragging them teeth for? You going crazy?"

Marty kept on pulling the string, and walking up and down nice and easy. "I ain't crazy no-ways," he told her. "I just lost my plug of tobacco in the grass, and this here's the best way to find it. If them teeth get near that plug, they know it so good they'll snap onto it quicker than a rat onto cheese."

The Quail Boy

Two friends were hunting in Georgia. This is dangerous business, because a careless shot is likely to knock a hole in somebody's still, and then there's the devil to pay. But they found a farm which looked like it might be covered with quail, and had no difficulty getting permission to hunt over it. But when they started to get the dogs out of the car the farmer objected.

"Why," they said, "these are the best two quail dogs in Georgia."

"Don't care if they're the best quail dogs in the world," the farmer said. "They can't find quail on this farm. Cover's too thick. But my boy here can find 'em for you."

The hunters estimated this to be an indirect method of collecting toll for allowing them to hunt, and they made no further objections.

But the boy turned out to be better than the dogs could have been. He swept the fields slowly, in careful arcs, sniffing the wind. Suddenly he stiffened and pointed.

"They's quail in that clump of bushes there," he whispered. "The way they're sittin' they'll go up to the right. Get set for a shot."

Then he went in and flushed the covey, and as usual in this sort of story the quail did just as he had predicted. It wasn't long before the team had its limit, and without wasting a shell.

The next year they came back and discovered to their pleasure that quail were reported to be so thick on the place that the coveys had to take day about to move around for feed.

"Can we get that boy of yours to go with us again?" they asked.

The farmer's face lengthened and he spoke sadly. "I'd forgot you were the fellows that hunted with him last year," he said. "No, he's not here now. We just don't mention that boy any more."

"Sorry," said one of the visitors. "We didn't mean to rake up anything unpleasant. He sure was a wonderful boy with quail."

"Yes, he was," the farmer agreed, shaking his head. "I reckon I might as well tell you, now that it's been brought up. It wasn't two months after you men were here, and I thought he was getting better, if anything. But the fact is, he got to chasing rabbits, and we had to shoot him."

Of course I know that one of the saddest sights in Georgia, which is saying a good deal, is to see a hitherto respectable quail dog suddenly dash through a quail field after a rabbit, flushing covey after covey out of gunshot. But in such parts of the South as I have inhabited, humanity would have dictated that this boy be sold up the river to somebody who could use him in a beagle pack.

The Knittingest Woman

[A stranger in the Kentucky mountains] commented to a mountain woman on her skill in knitting as she walked along the rough mountain roads or climbed the steep trails.

"Oh, that's nothing!" the woman exclaimed. "Now ther's Aunt Mandy. She's the *knittingest* woman ever I saw. She takes her yarn to bed with her every night, and ever' now and then she throws out a sock!"

Roast Duck

'Twas in the early fall an' pappy an' me hed been a-eatin' nothin' but fish all through the hot spell, then they stopped a-bitin' an' fer days an' days we had no meat vittles at all. The ducks was a-beginnin' to flap towards the south an' Pappy bein' a dead shot with "Jenny," that's the old muzzle loader, 'lowed as we might contrive to get ourselves a nice fresh duck. So we loads up old Jenny with powder and balls an' sets out. 'Bout ten rod from our doorstep we sees a big mallard duck come a-flappin' along 'bout ten feet high. When he sees us he riz up, but didn't change his direction none. Pappy waits till he has passed over an' then he ups and lets him have it right where he sets down; if he'd been a-settin' which he ain't.

When the black powder smoke clears so we can see a little, there ain't nary sign of that duck, 'ceptin' the innards which is a-danglin' graceful like from the limb of a big sycamore. Pappy 'lows he musta blowed him to bits; so we gives up a-huntin' fer the other parts. All the rest of the mornin' me and Pappy tramped the woods but nary wigglin' fowel or varmint did we see. Pappy's shootin' musta scairt 'em away. By this time we was plumb tired an' empty, so we come back to the cabin a-figgerin' we'd hafta be content with mush.

But when we opened the door the pleasentist smell come to our noses. Pappy looked at me an' I looked at him. . . . Then our eyes lit on the fireplace an' a-hangin' on the big hook, over the fire, was a duck, roasted to a nice gold brown. We figured the way it all happened was like this: Pappy's shot hit the mallard a-cleanin' him out from stern to stem an' knockin' him up in the air, where he fell down the chimney a-catchin' by one foot on the hook. He hung there a-turnin' an' turnin' while the feathers singed off. Then with the outsides off an' the insides out he jest natcherally couldn't do nothin' 'cept roast. Which same he did to a turn.

Lute Goins' Sawmill

Many's the man that's taken a good walnut log up to Lute Goins' mill to have sawed and got back a doughy old cottonwood plank or two. That Lute Goins would skin a louse for its hide and tallow.

One time I had me as pretty a hickory log as a man ever saw and I aimed to have it sawed up for my coffin boards. Well, sir, I started out for the sawmill one morning, aiming to get there in good time so's I could watch the log being sawed and get back before hog slopping. I would of made it, too, but the wagon broke down crossing Sugar Creek and it took me till nearly dusk dark to put the wheel back on. It was too late to go back home, so I just went on to the mill. Lute had gone home, but I had heared that a lot of funny business went on during the night, like switching logs around, and I aimed to stay close to make sure there was no skulduggery.

'Long about midnight my poor old eyes started to go shut on me in spite of all I could do. Still couldn't hear nothing but the sloshing of the water against the mill wheel and an old hoot owl asking, "Who, who, who are you?"

I was bound and determined that here was one log that would be sawed honest. I wropped my legs around the log and mounted it like a saddle horse. I'm a light sleeper and I knowed if anybody tried to fool with that log as long as I had a death grip on it I'd wake up sure as shooting.

I was up with the sun. Everything's all right, I told myself. Still got a good holt on the log.

Everything was all right in a pig's eye! There ought to be a whopping big government bounty on the pelt of that Lute Goins. You know what that scoundrel done to me? Sometime during the night he had snaked the log right out of the bark slick as a whistle and left me there setting with my legs wropped round the shell of my fine hickory log.

The Biggest Liar in McDonald County

Lee Carnell and I were sitting on a bench in front of Mildred's Hollywood Café in Pineville one Saturday afternoon. Along came a great big lummox of a man carrying a hundred-pound sack of ground corn chops over his shoulder, like it was a poke of post toasties. Well, I was sitting there with old Lee. Of course, Lee was pretty much the pure quill himself. He was the leading merchant of the town, but he was sort of taking it easy. We had just been talking along. So when this old boy came up and stopped with the hundred-pound sack of corn, he just fell into the conversation. Got to talking about mice. Got to talking about every time you caught a mouse you had to take the trap and boil it because mice had such a keen sense of smell that they never would touch a trap that had been touched by human hands or had a dead mouse in it before. So he went on and I have an idea old Lee was leading this feller out for my benefit, but we got to talking about fish. About what big fish had been caught in Big Sugar Creek, about how big gars got, and catfish and things of that kind.

Lee said, "Well, sir, we had quite a business back here a few years ago. Was this great big garfish in Big Sugar Creek. It was the grandpappy of all garfish. People tried to catch it but it just broke every hook and line. Just dangling those leaders out of his mouth like pea vines. Nobody could gig it. So a feller come in here from outside some place. He heard about it. He was bound that he was going to noodle that garfish out of Big Sugar Creek. Took him a hay hook. Well, sir, he took that there hay hook and filed it down to a needle point. Strapped it to his wrist. Well, we tried to talk him out of it. But he wouldn't listen. He was bound and determined he was going to noodle that old garfish out of the crik. 'Y God, he taken off his clothes and had that there hay hook strapped to his hand and he dove down under the rock shelf. There was that old garfish hiding under there and he socked that old hay hook into the garfish. The garfish took off down the stream. The feller hung on. Drowneded him dead. Well, sir, for four-five years we go out fishing and see that old gar with that feller's skeleton swimming up and down Big Sugar Creek. I don't know whatever did become of that old garfish."

Old Glade Kidd had been standing there just waiting to get his word in. He says, "I can tell you what become of that. I caught that big old gar."

Lee says, "You did?"

He says, "Yes, sir, I shore did. If you don't believe it I can take you right home and show you the knife I cut that skeleton off of him with."

So with that, old Glade Kidd turned and walked off with great dignity, placing the hundred-pound sack of ground corn chops on his shoulder. We just sat in silence and then Lee turned to me and gave me a kind of slow grin and said, "I guess you know who that was, don'tcha? That was Glade Kidd. He's the biggest liar in McDonald County."

Hogs and High Water

A rural Missourian was trying to sell his farm to a hillman from Arkansas.

"Does the river ever flood this here wood lot?" asked the hillman.

"Hell, no," replied the farmer, "we ain't had no high water in forty years."

The Arkansawyer noticed a ring of mud on every tree trunk, about six feet above the ground. "Then how did that mud git away up thar?" he asked suspiciously.

"Oh, it's them damn hawgs o' mine," said the Missourian, "they're always a-rubbin' ag'in the trees."

The hillman said no more, but prepared to take his departure.

"Well, do you aim to buy the farm?" asked the Missourian.

"Naw, I don't want the farm," said the hillbilly, "but I sure would like to git a start o' them hawgs!"

Hog-Wild

I

A cracker . . . lived in a shack in the pine barrens of South Georgia. He had a little land cleared for farming, and considered himself especially fortunate because a herd of tasty wild razorbacks ran "hog-wild" through the woods and sustained themselves on the nutlike pine mast. One day a Northerner happened to visit him, and suggested that he get rid of the razorbacks and start raising Poland China hogs.

"Why should I git shet of them hawgs?" asked the cracker suspiciously. "Ain't costin' me nary a cent to raise 'em."

"But think of the time!" exclaimed the Northerner. "You can fatten Poland Chinas in six months, while it takes two years for those razorbacks to get any meat on them."

The cracker expectorated with eloquent disdain. "Shucks," he said, "time don't mean a dadblamed thing to them hawgs."

II

Rome Nelson, a veteran of the War between the States, who lived near Crane, Missouri, was credited with developing a variety of razorbacks called the second-row strain. The idea is that any wild hog can reach through a rail fence and pull off ears of corn from the nearest stalks. But the Nelson hogs had such slender heads and long snouts that they could reach the second row of corn. . . .

I have heard also of razorback hogs with such long noses that they can drink buttermilk out of a jug. In dry times, the old folks say, a wild hog need not come to the creek for water. When he wants a drink, he just sticks his snout down a crawdad hole. These burrows are common in many places, and the hillfolk believe that a crawdad always digs till he strikes water, no matter how deep it may be. According to one old tale, a certain long-snouted sow always drank out of crawdad holes, even when plenty of surface water was available. Not only this, but she pumped water from the crawdad hole through her own body and out on the ground, so that all the other pigs could satisfy their thirst. In some versions of this yarn, the sow's owner trained her to pump enough water to irrigate his garden patch in dry weather.

One hears many stories of the razorback's ability to get food under difficult conditions. "One of them wild shotes," a hunter told me, "can hear an acorn drap a mile off, an' run fast enough to ketch it on the second bounce."

In Polk County, Arkansas, they told me of a man who found two or three wild hogs in his garden patch every morning, though it was fenced with wire and apparently hogtight. He had to open the gate and drive 'em out. One morning very early he hid in the brush and watched, to see how the razorbacks were getting past the fence. The pigs climbed up on a hillside, swung far out on a trailing grapevine, and let loose when they were directly over the garden. . . .

Some hillmen claim that the average razorback is so thin that he needs a ball of mud on his tail to preserve a proper balance, otherwise he'll pitch forward and stick his bill into the ground. The head is the heaviest part of an old-time hazel-splitter, anyhow, and that's why he can't root downhill.

Louis Hanecke, who used to run the Allred Hotel in Eureka Springs, Arkansas, is credited with a yarn about wild hogs that broke into a still-house and got gugglin' drunk; then they ran through the woods in packs, killing deer, cattle, and even bears. Some hillfolk near Hot Springs, Arkansas, declare that these whisky-maddened razorbacks climbed trees to pull down coons and bobcats. . . .

Not far from Eureka Springs, Arkansas, there are several round potholes in the bed of a little creek. It is said that the pioneers threw heated stones into these pits, and scalded hogs there. The place is known as Hog Scald to this day. An old-timer told me that he had lived near Hog Scald in the early 1880's. There used to be a bramble thicket near the potholes, he said, about where the road is now. "We used to git the water good an' hot," he explained, "an' throw the hogs in alive. They'd jump out a-squealin', an' run right through them bramble bushes. The thorns would take the bristles off slicker'n a whistle, so we didn't have to scrape 'em at all."

At Newport, Arkansas, some jokers were talking about the strange customs of the people in a nearby settlement called Oil Trough. The folks up that way, I was told, "never cut up their hogs at butcherin' time, and don't even bother to gut 'em. They just feed 'em nothing but salt and spices for a week, then shoot the critter an' smoke the whole hog!"

Tin Lizzie

A farmer in western Kansas put a tin roof on his barn. Then a tornado blew the roof off, and when the farmer found it in the next county, it was twisted and mangled beyond repair.

A friend of his advised him that the Ford Motor Company would pay him a price for the scrap tin, and the farmer decided he would ship the roof up to the company to see how much he could get for it. He crated it up in a big wooden box and sent it off to Michigan, marking it plainly with his return address so that the Ford Company would know where to send the check.

Weeks passed, and the farmer didn't hear from the Ford Company. Finally he was just on the verge of writing them to find out what was the matter, when he received a letter from them. It said, "We don't know what hit your car, mister, but we'll have it fixed for you by the fifteenth of next month."

The Laziest Man in Oklahoma

Probably the most unenergetic person I ever seen was a roustabout I used to have working for me. Went up on top the derrick one day to grease the crownblock, and when he got ready to come down he couldn't decide whether it'd be easier to use the ladder or slide down a guy-wire. He set up there so long—tryin' to figure out which would be the easiest—that the pecker-woods thought he was part of the rig and started pecking at his head. Fortunately, his head was of such a construction that he was not injured, and the pecker-woods got thicker and thicker. When winter come and it was time to go south, about a jillion of them caught ahold of him and taken him right along. Guess he seemed like home to 'em. Just as they sail away, I hear him speaking to these pecker-woods.

"Turn me on my back, fellers," he says, "when we pass through a cloud. I wanta get a drink."

The Stingiest Man

When Si Barton dug his deep well and put up a windmill, the neighbors were excited about it. He was considered the stingiest man for miles around Stringtown, it being said of him that he often sat out under the hackberry trees in his yard to save the shade on his porch.

Ed Lanson was, on the other hand, the jolliest man in the community. He was prosperous, too, and owned as good a quarter-section of black land as a crow ever flew over. One day he passed Barton's on his way to John Abner's store. Si was sitting in the shade of a tree reading the *Weekly Newser,* which a neighbor had given him. Ed saw him, and thought he would ask about the windmill, which at that moment was whirling merrily in the morning breeze.

"Hidy, Si!" he greeted. "How 'e maken it?"

"Purty porely, purty porely," grunted Si, without looking up from his paper.

"Yer know, Si," went on Ed, "I've been er thinken about putten me up er win'mill lack thet critter thar. I thank I need it."

"I woulden', no, I woulden'," answered Si, interested at last.

"Why?" asked Ed, surprised.

"Wall, yer see, it's this away, Ed. Thar mought not be ernough wind to turn 'em both."

Hogs and Woodpeckers

One day a stranger passed through the woods near a farmer's house in East Texas and saw three hogs running about as if crazy. They would dart up to a tree, stop suddenly, grunt, sniff at the tree a moment, then dash madly off towards another tree at a distance of perhaps fifty yards, repeat the strange actions, and dash off again. They kept up these antics until they were so exhausted that they could hardly take another step, then fell down apparently dead. Being very curious, and seeing a log house in a clearing nearby, the stranger walked up to the door and rapped with a stick on the facing. A tall, sad-faced, sandy-haired East Texan came to the door.

"Come in," he whispered.

The stranger stepped in.

"I notice you have a cold, friend," he said sympathetically.

" 'Tain't thet, stranger—'tain't thet, er tall," he whispered hoarsely. "It's thiserway. I uster raise a good pa'sel o' hogs, en I wud go out en call 'em in ter ther feed et night. I done thet ontil I lost my voice; then I'd knock on th' corner uv th' corn crib with a pine stick en they wud come to ther feed. But this spring thar come a eperdemic uv 'em thar red-head' woodpeckers inter these parts, en upter yisterday all my hogs 'cepten three hed run 'emselves ter death, en I 'low they's dead by this."

The Growing Salve

"Yes, sir," began old Uncle Noah, "them surgeons over in France did some right clever patchin' up of our soljers, but I'll bet if old Doc Goodfellow hadda gone over he'd beat the hull lot. Did I ever tell you about his wonderful growin' salve? No? The time he made his big hit at the Territorial Fair? Well, you see, some boys were puttin' a tame coyote into a pen when his tail caught in the door and was cut plumb off at the roots.

"I tell you them boys felt bad, and the coyote wasn't very cheerful himself. They sent for old Doc Goodfellow, of course, and the Doc rubbed some of his growing salve on the stub, and blame my cats if a new tail didn't grow right out while they was watchin' it.

"Then them boys had a fine idea, and rubbed some of the stuff on the cut place on the tail, and sure as I'm a truthful man, another coyote grew out of the tail, only"—here Uncle Noah spat reminiscently—"he was a wild coyote and they had to kill him."

Hotter 'n Hell

I listened to a discussion, last evening, on the comparative merits, or rather demerits, of the various military posts.

"Boys, did ever any of you hear of Fort Yuma?"

Not one of them.

"Well, Fort Yuma is clear over beyond Arizona, where nothing lives, nor grows, nor flies, nor runs. It's the hottest post, not only in the United States, but in all creation, and I'll prove it to you. You see I was ordered to Fort Yuma six years ago, and hadn't been on duty two weeks in the month of August, when two corporals took sick. Well, they both died, and where do you think they went?"

No one could possibly imagine.

"Why, I'll tell you; they both went straight to hell!"

Profound astonishment in the auditory.

"Yes, but they hadn't been gone forty-eight hours—hardly time to have their descriptive-lists examined and put on fatigue duty down below—when, one night at twelve o'clock, the hospital steward at the Fort was waked up in a hurry, and there he saw the two corporals standing by his bedside. 'What do you want?' says he. You know them hospital stewards always get out of temper at a soldier's ever wanting anything. 'What do you want?' says he. 'We want our blankets,' says they!

"After that, you needn't talk to me about any post being hot as Yuma!"

John Hance's Fog Yarn

One of [Grand Canyon guide John] Hance's favorite stories was the fog yarn. At rare times the Canyon will be filled with clouds. Both rims will be clear, but the depths will be concealed by a sea of fog temporarily locked within the walls. Hance would then bring out his snowshoes and casually approach whatever tourists might be at the rim.

"Well," he'd say to himself, "she's just about right to cross."

Inevitably somebody would ask him what he meant.

"Oh, don't you know? Strangers here, eh? Well, say, too bad I haven't got another pair of snowshoes or you could join me."

"What are you going to do?"

"Whenever she fogs up good and solid like this, I always put on my snowshoes and take a walk across to the North Rim."

The startled visitors looked aghast, but hesitated to call the bluff, for Hance was busy strapping on his snowshoes. He'd test them gingerly and add, "Yep, just right," and before the bewildered audience he would walk to the rim, stick a foot into space, and say, "Ah, that's just fine!" Then he'd stroll along the rim and call back to his audience, "It's a lot shorter if I start from Yaki Point. You just keep watching and tonight when you see a fire over on the North Rim you'll know I made it." And off he would go, disappearing along the rim walk in the direction of Yaki Point.

The next day he would be "back."

"See my fire last night?" he'd ask.

Once in a while somebody would say yes, and Hance would merely nod matter-of-factly. But as the answer was usually in the negative, he would say, "Well, the danged fog rose and blotted it out for you. I couldn't see your lights over here either. You know that blasted fog pretty near fooled me? It was good and thick goin' over but when I come back it was so thin that I sagged with every step. Once I thought I was goin' to hit bottom. Just like walkin' on a featherbed, only worse. Plumb wore myself out gettin' back. You want to try it some time. Stay around a while and I'll lend you my snowshoes next time she fogs good and solid."

The Belled Burro

A prospector over at Quartzsite, Arizona, that's spent twenty-six years out here in the desert, six years huntin' gold, and twenty years huntin' his three dad-burned burros, told me this story today.

"Years ago," said he, "I put a bell on Sappho, my pet burro, and turned her loose to feed nights with Frankey and Johnny, a pesky pair of blues, the bell so's I can locate them in the mornin', they stayin' together. Well, lots of times I couldn't hear that bell and after spendin' most a day lookin' for 'em would find their tracks close by. I thought maybe I might be gettin' deaf, till one day after trampin' for miles, I found out how them pesky burros had been a-trickin' me these years. I returned to camp and looked down into a canyon close by; there was Sappho, her head motionless over a large rock, and Frankey and Johnny bringin' every other mouthful of grass over to her rock, so's she wouldn't move her head and ring that tell-tale bell."

Death Valley Scotty's Heroism

One night as we sat in the patio of [Death Valley] Scotty's palace, a feminine tourist turned wide eyes toward our host.

"Oh, Mr. Scott," she twittered, "you have saved *so* many lives here on the desert, won't you *please* tell us one real story of your heroism?"

Scotty scratched his head. "Well, lemme think—"

"How about the old couple that were lost up Sure Death Canyon?" I suggested.

"Them? That warn't nuthin'." Scotty grunted and shifted in his chair. "Well, I was out prospectin' when I come across an old man an' woman. They'd driv up in their auto an' th' damn thing had broke down. They hadn't et or had a drop o' water fer two days. Must 've bin all of a hundred and fifty miles from anywhere.

"Well, I only had my burros, but I give 'em what water and grub I had an' started back to git help. Then I got to thinkin'. Time I got back them two would be dead. An' they'd sure have suffered to beat hell. Took me quite a spell to figger out what to do."

Scotty stopped.

"Oh, Mr. Scotty," the woman begged, "what happened?"

"Went back an' shot 'em!" Scotty wiped his eyes. " 'Twas th' only Christian thing to do."

"Whispering" Thompson and His Pet Trout

[Oregon's freighter hero, J.G. ("Whispering") Thompson caught a trout in the Umatilla River and took it home to his ranch. While admiring it, he recalled that he had never heard of anyone's trying to teach fish tricks of any kind. He decided, therefore, to experiment.]

"So [he said], I got me a bar'l and filled it with water and put the fish in it. That blamed fish would swim around and around crazy as a loon, and I stood thar talkin' to him and tryin' to quiet him down. Soon he got over most of his skittishness and in three or four days he got real gentle and would stick his head out of the water for food, grasshoppers and sich, I'd gathered for him.

"Purty soon he got in the habit of showin' off and would swim around that bar'l a mile a minute. One day, while circling around at a great rate, he gave an extra flop and fell out on the floor. I was skeered he'd busted hisself and picked him up pronto and put him back in the water. Howsomever, he was so tickled to get out of the bar'l he did it again in a couple of minutes. He kept doin' this till I calkalated I'd leave him out of the water long enough for him to find out the need of bein' in it.

"But, skin me for a polecat, that thar fish seemed to like it out thar, and began to wiggle. I'll be etarnally switched if he didn't soon learn to wiggle hisself across the floor just like a snake. In a few days he could get around the house real pert, and as the doorstep was low he soon pushed hisself out into the yard. The little feller had a lot of fun wiggling around through the grass and catchin' bugs and worms. I didn't have to catch him any more grasshoppers, he jest fed his ownself.

"One day while that thar fish was out chasin' bugs, I saw a cow in my garden jest over the crick. Runnin' across a foot log, I was about to pick up some rocks to throw at that thar blamed cow when I looked back at the crick. Thar was that fish wiggling along the log. Afeared I was gonna lose him, I forgot all about the cow and gallivanted back to the log, but afore I could get him he slipped from the log into the water, and afore I could get him out, I'll be damned if that fish didn't drown afore my eyes.

"Why, I wouldn't have taken a thousand dollars for the derned leetle cuss!"

☞ 8 ☜

"The Gospel According to Joe Miller"

A certain minister was fired by the board of deacons and, protesting his dismissal, he said to the board, "Didn't I argufy? Didn't I magnify? Didn't I glorify?" "Yes," they agreed, "you argufy, magnify, and glorify, but you don't tell us wherein. We want a preacher who will tell us wherein."

ALBEN W. BARKLEY

Introduction

From the medieval *exemplum* to the Southern preacher tale, the illustrative story has been a powerful aid to the sermon. With "twenty minutes to wake up the dead," in Henry Ward Beecher's words, the preacher also has had to combat the evils of listlessness and sleeping in church by preaching the "gospel according to Joe Miller," as Beecher was accused of doing. When a funny story failed to keep the congregation awake, plain-speaking Yankee parsons often resorted to ingenious stratagems. "In our church," Beecher observed once, "we have had for some years an able-bodied committee whose duty it is, whenever anyone is discovered asleep in the congregation, to go at once into the pulpit and wake up the pastor."

Amidst the primitive, challenging conditions of the backwoods camp meeting, the pioneer preacher needed no waking. His lively art of dramatic storytelling was a natural accompaniment to his impromptu, ejaculatory eloquence, and of a piece with the homely vernacular style of folk sermon and spiritual.

"Look at that boy," preached the evangelist in the Ohio River country, dangling the vivid allegory of the Prodigal Son above the rostrum for all to see. "Knows more than his Pap. Wants his portion of the estate. Dad sells off the steers and gives him his share. Now look at him. See that deck o' cards in the upper-left coat pocket. A plug o' terbaccer in one hip pocket and a six-shooter in the other. And watch him as he goes to that far-off country. He wanted to get money in a hurry—not make it, mind you, *get* it. He went to gambling and was going to make a hundred thousand dollars and then go home and lord it over the folks. But every time he played he lost. Kept on losing. Got down to his last dollar. Then had no dollar at all. Would have starved to death if he hadn't got a job feeding hogs. At last he had to eat what the hogs left." And when the preacher wound up with the Prodigal Son's return—"Dad . . . killed the fatted calf and put a ring on his finger"—Uncle George burst out laughing. "That was the wrong place to put the ring. He oughter a put it in his nose."

Thus the preacher's audience enriched anecdotal humor with stories about pastors and their flocks—from the pranks and tricks of eccentric Peter Cartwright and "Crazy" Lorenzo Dow to "talking back" to the preacher, as in J. Mason Brewer's story of the Negro minister who was telling off the "good-for-nothin' young generation." "Yeah, dey's goin' to hell in Cadillacs; dey's goin' to hell in Packards; dey's goin' to hell in Buicks; dey's goin' to hell in Dodges." "Well," spoke up Sister Flora, "mah boy'll be back, 'caze he's goin' in a T-model Fo'd."

"P.C."

A young farmer who had been converted at one of the revivals went before the next conference and asked for a license to be a preacher. "I know I am born to preach the word," said the applicant, "for I have had three visions all the same, and it has made a lasting impression on me." "What was your vision?" asked a bishop. "Wal, I saw a big, round, blue ring in the sky, and inside, in great gold letters, were 'P.C.' It meant, 'Preach Christ,' and I want to join the conference."

The argument was about to carry when an old pastor stood up in the back part of the hall and said, "Young man, we don't doubt your intentions, nor do we doubt that you saw the vision with the golden 'P.C.'; but I am of the opinion that the 'P.C.' meant 'Plough Corn.'"

The convert is still a farmer.

Horse-Trading Preacher

There [was] a traveling preacher whose opinions with regard to horse-flesh were quite as ready and orthodox as were the views of scriptural doctrine with which he enlightened his backwoods audiences. This preacher once stopped at the house of a brother of the same faith, who had reared a beautiful colt. Between the two services on Sunday the two ministers visited the barn of the resident preacher, where the latter introduced his promising colt to his traveling brother. The guest was so much delighted at the fine points of the animal that he could not restrain himself, and he immediately blurted out the question: "Suppose it were not the Sabbath, Brother S., how would you trade?"

Raising the Minister's Salary

A New Hampshire farmer, going to a parish meeting, met his minister, and told him that [the] society thought of increasing his salary. "I beg you not to think of any such thing," said the minister, "for it is about as much business to collect my present salary as I wish to attend to; if it should be increased, I should be obliged to devote my whole time to collecting it."

The Skinflint

In a certain [Maine] community there was a well-to-do man who had plenty of money, but he was unbelievably close, with the reputation of being a skinflint. One day a community gathering was being held to raise a fund to repair the church. The members were offering their somewhat meager sums and they were all wondering what the wealthy skinflint would do, who meantime was saying nothing. All of a sudden a piece of plaster from the dilapidated ceiling fell and hit him on the head. He leaped to his feet and said, "I will give twenty-five dollars!" An old woman in the congregation shouted, "Oh, Lord, hit him again!"

Soaping the Preacher's Horn

There was no bell in the [Oak Bluffs] Camp Ground at the time, and when it was time for the congregation to assemble, a lusty-lunged clergyman would blow a huge fish-horn from his position in the high pulpit. As the majority of the people knew when the service was to begin, they would have the seats well filled before the blast shook the air, and only the stragglers would come trooping in at the summons. One day, a wearied soul, albeit somewhat venturesome, filled this horn with soft soap. The clergyman mounted to the pulpit, filled his lungs and blew mightily upon the horn. The blast of sound was somewhat muffled, but it was followed by shrieks and cries as the gathering received the spray of soap. Confusion followed and an investigation started that went on and on, but no clew to the culprit could be uncovered.

The sequel occurred some time later. One evening the mourner's bench was crowded with repentants, and among them was one man who seemed to be in great mental distress. He moaned loudly, called upon God for help, and gave other manifestations of a deeply troubled soul. The lusty-lunged clergyman before-mentioned descended to the bench and bent above the man.

"Tell me your trouble, brother," he said. "Let me help you to wrestle with it."

"Oh, it is awful," moaned the sinner. "I can't tell you!"

"But brother, if you will unburden your soul you may find peace. Otherwise it will continue to gnaw and destroy," warned the clergyman, warming up to his work.

"It's killing me, but I can't tell," groaned the man. "It's too, too awful!"

"Have you stolen, brother?" questioned the clergyman gently.

"Oh, 'tis worse than that!" was the agonized answer.

"Have you been loose-living; is it adultery?"

"Oh worse, much worse than that!"

"Is it—is it murder?" almost gasped the clergyman, now fully shocked at the behavior of the man.

"Oh, worse, much worse than that!"

The clergyman sprang to his feet. "Brother Smith, come here and hold my coat!" he shouted. "I've found the man who soaped that horn!"

"Schooner Ashore!"

[In 1876 it was still a misdemeanor in Massachusetts to perform any labor on Sunday, except work of necessity or charity, including the preservation of property which might be lost by delay.] A [Cape Cod] clergyman was once holding forth to his congregation on Sunday morning—on the vanity of human riches, perhaps—when a man rushed in with the alarm, "Skewner ashore!" The audience arose *en masse*, and made a stampede for the doors, but were arrested by the voice of their shepherd, who exclaimed in stentorian tones, "Brethren, before you leave, I've one last word to give ye," at the same time descending the pulpit stairs and walking deliberately down the aisle, "and that is," continued he, as he joined the crowd at the door, "let's all start fair!" and off he went like arrow from bow, and was the first man on the scene of "accessible value."

The Millerite

Up in Peekskill, [New York], we had at one time that Millerite excitement, which went over the country, when Miller predicted that on a certain night, at twelve o'clock, the world would come to an end. A very good and pious man, a shoemaker of our village, believed in Miller's doctrine. He left his business early on the last day, locked up his store and prepared himself and family for the dread event. When twelve o'clock had passed, and it got to be one o'clock, the shoemaker felt that he must appeal to some higher power than Mr. Miller. He said, "O Lord, if the millennium is to come, let it come now, and then I shall be translated at once to a land where the people wear no shoes and shoemakers are happy in doing nothing; but if it is to be postponed, let me know now, because I must get ready Mrs. Brown's shoes for Sunday morning church or lose the best customer I have."

Watch and Pray

Nicholas Waln, though a regular Quaker preacher, was a great wag, and many are the good things said by him which are still current in certain Philadelphia circles. He was once traveling on horseback in the interior of Pennsylvania in company with two Methodist preachers. They discussed the points of difference in their respective sects, until they arrived at the inn where they were to put up for the night.

At supper, Waln was seated between the two Methodists, and before [the three of] them was placed a plate containing two trout. Each of the circuit-riders placed his fork in a fish and transferred it to his plate, after which each shut his eyes and said an audible grace before meat. The Quaker availed himself of the opportunity to transfer both of the trout to his own plate, merely remarking, when the others opened their eyes, "Your religion teaches you to pray, but mine teaches me both to watch and pray."

The Quaker's Veracity

When the first summer schools were held at the end of the last century, an elderly Friend was disturbed over what seemed to him new and upsetting ideas. Upon his return home, he arose in meeting and said, "I have been greatly distressed over the new views which are being taught in these summer schools and I have heard of an instance which shows how dangerous it is to hold unsuitable views. A young man who had lost his faith went out sailing with a friend of his. A storm came up, and the man who had lost faith was drowned." The Friend sat down and seemed somewhat uneasy, clasping and unclasping his hands and crossing his knees. Finally he got up a second time and said, "For the honor of truth, I think I should say that the other young man was drowned also!"

A Letter to the Lord

[During the Depression] a Virginia mountaineer complained grievously to his minister about the hard times that had been visited upon him. "Things have been going from bad to worse," brooded the man. "I'm behind with taxes, and there's a mortgage due. I'll have to have help or lose the place."

The minister sought to bear up the man's spirit, and suggested that he take his troubles to the Lord. The farmer, simple soul, trudging homeward over his rough acres, suddenly got a bright idea. He would write a letter to the Lord, setting forth his case in detail, and plead for help to carry on the farm. He would need, of course, a few hundred dollars to make a payment on the mortgage, but he would be moderate in his petition, putting down the figure at five hundred.

Having carefully written the letter, he addressed it to "The Lord." For a street address he wrote, "On High," and being not far from the capital, he penned "Washington, D.C." as the last line.

In due course of time the letter, which bore no return address, landed at the Dead Letter office. Amused, the clerk in charge referred the letter to a friend, who, his curiosity whetted, opened the envelope and read the letter. And as he read, he was deeply touched by the simple faith and the sad plight of the mountaineer. Half in humor, half inspired by sympathy, he passed the letter on to a wealthy officeholder, with a suggestion. As a result, the letter went through a number of hands, and a total of three hundred dollars was subscribed to the cause of the mountaineer. This sum the clerk mailed, in three one-hundred dollar bills, to the address given, without comment.

A few days later the mountaineer met the minister, who asked as to his affairs.

"Well, you know what you said about taking my troubles to the Lord," said the man.

"Yes, yes," answered the minister eagerly.

"I did just that, Reverend," continued the man. "I thought it would be easier to get in all facts if I wrote my troubles in a letter. So I told the Lord I needed five hundred dollars, and I got my answer only yesterday."

"Of course, the Lord would answer your prayers," said the minister confidently.

"Yes," agreed the mountaineer, "and it was postmarked Washington, all right, but when I looked in the letter, I found that them crooked politicians over there had opened the envelope and taken out two hundred dollars."

Going to Heaven by Land

There were two brothers who had confessed Christ and were ready to be baptized. The preacher took one of them by the hand and led him down into the water. He said, "My son, I baptize you in the name of the Father and the Son," and he plunged him under. The boy slipped out of the preacher's hand and was drowned before he could be saved. So it was the second boy's turn to be baptized. The preacher called him, but he said, "Mister, my brother may have gone to heaven by water, but I am going by land," and he wouldn't allow the preacher to baptize him.

The Holy Ghost

One time a Negro preacher wishing to convince his congregation of the power of the Lord tied a string around a white pigeon's leg, and giving it to a little Negro boy, sent him up in the loft of the church.

After the sermon was over, the preacher said, "Now, bruthern an' sistern, I's gwine ter kneel an' pray an' when I's finished, de holy ghost, in de form of a white dove, is gwine ter descen' on my haid lak it did on de Lawd's haid."

He prayed and prayed and still no holy ghost descended. After another long prayer the little Negro stuck his head out of the loft and exclaimed, "Lawd, Marse Preacher, de cat done eat de holy ghost!"

Praying to the Lord

One of the older Negroes, Uncle Ben we called him, used to pray nightly from his cabin. He prayed so earnestly and with such feeling that his neighbors and any who chanced to hear him could not resist the temptation to linger and listen to his invocations. The theme of his prayer usually took the turn of an entreaty to God to come and get him, to descend and take him home to Heaven. He avowed that he had had enough trials and tribulations. He told God he wanted to be "transferred." A group of the colored boys had accumulated upon his threshold one night when he was praying with more energetic fervor than usual. He at last came to the point where he called upon God to come and "transfer" him at once. Then one of the boys rapped upon his door. "Who's dat?" he called. His voice trembled with fear and emotion. "It's the Lord," the boy replied. "The Lord you've been prayin' to." In a flash the old man replied, "You needn't come in, Lawd! There ain't nobody home."

The Preacher and the Bear

The Reverend Adoniram Jackson, who died recently in his native town, in South Carolina, was one of the most prayerful old colored men to be found in all the Sunny South. His congregation idolized him, but that is not saying that they followed all his teachings. One sultry Sabbath day the reverend gentleman had preached at length, concerning his favorite subject of "prayer," to another of his congregations in a town ten miles distant from his home. "Now to conclude, bredern an' sistern," he said, as he approached the end of his discourse, "when yo' wants anything real bad, pray fo' it. I wouldn't pray fo' Inkwell White dah in de back pew to wake up. I jes says, 'Wake up dar!' in a voice lak dat. Don't yo' go to sleep again, Mistah White! But ef yo' wants anything real bad, bredern, lak a melon or a side ob bacon or a chicken, jes pray fo' it. An' ef yo' is in danger, pray to have it removed; pray, an' I bets it will scoot away!"

That afternoon the minister was trudging along the highway on his ten-mile homeward walk when a large black bear crashed out of the underbrush. The prayerful Divine did not pray for the danger to disappear; he took to his heels and the tall timber. In that tall timber he found a very tall tree, and the way he forgot his rheumatism and skinned up it to roost on the topmost branch and pray took away the bear's breath. So the animal sat down at the foot of the tree to wait. It was still stationed there an hour later, when a couple of the Reverend Mr. Jackson's late congregation came along and heard him praying in this wise: "I's not 'fraid ob danger, but I is a cautious man an' a preacher dat's needed yere. Yo' tooked Daniel out ob de lion's den an' yo' helped Jonah out ob de big fish's mouth, so help me down dis tree. But ef yo' don't want to help me, Lawd, please then don't help de b'ar. An' don't shake de tree, whatever happens!"

The Hard-Shell Kernel

A Hard-Shell preacher wished to bring forth a good illustration, as he thought, and hence he took a walnut, as he called it, into the pulpit with him, and something to crack it with. On holding it up, in the course of the sermon, he said:

"My friends, you see this walnut—well, this outer hull here is like the Methodists, soft and spongy, with no strength into it; see, I even break it with my fingers," and suiting the action to the words, he disclosed the nut [inside] and said: "This is like the Missionary Baptists, hard and dry, with no substance in it; but the kurnul—the kurnul, my friends, is like the good old primitive Hard-Shell Baptist faith, full of fatness and sweetness."

He then proceeded to crush the walnut and give his hearers an ocular demonstration of his illustration, but behold, it was [spoiled]; and, to the utter astonishment of his hearers, he cried out: "By jinks! It's rotten."

In Partnership with the Lord

A Negro preacher . . . called on a hard-working parishioner, a farmer, each year, soliciting increasingly larger contributions for the church. One year, when he got the proposed levy past a point which the farmer thought he could bear, the preacher sought to persuade him by arguing, "Your farm's been good to you, and the Lord's been good to you. Part of this land belongs to the Lord. You're in partnership with Him, so you ought to give Him His share." To which the farmer replied, "I acknowledges that the farm is paying off, that the Lord's been good to me, and that He is my partner. But did you ever see this place when the Lord was looking after it Hisself?"

The Language of Appreciation

[A] fellow . . . came up to the preacher and said, "Reverend, that was a damn good sermon you preached this morning!"

The minister replied, "I appreciate your compliment, but not your language."

"Yes, sir," the fellow went on, "it was such a damn good sermon that I put a hundred dollars in the collection plate."

"The hell you did!" said the minister.

The Preacher and the Cat

There was a preacher stayed one night in an old vacant house. He built a fire and he set in front of the fire reading a book, and he told himself, "The' aint no such thing as a ghost!"

Well, a little cat—just a kitten—passed by, and the preacher he didn't pay it any mind. Well, the' come a cat then, he was three, four feet high. Cat said, "Yes, sir! The's two of us, tonight."

Preacher said, "Yeah, and in a minute, the' won't be but one." And he streaked out and he ran! Got to a log by the creek and set down to rest. That big old cat sidled up. He said, "We sure had a good race, didn't we?"

Preacher looked at that monstrous big cat and he said, "Yeah, and we damn sure gonna have another one, right now!"

A Religious Captain

[An] old couple wanted to go down river with a captain who was a religious man. They went to a old hell-raisin' Cap in St. Paul and said they heard he was a religious man. "The hell you have," the Cap said, and when he wrote home his letters burned up the mail bags. "Get out, you blankety-blank so-and-so's! More lunatics come to me than any dash-dash captain on the river."

The old lady whispered to her old man, "He's not very religious, do you think?" The old man said, "Well, I dunno. This is out west, Mama. He swears, but he looks like a man to depend on in a storm. I guess religion out here has got to be kind of sketchy and useful. We'll go by his boat and if he don't swear any harder than he just done, mebbe Providence will let him squeeze through on the down trip and sink him when he comes up!"

Denominational Differences

It is related that Professor [George Washington] Gale [of Knox College] putting up at an early tavern was inquired of by the landlord thus: "Stranger, I perceive you are a clergyman; please let me know whether you are a Presbyterian or a Methodist."

"Why do you inquire?" said the traveler.

"Because I wish to please my guests, and I have observed that a Presbyterian minister is very particular about his own food and bed, and a Methodist about the feed and care of his horse."

"Very well," said the professor, "I am a Presbyterian, but my horse is a Methodist."

The Same Three Fellows

"The only schooling I ever had [said Abraham Lincoln] was in a log schoolhouse when reading-books and grammars were unknown. All our reading was done from the Scriptures, and we stood up in a long line and read in turn from the Bible. Our lesson one day was the story of the faithful Israelites who were thrown into the fiery furnace and delivered by the hand of the Lord without so much as the smell of fire upon their garments. It fell to one little fellow to read the verse in which occurred, for the first time in the chapter, the names of Shadrach, Meshach, and Abed-nego. Little Bud stumbled on Shadrach, floundered on Meshach, and went all to pieces on Abed-nego. Instantly the hand of the master dealt him a cuff on the side of the head and left him wailing and blubbering as the next boy in line took up the reading. But before the girl at the end of the line had done reading he had subsided into sniffles, and finally became quiet.

"His blunder and disgrace were forgotten by the others of the class until his turn was approaching to read again. Then, like a thunderclap out of a clear sky, he set up a wail which even alarmed the master, who with rather unusual gentleness inquired, 'What's the matter now?'

"Pointing with a shaking finger at the verse which a few moments later would fall to him to read, Bud managed to quaver out the answer: 'Look there, marster—there comes them same damn three fellers again.' "

Nearly Out of Bible

A wandering Methodist preacher tried to sell a Bible to a backwoods housewife struggling with mean surroundings and a lot of ragged children. She was polite to begin with, but resented his aggressiveness in trying to make a sale. Shouldn't every home have a Bible? Did they have a Bible in this home? The harassed housewife said of course they had a Bible. The preacher wanted to know where it was. She called the children and they organized a hunt for the missing Bible. At last one of the children dug up a few torn pages of Holy Writ. The woman took the pages and held them up in triumph. The preacher argued that this was no Bible. The woman argued it was, adding, "But I had no idea we were so nearly out."

"Done with the Bible"

A country meeting-house, that was used once a month, was quite a distance from any other house. The preacher, an old-line Baptist, was dressed in coarse linen pantaloons, and shirt of the same material. The pants, manufactured after the old fashion, with baggy legs, and a flap in the front, were made to attach to his frame without the aid of suspenders. A single button held his shirt in position, and that was at the collar. He rose up in the pulpit, and with a loud voice announced his text thus: "I am the Christ whom I shall represent today."

About this time a little blue lizard ran up his roomy pantaloons. The old preacher, not wishing to interrupt the steady flow of his sermon, slapped away on his leg, expecting to arrest the intruder, but his efforts were unavailing, and the little fellow kept on ascending higher and higher. Continuing the sermon, the preacher loosened the central button which graced the waistband of his pantaloons, and with a kick off came that easy-fitting garment.

But, meanwhile, Mr. Lizard had passed the equatorial line of the waistband, and was calmly exploring that part of the preacher's anatomy which lay underneath the back of his shirt. Things were now growing interesting, but the sermon was still grinding on. The next movement on the preacher's part was for the collar button, and with one sweep of his arm off came the tow linen shirt.

The congregation sat for an instant as if dazed; at length one old lady in the rear part of the room rose up, and, glancing at the excited object in the pulpit, shouted at the top of her voice, "If you represent Christ, then I'm done with the Bible."

On the Lord's Side

Abraham Lincoln was one day chatting with a delegation of church-men who had called upon him, offering him spiritual guidance. "The Lord is on our side," the spokesman reassured the President. Lincoln merely nodded silently. "But, Mr. Lincoln, don't you believe that the Lord is always on the side of the right?" "Yes," the President answered, "and, therefore, it is my concern to see that this nation and I stay on the Lord's side."

Padre Martinez and the Storekeeper

The small village of San José [New Mexico] baffled all [Padre Marti-nez'] efforts for revenue. The people there never killed a chicken or goat to feed him, but gave grudgingly of their ordinary fare. Though he worked hard at his sermons, the people listened without interest, and the collection box came back almost empty. The padre, not lik-ing this meager harvest for his labors in the vineyard, consulted with the local storekeeper about his failure.

"Your trouble, Padre," said the man, "if I may speak as one busi-nessman to another, is that the people of San José do not like your sermons." Padre Martinez protested that he preached his best ser-mons in that parish, the kind of sermons that made others turn out their pockets.

"That may be so," replied the storekeeper, "but you don't get re-sults, do you? And the trouble is that you stand up in the pulpit and never mention good old San José, our patron saint. You preach and preach about Jesus and Mary, and a dozen saints, while our own San José stands there behind you. He is the only one who understands us, the only one who does anything for us. It makes us angry to have him neglected. We want to hear about San José."

A hint was enough for Padre Martinez, and the next time he came to the village he placed the image of San José in the pulpit and stood aside. "Perhaps you wonder," he began, "why I have placed San José in the pulpit. It is because, without speaking, he can preach a better sermon than I. This is the feast day of the greatest of saints, your own patron, San José. He didn't preach to birds like San Francisco, but spent his time helping people. You should all pray to San José. He will find a good mate for you. He will help your crops to grow. San José will help you all through purgatory. San José is the only saint who is worth talking about. San José . . ."

At this point the storekeeper, who had been passing the collection box, came up to him and whispered, "Padre, stop now. The box is full of money, so don't mention San José again, or there won't be any money left in the village tomorrow . . . and remember, I am the storekeeper."

Lorenzo Dow and Gabriel

Some of the American preachers of the past have delivered sermons more startling than edifying, and have condescended to singular tricks to arrest and take the attention of the audience. Lorenzo Dow, one of these preachers, it is said, was on his way to preach in South Carolina, under a large spruce tree, when he overlooked a colored lad who was blowing a long tin horn, and could send forth a blast with rise, and swell, and cadence, which waked the echoes of the distant hills. Calling aside the blower, Dow said to him, "What's your name, sir?" "My name—Gabriel, sir," said the brother in ebony. "Well, Gabriel, have you been to Church Hill?" "Yes, massa, I'se been dar many a time." "Do you remember a big spruce pine tree on that hill?" "Oh, yes, massa, I knows dat pine." "Did you know that Lorenzo Dow had an appointment to preach under that tree tomorrow?" "Oh, yes, massa, everybody knows that." "Well, Gabriel, I am Lorenzo Dow, and if you'll take your horn and go tomorrow morning, and climb up into that pine tree and hide yourself among the branches before the people begin to gather, and wait there till I call your name, and then blow such a blast with your horn as I heard you blow a minute ago, I'll give you a dollar. Will you do it, Gabriel?" "Yes, massa, I takes dat dollar."

Gabriel, like Zaccheus, was hid away in the tree top in due time. An immense concourse of persons, of all sizes and colors, assembled at the appointed hour, and Dow preached on the judgment of the last day. By his power of description he wrought the multitude up to the opening of the scenes of resurrection and grand assize at the call of the trumpet peals which were to wake the sleeping nations. "Then," said he, "supposing, my dying friends, that this should be the hour. Suppose you should hear at this moment the sound of Gabriel's trumpet?"

Sure enough, at that moment the trumpet of Gabriel sounded. The women shrieked, and many fainted; the men sprang up and stood aghast; some ran; others fell and cried for mercy; and all felt for a time that the judgment was set, and the books were opened. Dow stood and watched the drifting storm till the fright abated and someone discovered the colored angel who caused the alarm quietly perched on a limb of the old spruce and wanted to get him down to whip him, and then [Dow] resumed his theme, saying, "I forbid all persons present from touching that boy up there. If a colored boy with a tin horn can frighten you almost out of your wits, what will ye do when ye shall hear the trumpet thunder of the archangel? How will you be able to stand in the great day of the wrath of God?"

Lorenzo Dow Raises the Devil

At one time when Mr. Dow was traveling in the South, he asked permission to remain overnight. The woman of the house informed him that her husband being from home, he could not stay. He insisted that she should grant him permission as there was no other house near to which he could go; but she positively refused, until he told her he was a preacher, and would sleep in the stable if he could do no better. This information, together with his long beard, at once suggested to her who he was, and she accordingly inquired if he was Lorenzo Dow. Being answered in the affirmative, she waived her objections, and concluded that he might stay—probably more out of fear that evil might befall her if she turned him off, than out of a wish to have him in the house.

Accordingly Mr. Dow put up; and about the usual hour retired to bed in a back room, where he had not lain long until he heard a man arrive, who he soon discovered was not the woman's husband. A series of jokes commenced between the woman and the man, which continued with a good deal of pleasantry till about midnight, when, all of a sudden, their pleasures were disturbed by a rap at the door, which announced that the husband had returned. Alarm and consternation followed. There was but one door, and at it stood the husband. To be caught there at that hour of the night would, to say the least of it, insure him a sound thrashing. To escape seemed impossible. At this critical juncture, when the ingenuity of man had failed, the quick perception of woman, as in most cases of emergency, found an expedient. At the foot of the bed stood a large gum full of raw cotton, in which she concealed the visitor. Then turning round very composedly, opened the door and received her husband.

But his lordship had been at the grogshop, and was in what the Irish schoolmaster called an "uproarious mood." "Hush, hush," said the wife, as the husband blundered in, and roared out, "Thunder and potatoes, Mag, and why didn't you open the door?" "Hush, my dear, hush! Lorenzo Dow is in the house." "O blood and tobacco! And is it Lorenzo Dow, the man who raises the Devil?" "Sure it is, and why don't you be still?" "Oh, by Saint Patrick, he shall come forth, and you shall see the Devil before you sleep." So blundering into the bedroom, Mr. Dow was compelled to come forth, and nothing would satisfy the husband but that Lorenzo must raise the Devil.

Mr. Dow protested and urged his inability to perform such wonders; but no excuse would satisfy the uncompromising husband—he had heard that Dow could raise the Devil, and now that he had him in his house, he determined that he must. At length, said Mr. Dow, "If you will stand in the door and give him a few thumps as he passes, but not so hard as to break his bones, I will see if I can raise him." So saying, he took the candle in his hand, and walking up and down the room, Lorenzo touched the candle to the cotton, and said, "Come forth, old boy." Out jumped the hidden gentleman all in a blaze, and breaking for the door like a mass of living fire made good his escape, but not without first receiving a good rap over the shoulder from the husband's cudgel as he passed the threshold. The job was now done, Lorenzo had raised the Devil, and the husband thought it a real wonder performed by the Yankee preacher.

On Wings of Song

An old lady in one of the parishes of Peter Cartwright, an early Methodist pioneer, often annoyed him by being more noisy than pious and by often going off on a high key. In a class meeting one day, when her soul was filled with ecstatic emotions, she rapturously cried out, "If I had one more feather in the wing of my faith, I would fly away and be with my Saviour!"

"Stick in the other feather, Lord," interjected Cartwright, "and let her go!"

Holding the Gun All Over the Tree

While no man ever preached with more concentration and conciseness, sometimes [Sam Jones] would realize that there was a possibility of his crowd not following him closely; then he would leave his thread of argument and stay with his crowd. This frequently led him to say, "I may not always stick to my text, but I'll stick to my crowd." The story told him by Brother Richardson illustrated the point rather forcefully.

"There is nothing like holding the gun all over the tree," he would say. "As with the old, palsied father who went out with his son squirrel hunting, the old man's part was to shake the bush, and he had but to take hold of the bush and it would shake without any effort. On one occasion when he was to shake the bush and turn the squirrel, after he had turned the squirrel for four or five different shots for his son, all of which failed of their mark, the old man said, 'Give me the gun, and you shake the bush.' The boy gave up the gun and shook the bush and turned the squirrel. The old man held up the gun in his palsied hands, and as it wobbled all over the tree, bang went the gun and down came the game, at which the old man remarked joyfully, 'I told you I'd git him.' The boy replied, 'Anybody could kill a squirrel up a tree who would hold a gun all over it, as you did.'"

From a Preacher's Joe Miller

Maybe the city parson has little need of a joke book, but if you're going to preach in the country you'd better have a stock of stories on hand, and funny ones at that. There's nothing like a good story to illustrate a point or to wake up a tired farmer in the pew. Henry Ward Beecher used to say that the sermon period was "twenty minutes in which to wake the dead." I've found that good stories waken them up quicker than anything else, so I've made a study of the art of story-telling in the pulpit as well as on the platform.

I've discovered that the first rule is that the story must be relevant and should always have some connection with the thing you're talking about. . . .

TAKING UP WHERE HE LEFT OFF

There are occasions when a speaker, going back to a place for the second or third time, wants to take up where he left off. I've often used the following story to prepare my listeners for that.

In a farmer's family were two boys, both of whom he wanted to send to college. They were twins, so the none-too-rich parents hit on a happy scheme to get that college education for both their sons. George went to college first. He would go for one term, then send the work and the exams back to brother John. Then John would go for a term and send the work and exams back home to George.

So John went up the second term, and his father said to him, "Now, John, don't let them rattle you. You just take up where George left off." John kept thinking of that, when he arrived on the campus. It worked perfectly. He went into George's class, into George's fraternity, into George's outside activities. He even decided to pay a call on George's girl, who lived down on Faculty Row. Dressed in his Sunday best, he mounted the professorial porch and rang the bell. The door burst open and out rushed a beautiful girl. She flew into his arms with "Oh, George, George, I thought you were never coming to see me again."

John made the most of that moment. "I know, I know," he cried, taking her in his arms. "I'm not George, but I'll begin right where George left off."

JACK OF ALL TRADES

Many times, when I am introduced, the host will speak of my numerous occupations—farmer, minister, barber, and so forth. That always gives me a chance to tell of the barber who cut his customer all over the face, and then tried to patch up the cuts with pieces of brown paper. The man looked at himself in the glass when the torture was over, and he was so mad that the barber feared for his life.

"I'm sorry," said the barber. "I had bad luck with you."

The customer pulled out a dollar bill and passed it over. The barber started to give back his change, but the customer roared, "Keep the change, man, keep the change. It's the first time I've ever met a man who was a barber, a paperhanger and a butcher at the same time."

THE CLERGYMAN'S DYING MESSAGE TO HIS VESTRYMEN

Stories on the various denominations always go over well at any sort of gathering, but especially at a church one. The minister who can crack a joke on his own denomination gets off to a good start. I've done it many a time by telling about the Episcopal clergyman who was fatally ill. It seemed fitting for him to leave a message to his vestrymen. They brought him a pad and a pencil and with trembling fingers he wrote:

> Go tell the vestry that I'm dead,
>   But they need shed no tears;
> For though I'm dead I'm no more dead
>   Than they have been for years.

THE FARMERETTE AND THE GARDENER

City people coming out to the country always know a lot more about farming than the native, and they often provide good illustrative material for the country preacher. I know of one city woman who came out our way and sent for a native to help her make a flower garden. He dug out a bed, rounding it up nicely and smoothing it down with a rake. Then he asked, "What are you planning to plant here, ma'am?"

"I plan to put salivas in here," she replied proudly.

"Salivas? Salivas?" repeated the old farmer. "You don't mean salvias, do you?"

"I mean what I say. Do as you're told."

He did as he was told.

Then the city farmerette said, "Samuel, what would you suggest as a border around this bed?"

"Well, I'll tell you, ma'am," came the quick answer. "If you're going to have this great big bed of salivas here, I would suggest that you have a mighty wide border of spittoonias around the outside."

Oil Strike in Hell

[This is what happened to the story of the gold miner in heaven when the] story came to Texas, and took on a Texas character. A speculator in leases on oil lands—in the vernacular, a lease-hound—died and went to heaven, only to find the place so crowded that he could barely find standing room inside the door. The lease-hound hit upon a trick which he hoped would relieve the congestion. He produced a scrap of paper and pencil from his pocket and scribbled the following note, "Oil discovered in hell," which he dropped on the floor. Presently the note was picked up and read. The man who read it whispered to a few other persons and slipped away. Those in whom he had confided similarly whispered to others and followed him. There was a regular exodus in the direction of the reported strike.

Watching the procession, the man who had started the rumor grew more and more restive. At length he could stand it no longer, and muttering, "There may be something in this thing—I guess I'd better look it over," he joined the stampede.

Biblical Wildcatting

It seems that a director of Standard Oil Company was reading his Bible one day and came upon Exodus 2:3, which states, ". . . and daubed it with slime and with pitch."

Now the director reflected that where there is pitch there is usually oil. So Standard Oil engineers went to work and today they are pumping vast quantities of oil out of the ground near Moses' home town in Egypt.

☞ **9** ☜

Heroes Without Haloes

After [Charles Farrar] Browne [better known as Artemus Ward] had created immense enthusiasm for his lectures and books in the Eastern states, which filled his pockets with a handsome exchequer, he started, October 3rd, 1863, for California, a faithful account of which trip is given by himself. . . . Previous to starting, he received a telegram from Thomas Maguire, of the San Francisco Opera House, inquiring what he would "take for forty nights in California?" Mr. Browne immediately telegraphed back: "Brandy and water. A. Ward."

MELVILLE D. LANDON
(*"Eli Perkins"*)

Introduction

A cracker-barrel history of America could be compiled from grapevine gossip and canards about our historical and headline heroes. Such apocryphal biography—hidden or buried history—comes close to the original meaning of the word anecdote as "things unpublished" or "secret history." It brings to light not only lost or suppressed chapters in the lives of great men but the equally fascinating stories of the "lost men" of history. Here, as elsewhere in popular tradition, the authenticity of the anecdote is less important than its color. All that matters is that "it makes a good story."

On another and far less interesting level of tradition are the retouched or embellished historical and biographical anecdotes that are the stock-in-trade of almanacs, readers and speakers, books of ana, edification, and inspiration. Being written rather than told, these pious anecdotes have acquired some of the stuffiness as well as the sacredness of print, and the heroes are, correspondingly, stuffed shirts.

Between these two extremes is a body of eye-witness or contemporary anecdotes which, even in print, have not lost their vernacular flavor and the fresh juices of life. If these stories are often irreverent, so were the heroes.

"Out of their own mouths" comes the strong language of Ethan Allen, revealing a streak of profanity in northern New England eloquence less well known than its restraint. Before he uttered his immortal words at the surrender of Fort Ticonderoga, "In the name of the Great Jehovah and the Continental Congress," Allen is reported to have said, "Come out of here, you damned old rat," or, more trenchantly, "you sons of British bitches." As Stewart H. Holbrook tells the story of Ethan Allen's dying words, the parson soothingly said to him on his deathbed, "General Allen, the angels are waiting for you." "Waiting, are they?" said Allen. "Waiting, are they? Well, God damn 'em, let 'em wait!"

From Pennsylvania German almanacs of the closing decades of the last century, Arthur D. Graeff has unearthed this intimate, juicy little story of henpecked Abraham Lincoln. One night as Abraham was leaving to join his friends, his wife warned him that she was going to bed promptly at ten and would not get up to open the door for him if he was late. At eleven o'clock Abraham rapped on the door—once, twice, three times, until at last a window on the second floor was opened and Mrs. Lincoln stuck her head out. "Who is there?" "I am." "You know what I said, Abraham." "Yes, but, dear wife, I have something wonderful to tell you. Let me come in." "I need hear nothing. Probably more political nonsense." "But, wife, it is important. I have a telegraphic message that I have been elected President." "Oh, Abraham! This is terrible. I never would have believed that you would drink too much, but now I know it is true. Go your way and sleep off your drunk at the place where you drank the stuff!" And down came the window with a clatter.

"Old Wolf" Tests the British Major's Courage

In the time of the old French [and Indian] War much jealousy existed between the British and provincial officers. A British major, deeming himself insulted by General (then Captain) Putnam, sent him a challenge. Putnam, instead of giving him a direct answer, requested the pleasure of a personal interview with the major. He came to Putnam's tent, and found him seated on a small keg, quietly smoking his pipe, and demanded what communication, if any, Putnam had to make. "What you know," said Putnam. "I'm but a poor miserable Yankee that never fired a pistol in my life, and you must perceive that if we fight with pistols you have an undue advantage of me. Here are two powder kegs. I have bored a hole, and inserted a slow-match in each. If you will be so good as to seat yourself there, I will light the matches, and he who dares to sit the longest without squirming shall be called the bravest fellow."

The tent was full of officers and men, who were heartily tickled with the strange device of the "Old Wolf," and compelled the major by their laughter and exhortation to squat. The signal was given, and the matches lighted. Putnam continued smoking, quite indifferently, without watching at all the progressive diminution of the matches—

but the British officer, though a brave fellow, could not help casting longing and lingering looks downwards, and his terrors increased as the length of the match diminished.

The spectators withdrew, one by one, to get out of the expected explosion. At length, the fire was within an inch of the keg. The major, unable to endure longer, jumped up, and drawing out his match, cried out, "Putnam, this is wilful murder; draw out your match; I yield." "My dear fellow," cried Putnam, "don't be in such a hurry. They're nothing but kegs of onions!" The major was suddenly missing, having sneaked off.

Franklin and the Stamp Act

Dr. Franklin's peculiar talent was that of illustrating subjects by apposite anecdotes. When he was agent for the province of Pennsylvania he was frequently applied to by the ministry for his opinion respecting the operation of the Stamp Act; but his answer was uniformly the same, "that the people of America would never submit to it." After news of the destruction of the stamp papers had arrived in England, the ministry again sent for the doctor to consult with; and in conclusion offered this proposal, "that if the Americans would engage to pay for the damage done in the destruction of the stamped paper, etc., the parliament would then repeal the act." The doctor, having paused upon this question for some time, at last answered as follows:

"This puts me in mind of a Frenchman, who, having heated a poker red-hot, ran furiously into the street, and addressing the first Englishman he met there, 'Hah! Monsieur, voulez-vous give the plaisir, de satisfaction, to let me run this poker only one foot into your body?' 'My body!' replied the Englishman. 'What do you mean?' 'Vel den, only so far,' marking about six inches. 'Are you mad?' returned the other. 'I tell you, if you don't go about your business, I'll knock you down.' 'Vel den,' said the Frenchman, softening his voice and manner, 'vil you, my good sir, only be so obliging as to pay me for the trouble and expense of heating this poker?' "

Revising the Sign

When the Declaration of Independence was under the consideration of Congress, there were two or three unlucky expressions in it, which gave offense to some members. The words "Scotch and other auxiliaries" excited the ire of a gentleman or two of that country. Several strictures on the conduct of the British King, in negativing our repeated repeals of the law which permitted the importation of slaves, were disapproved by some Southern gentlemen, whose reflections were not yet matured to the full abhorrence of that traffic. Although the offensive expressions were immediately yielded, those gentlemen continued their depredations on other parts of the instrument. I [Thomas Jefferson] was sitting by Dr. Franklin, who perceived that I was not insensible to the mutilations.

"I have made it a rule," said he, "whenever it is in my power, to avoid becoming the draughtsman of papers to be reviewed by a public body. I took my lesson from an incident which I will relate to you. When I was a journeyman printer, one of my companions, an apprentice hatter, having served his time, was about to open shop for himself. His first concern was to have a handsome signboard, with a proper inscription. He composed it in these words: 'John Thompson, *Hatter, makes and sells hats for ready money,*' with the figure of a hat subjoined. But he thought he would submit it to his friends for their amendments. The first he showed it to thought the word 'hatter' tautologous, because followed by the words 'makes hats,' which shew he was a hatter. It was struck out. The next observed that the word 'makes' might as well be omitted, because his customers would not care who made the hats; if good and to their mind, they would buy, by whomsoever made. He struck it out. A third said he thought the words 'for ready money' were useless, as it was not the custom of the place to sell on credit—everyone who purchased expected to pay. They were parted with and the inscription now stood: 'John Thompson sells hats.' Sells hats? says his next friend; why, nobody will expect you to give them away. What then is the use of that word? It was stricken out, and 'hats' followed it, the rather as there was one painted on the board; so his inscription was reduced ultimately to 'John Thompson,' with the figure of a hat subjoined."

Astronomical Toasts

At the close of the American Revolutionary War, Dr. Franklin, the English ambassador, and the French minister, Vergennes, were dining together. They agreed that each should offer a toast. The English ambassador began: "George the Third, who, like the sun at noonday, spreads his light and illumines the world."

The French minister followed with: "His Majesty, Louis the Sixteenth, who, like the moon, fills the earth with a soft, benevolent glow."

Franklin gave the following: "George Washington, General of the armies of the United States, who, like Joshua of old, commanded both the sun and the moon to stand still, and both obeyed."

Franklin's Advice

"Friend Franklin," said Myers Fisher, a celebrated Quaker lawyer of Philadelphia, one day, "thee knows almost everything; can thee tell me how I am to preserve my small-beer in the backyard? My neighbors are often tapping it of nights."

"Put a barrel of old Madeira by the side of it," replied the doctor. "Let them but get a taste of the Madeira, and I'll engage they will never trouble thy small-beer any more."

Farmer-Governor Chittenden

[Vermont's] first Governor was Thomas Chittenden, born and brought up in Salisbury in Western Connecticut, close to the New York line. He was elected . . . at a time when other American governors wore brocaded waistcoats, coats of broadcloth or silk, lace ruffles, silk stockings. They rode in coaches with a liveried driver on the seat. Their wives wore silk dresses, never cooked a meal or washed a dish.

Governor Chittenden was a working farmer. He wore homespun clothes and a loose farmer's smock-frock. Once a finely dressed gentleman on horseback came along the road. A load of hay blocked the way. To the elderly farmer on the load the traveler called out, "Can you tell me where Governor Chittenden's house is?"

The farmer called back, "I'm goin' right there now."

The man on horseback followed the hay wagon till it turned into a barnyard. The gray-haired farmer slid down, handed the reins to a waiting boy, dusted off his hands, and said pleasantly, "Now what can I do for you? I am Governor Chittenden."

Ethan Allen's Wife

[Ethan Allen's] first wife was the kind of woman now called a pill, a lemon, a sour-puss. In Sunderland they said she got out of bed the wrong side every morning of her life. Somebody, passing by the Arlington burying-ground and seeing the gravedigger at work, asked him who the grave was for. "For Mrs. Allen," said the digger with a neutral intonation. He added reflectively, "I never dug a grave I enjoyed more." I also was brought up on the story that when plans were being made for transporting her coffin to the church, a Sunderland man made a cordial offer of help in these words: "You could call on any of the neighbors. There's not a man in town wouldn't be glad to help out."

Ethan Allen never pretended his wife's character was different from what everybody knew it to be, but he never philandered with other women. He was an affectionate father to his children. Only once (as far as I have ever heard) did he speak of his bad-tempered wife. That was at two o'clock at night, on the road between my great-grandmother's home and the old burying-ground of Arlington.

This is the way that story goes: Ethan Allen had ridden down to Bennington to pass a cheerful evening with tavern cronies. Some of the lively Arlington boys, in the horseplay years of their teens, made themselves weirdly tall by draping sheets from broomsticks held up over their heads, and hid behind the marble tombstones. When Ethan came along, these eight-foot-tall, white specters ran out to the road, screeching that they were devils come to carry him off to hell.

Ethan Allen waited composedly till his voice could be heard, and said, "Go back to your master Beelzebub, and tell him I said, 'I fear him not, for I married his sister.'"

Washington's Guard

An Englishman in Philadelphia, speaking of President Washington, was expressing a wish to an American to see him. While this conversation passed, "There he goes," replied the American, pointing to a tall, erect, dignified personage, passing on the other side of the street. "*That* General Washington!" exclaimed the Englishman. "Where is his guard?" "*Here*," replied the American, striking his breast with emphasis.

Jefferson and the Landlord

When Thomas Jefferson was Vice-President of the United States, the landlord of the main hotel in Baltimore was a man named Boyden. The hotel at a later date was owned by a German named Belzhuber.

One day Jefferson, unattended by servants, arrived at the hotel on horseback. The rider dismounted and, whip in hand, entered the barroom, where a number of persons were assembled. Boyden surveyed the newcomer from head to foot and surmised that he was a farmer, a low country person who would not be a credit to his establishment. Boyden said curtly, "We have no room for you, sir." Jefferson, not appearing to have heard the remark, asked whether a room could be had. The proprietor repeated his statement. Jefferson turned around, called for his horse, and departed.

Soon afterwards a very wealthy gentleman came to the hotel and informed Boyden that the departing guest was Thomas Jefferson, Vice-President of the United States.

"Vice-President of the United States!" Boyden was overcome with amazement.

"Yes, and the greatest man alive," reasserted the [other].

"Murder and death, what have I done! Here, Tom, Jim, Jerry, Jack —where are all of you? Run and tell that gentleman that he may have forty rooms if he wishes. Tell him to come back. He can have my wife's bedroom—my own—what have I done! Here, Harriet, Mary, Julie—clear everything; he shall have the best of everything!"

Meanwhile, Jefferson had ridden to Market Street, where he met several old acquaintances, and from there to the Globe Hotel, which stood near the corner of Mary and Charles streets. Here Boyden's servants found the Vice-President and conveyed their master's message.

"Tell him I have engaged a room," said Jefferson. "Tell Boyden that I value his good intentions highly, but if he has no room for a dirty farmer he shall have none for the Vice-President."

Rum and Rain

Some talk got out about the Justices of the Supreme Court drinking too much. They all lived at the same house in Washington. They did not bring their wives to Washington with them, as the accommodations were frightful. They boarded together at 2-½ Street, called Marshall Place. That house still stands. They lived together like a sort of family and discussed their cases all the time; but they had every Saturday as "consultation day" at the capital.

There came to be a little talk about the Justices drinking too much, even then. So [John] Marshall said . . . , "Now, gentlemen, I think that with your consent I will make it a rule of this Court that hereafter we will not drink anything on consultation day—that is, except when it rains."

The next consultation day—I think the Court went on the water wagon during the week—when they assembled, Marshall said to Story, "Will you please step to the window and look out and examine this case and see if there is any sign of rain." Story looked out the window, but there was not a sign of rain. . . . He came back and seriously said to the Chief Justice, who was waiting for the result, "Mr. Chief Justice, I have very carefully examined this case, I have to give it as my opinion that there is not the slightest sign of rain." Marshall said, "Justice Story, I think that is the shallowest and most illogical opinion I have ever heard you deliver; you forget that our jurisdiction is as broad as this Republic, and by the laws of nature, it must be raining some place in our jurisdiction. Waiter, bring on the rum."

John Marshall, Errand Boy

[A gossipy Richmond tradition] tells of how, later in life, [John Marshall] was standing at the entrance of the Market House when a young man, lately come to town, addressed Judge Marshall as "old man" and asked if he would "like to make a ninepence by carrying a turkey home for him?" It was just the sort of prank Marshall enjoyed, and he took the turkey without a word and followed the stranger to his own door.

"Catch!" said the hirer, on their arrival there, tossing ninepence to his hireling.

Marshall caught the coin and pocketed it. . . . The young man before he had entered his house saw a better-known citizen, in passing, lift his hat with deference to the retreating figure, and asked, "Who is that shabby old fellow?"

"The Chief Justice of the United States."

John Randolph and the Landlord

[John Randolph] was traveling through a part of Virginia in which he was unacquainted; during the meantime, he stopped during the night at an inn near the forks of the road. The innkeeper was a fine gentleman, and, no doubt, one of the first families of the Old Dominion. Knowing who his distinguished guest was, he endeavored during the evening to draw him into a conversation, but failed in all his efforts. But in the morning, when Mr. Randolph was ready to start, he called for his bill, which, on being presented, was paid.

The landlord, still anxious to have some conversation with him, began as follows: "Which way are you traveling, Mr. Randolph?"

"Sir?" said Mr. Randolph, with a look of displeasure.

"I asked," said the landlord, "which way are you traveling?"

"Have I paid you my bill?"

"Yes."

"Do I owe you anything more?"

"No."

"Well, I'm going just where I please, do you understand?"

"Yes."

The landlord by this time got somewhat excited, and Mr. Randolph drove off, but to the landlord's surprise, in a few minutes, sent one of his servants to inquire which of the forks of the road to take. Mr. Randolph not being out of hearing distance, the landlord spoke at the top of his breath: "Mr. Randolph, you don't owe me one cent; just take which road you please."

It is said that the air turned blue with the curses of Randolph.

Daniel Webster's First Defense Plea

A woodchuck had dug its hole near the garden of the Webster homestead. Daniel Webster, aged ten or twelve, together with his brother Ezekiel, had set a trap and one morning the animal was captured.

Ezekiel wanted to kill the animal at once, but young Daniel pleaded for its life. A dispute ensued and Ebenezer Webster, the father, decided to act as judge. Pointing to the woodchuck, he said to his sons, "There is the prisoner. Ezekiel, you take the part of the plaintiff, and you, Daniel, will be the defendant."

Ezekiel then reviewed the misdeeds of the beast; reminded the judge of the damage he had done to the garden; predicted that if the culprit were given his life and freedom he would resume his thieving ways but would be too shrewd to be caught in a trap the next time. Furthermore, argued Ezekiel, the animal's fur could be sold to redeem, in part, the losses which his depredations had occasioned. He concluded his argument by demanding the death of the criminal.

The father was proud of his son (Ezekiel Webster later became a distinguished jurist), then turned to Daniel with these words: "Now, Dan, it is your turn. Let me hear what you have to say."

Daniel, unperturbed by the impression which his brother's argument had made on his father, fixed his black eyes upon the cage where the prisoner cringed and began:

"God created the woodchuck so that it might enjoy the sunshine and the free air in forest and field. God creates nothing without purpose, and the woodchuck has the same right to life that other creatures have. It is no thief like the fox or the wolf; it feeds upon meager fare, of which we have more than we need; it takes nothing from us except that which it needs to live. God gave to us all we have and should we not be willing to share this small portion? The woodchuck has merely followed its God-given instinct and we have no right to deny it its life and freedom when it follows that instinct."

During this plea tears welled in the elder Webster's eyes. He felt that God had blessed him with two sons, more than other men were blessed. Each speech had awakened his sympathies to the extent that he forgot his role of judge, and before Daniel had finished his speech the father called out to his older son, "Ezekiel, let the woodchuck go!"

Daniel Webster at School

When quite young, at school, Daniel [Webster] was one day guilty of gross violation of the rules. He was detected in the act, and called up by the teacher for punishment. This was to be the old-fashioned "feruling" of the hand. His hands happened to be very dirty. Knowing this, on his way to the teacher's desk, he spit upon the palm of his right hand, wiping it off upon the side of his pantaloons. "Give me your hand, sir," said the teacher, very sternly. Out went the right hand, partly cleansed. The teacher looked at it a moment, and said, "Daniel, if you find another hand in this schoolroom as filthy as that, I will let you off this time!" Instantly from behind his back came the left hand. "Here it is, sir," was the ready reply. "That will do," said the teacher, "for this time; you can take your seat, sir."

Webster and the Stage Driver

On one occasion [Daniel] Webster, the American senator, was on his way to Washington, and was compelled to proceed at night by stage from Baltimore. He had no traveling companion, and the driver had a sort of felon look which produced no inconsiderable alarm in the senator. "I endeavored to tranquillize myself," said Webster, "and had partly succeeded, when we reached the dark woods between Bladensburg and Washington—a proper scene for murder or outrage—and here, I confess, my courage again deserted me. Just then the driver turned to me, and, with a gruff voice, inquired my name. I gave it to him. 'Where are you going?' said he. The reply was, 'To Washington. I am a senator.' Upon this the driver seized me fervently by the hand, and exclaimed, 'How glad I am! I took you for a highwayman.'"

Why Johnny Appleseed Punished His Feet

Shortly after the War of 1812, [John Chapman] stopped at the Amariah Watson House in Washington Township, [Ohio], walked in without knocking, and accosted Mrs. Watson who, not recognizing him and being nervous from the recent Indian scares, was quite frightened.

"Madam," the barefooted caller said, straightening up and assuming considerable dignity, "God bless you—fear no evil—I am Johnny Appleseed!"

Mr. Watson came in presently and asked why he went barefooted.

"Sir," he said, holding out a foot, "this one had been guilty of offense in treading unmercifully upon one of God's dear creatures"—a snake—"and as a corresponding punishment I am now exposing it to the inclemency of the weather."

Crockett and the Fur Hat

Crockett was on an electioneering tour. It was about that time in the summer when the farmers had "laid by" their crops. Due notice had been given Crockett was to speak at Lawrenceburg, a small village in Lawrence County, Tennessee. At the time appointed there was a goodly number of country people present. Our hero was on hand early, and according to his custom, he, for an hour or so before taking the stand, amused the "boys" by "telling yarns," etc. In the crowd of men who were thus enjoying Davy's eccentricities there was a good-natured, though rather verdant, country chap, about twenty-one. He was clad in the plainest "homespun"—copperas pants and coarse cotton shirt. In striking contrast with this unpretending costume, he wore a bran-new fur hat; and the peculiar manner in which he bore himself under this covering showed that he was not only very proud of it, but that it was the first article of the kind that he was ever master of.

Crockett, at the conclusion of a hearty laugh over one of his stories, took occasion to compliment the new fur hat of our friend.

"And now, Jim," said Davy (he had heard the chap addressed by that familiar name), "what would you think if I were to say that I could take that hat, cut it into two pieces, and then put it together so that it would be as perfect as ever?"

"Oh! you couldn't do anything of the kind," replied the countryman.

"I'll bet you a quart of whisky on it," says Crockett.

"Done," says the proprietor of the fur hat.

Hereupon Davy took the hat, and with his pocket-knife cut directly through the brim and crown, dividing it in twain. Then taking a half of the hat in each hand, he exposed the divided chapeau to the spectators, in order that there should be no mistake about the matter. "You see, gentlemen," said he, "that there is no cheating. You see that the hat is cut clear open."

"Yes," they all responded.

The crowd looked on with intense anxiety to see how this thing was to end; most of them, however, knowing, from Crockett's character, that he would come out victorious and give them a good laugh. Our green country friend, meanwhile, was already laughing at the prospect of winning his wager.

Crockett then commenced blowing his breath upon those parts of the divided hat which he proposed to reunite, and at the same time uttering some mysterious words, and attempting some peculiar manipulations, which, he contended, were to accomplish the magical work. All at once he ceased his efforts, and, looking round upon the crowd, said, in a very serious tone, "Gentlemen, upon my word I have forgotten how. Jim has won the whisky."

Crockett on Washington

As a boy of fifteen, Uncle Turner had once stayed overnight in Raleigh. Early in the evening he had gone out upon the public square to see a bear which one of the natives had captured and was exhibiting in an enclosure near the statehouse. While looking at the bear, who should walk up but Davy Crockett. A small coterie was already following the popular idol to observe him at close range. My uncle joined them.

Crockett, according to my uncle, was all that he had been pictured and described by the press. A striking, powerful figure, the Tennessean wore his celebrated coonskin cap. And, to the delight of the crowd, he began making witty remarks about the bear, soon drifting into accounts of some of his own hunting experiences in the Appalachian Mountains. He said that, upon his first return from Washington to his home, several of his constituents wanted to know what the people of the capital were like. He had answered by telling them that the chief difference was the way in which they ate their meals. "For instance," Crockett said, "they have breakfast when the sun is one or two hours high, or when you fellows have done practically a half a day's work. About one or two o'clock in the day they have what they call lunch, and 'way in the night, they have their dinner." When a constituent asked, "Davy, when do they eat their supper?" Crockett had told them, "They don't get that until the next day."

Polite Phillips

In the days of the great Abolition furor, Wendell Phillips was accosted on a lecture tour by a minister who hailed from the state of Kentucky, a place with very different views concerning the ideas of the Abolitionists.

The clergyman, who was more militant on behalf of his prejudices than on behalf of his creed, said, "You're Wendell Phillips, I believe."

"Yes, I am."

"You want to free the slaves, don't you?"

"Yes, I do."

"Well, why do you preach your doctrines up North? Why don't you try coming to Kentucky?"

Phillips began to counter-question the man. "You're a preacher, are you not?"

"Yes I am, sir."

"Are you trying to save souls from Hell?"

"Why yes, sir. That is my business."

"Why don't you go there then?" suggested Mr. Phillips.

Greeley's Handwriting

[Many stories are told of Horace Greeley's illegible handwriting.] Some time before the [Civil] War he wrote a note to a member of the [New York *Tribune*] staff, discharging his employee for gross neglect of duty. The expelled journalist went to California, and returning after several years, he encountered Mr. Greeley in Printing House Square. The chief recognized him and inquired, with customary cordiality, where he had been and how he had gotten along. "Let me see," he continued, "didn't I get mad at you and send you off?" "Oh, yes. You wrote me a note telling me to clear out. I took it with me. Nobody could read it; so I declared it a letter of recommendation, gave it my own interpretation, and got several first-class situations by it. I am really very much obliged to you."

Stonewall Jackson in Heaven

[Thomas J.] Jackson . . . was the greatest military genius the world has ever seen. With a handful of barefooted men he flanked large armies and whipped three or four armies in a day. His genius was displayed oftenest in that flank movement.

When he died, St. Peter sent two angels for him. They searched the field, the hospitals—the whole army, but could not find him. They returned and told this to St. Peter. Said he, "Why, he has flanked you both and has been here six hours."

Short Rations

During the latter part of the [Civil] War, General [Robert E.] Lee lived exclusively on cabbage boiled in salt water, and allowed himself the luxury of middling [meat] only twice a week. One day, while in camp, he invited a number of distinguished guests to dine with him. When the table was set, behold a great pile of cabbage and a piece of middling about as big as the palm of your hand. Out of politeness, the guests all declined middling. Next day the general called for it. "Marse Robert," said his servant, "Marse Robert, de fac' is, dat ar was borrid middlin', an' I done 'turn'd it to de man whar I borrid it fum." General Lee heaved a deep sigh of disappointment, and pitched into his cabbage.

Lincoln and the Whetstone

In 1834 when Lincoln was a candidate for the legislature, he called on a certain farmer to ask for his support. He found him in the hay field, and was urging his cause when the dinner bell sounded. The farmer invited him to dinner, but he declined politely, and added, "If you will let me have the scythe while you are gone I will mow round the field a couple of times."

When the farmer returned he found three rows neatly mowed. The scythe lay against the gate post, but Lincoln had disappeared.

Nearly thirty years afterward the farmer and his wife, now grown old, were at a White House reception, and stood waiting in line to shake hands with the President.

When they got near him in the line . . . Lincoln saw them, and calling an aide, told him to take them to one of the small parlors, where he would see them as soon as he got through the handshaking. Much surprised, the old couple were led away. Presently Mr. Lincoln came in, and, greeting them with an outstretched hand and a warm smile, called them by name.

"Do you mean to say," exclaimed the farmer, "that you remember me after all these years?"

"I certainly do," said the President, and he went on to recall the day he had mowed around the farmer's timothy field.

"Yes, that's so," said the old man, still in astonishment. "I found the field mowed and the scythe leaning up against the gate post. But I have always wanted to ask you one thing."

"What is it?" asked Mr. Lincoln.

"I always wanted to ask you, Mr. President, what you did with the whetstone?"

Lincoln smoothed his hair back from his brows a moment, in deep thought; then his face lighted up.

"Yes, I remember now," he said, "I put that whetstone on top of the high gate post."

And when he got back to Illinois again, the farmer found the whetstone on top of the gate post, where it had lain for more than twenty-five years.

The Uglier Man

Lincoln was, naturally enough, much surprised one day when a man of rather forbidding countenance drew a revolver and thrust the weapon into his face. In such circumstances "Abe" at once concluded that any attempt at debate or argument was a waste of time and words.

"What seems to be the matter?" inquired Lincoln, with all the calmness and self-possession he could muster.

"Well," replied the stranger, who did not appear at all excited, "some years ago I swore an oath that if I ever came across an uglier man than myself I'd shoot him on the spot."

A feeling of relief evidently took possession of Lincoln at this rejoinder, as the expression upon his countenance lost all suggestion of anxiety.

"Shoot me," he said to the stranger, "for if I am an uglier man than you I don't want to live."

Lincoln on Bagging Prairie Chickens

"Every man has his own peculiar and particular way of getting at and doing things," said President Lincoln one day, "and he is often criticized because his way is not the one adopted by others. The great idea is to accomplish what you set out to do. When a man is successful in whatever he attempts, he has many imitators, and the methods used are not so closely scrutinized, although no man who is of good intent will resort to mean, underhanded, scurvy tricks.

"That reminds me of a fellow out in Illinois, who had better luck in getting prairie chickens than any one in the neighborhood. He had a rusty old gun no other man dared to handle; he never seemed to exert himself, being listless and indifferent when out after game, but he always brought home all the chickens he could carry, while some of the others, with their finely trained dogs and latest improved fowling pieces, came home alone.

" 'How is it, Jake?' inquired one sportsman, who, although a good shot who knew something about hunting, was often unfortunate, 'that you never come home without a lot of birds?'

"Jake grinned, half closed his eyes, and replied, 'Oh, I don't know that there's anything queer about it. I jes go ahead an' git 'em.'

" 'Yes, I know you do; but how do you do it?'

" 'You'll tell.'

" 'Honest, Jake, I won't say a word. Hope to drop dead this minute.'

" 'Never say nothing if I tell you?'

" 'Cross my heart three times.'

"This reassured Jake, who put his mouth close to the ear of his eager questioner, and said, in a whisper, 'All you got to do is jes to hide in a fence corner an' make a noise like a turnip. That'll bring the chickens every time.' "

Lincoln Shorts

The bevy of bright young ladies to which Miss Todd belonged before her marriage to Mr. Lincoln used to have a good deal of sport at this awkward young man's expense. One evening at a little party Mr. Lincoln approached Miss Todd, and said, in his peculiar idiom, "Miss Todd, I should like to dance with you the worst way." The young lady accepted the inevitable and hobbled around the room with Mr. Lincoln. When she had returned to her seat, one of her mischievous companions said, "Well, Mary, did he dance with you the worst way?" "Yes," she answered, "the very worst."

In the summer of 1862, General McClellan wrote from the Peninsula a long letter to Mr. Lincoln (then President) giving him advice as to the policy that should be pursued in relation to the rebellion, etc. "What did you reply?" asked someone of Mr. Lincoln. "Nothing. But it made me think of the Irishman whose horse kicked up and caught his foot in the stirrup. 'Arrah!' said he. 'If you are going to get on I will get off.' "

After a state election in New York in which the Republican party was defeated, while Mr. Lincoln was President, he was asked how he felt after having heard the news. He replied, "Somewhat like the boy in Kentucky who stubbed his toe when running to see his sweetheart. He said he was too big to cry, and too badly hurt to laugh."

Mr. Lincoln said once that the best story he ever read in the papers of himself was this: "Two Quakeresses were traveling on the railroad, and were heard discussing the probable termination of the war. 'I think,' said the first, 'that Jefferson [Davis] will succeed.' 'Why does thee think so,' asked the other. 'Because Jefferson is a praying man.' 'And so is Abraham a praying man,' objected the second. 'Yes, but the Lord will think Abraham is joking,' the first replied conclusively."

Grover Cleveland's Advice

A lean, ragged man came to the White House lawn and got down on his hands and knees and was chewing at the grass. President Cleveland from a front window saw the man and asked, "What are you doing?" When the man said, "I'm hungry and have to eat grass," Cleveland told him, "Why don't you go around to the back yard where the grass is longer?"

Teddy Roosevelt and Moses

We were at Winton, North Carolina, during a term of court. The place where everybody foregathered in the evening was the old Parker and Jordan Tavern, now gone. The lobby or lounging room was a great big room about thirty feet by twenty, and there was a large fireplace at either end of the room.

On this particular evening—it must have been in 1900 or along there—a number of us were sitting around talking about everything under the sun, when Mr. [W. D.] Pruden turned to me and said, "Whom are you Republicans going to nominate for President this time, Mr. Meekins?" "Theodore Roosevelt, I hope," was my reply. Mr. Pruden was an admirer of Mr. Taft, whom he considered a great lawyer. Then he asked why I wanted Roosevelt. "Because," I said, "I think Mr. Roosevelt is the biggest man in this country. I'd go further and say I think he is the biggest man in the world today."

Mr. Pruden said, "Well, I expect you think he is the greatest man that ever lived."

I said there were few in history who were any greater, barring, of course, the Saviour.

"Do you think he is a greater man than Moses was?"

I said, "Well, I don't know that I would say that. Moses was a wonderful leader."

And at that point another man in the crowd spoke up and said, "Well, I don't know if Teddy is a greater man than Moses, but I'll bet one thing—if Teddy had been leading the children of Israel I'll be durned if it would have taken 'em forty years to get out of the wilderness!"

How Taft Stopped a Through Train

In most small towns the ability to stop a through train was the surest indication of a leading citizen. It meant that one knew a director of the road or stood well at the bank which held stock in the line. Outsiders, even if famous, were not always able to do it. The late William Howard Taft, portly and dignified, could not persuade the station agent to stop the through train at a prairie town where the next local was not due for sixteen hours. Finally, with an eye to his three hundred pounds, he had an inspiration. "Tell them to stop for a large party," he said.

Silent Cal

[Calvin Coolidge] could, at an occasion that demanded a speech from him as a dignitary who had just broken the ground for the cornerstone of a public building, think briefly, then point to the new sod and, in the voice of Vermont, curiously intone, "There's—a—mighty—fine fishworm," and go hence, leaving many people thunderstruck.

Also, he could walk, wordless and blank, through miles of glassed-in tropical fruits and rare, exotic flowers all blooming in spite of the young strength of a Delaware winter, to point suddenly to a familiar growth with the single word, "Bananas."

Then there were the reporters who sought to draw him [out] on the subject of a biography of George Washington that seemed, to some, to contain actionable slander against the Liberator. Mr. Coolidge had listened patiently. Then, after a recital of enormities, he had gone to a window and pulled aside the curtain. Through it the reporters had beheld the rigid, uplifted finger of a famous monument. "I see it's still there," had murmured the thirtieth President.

Of course, a few individuals who pretended to understanding, and who proclaimed the universal eminence of Mr. Coolidge, were occasionally subjected to mockery when, almost consciously, the President refuted them. One such, talking to a friend aboard the *Mayflower*, with the Chief Executive only a few feet distant, pointed to an airplane that had flown into their ken and declared that so excellently wise was Cal, and so thoroughly conversant with everything in [the] matter, that he could without doubt identify the tiny air-swept blot as a land or sea plane. There fell a little pause during which the President drew near. He looked at the plane. Then he said to his admirer, "Guess that gull must be dead. It hasn't moved for quite a spell."

The Art of Making Enemies

Franklin D. Roosevelt was asked by his secretary whether he had heard that one of Roosevelt's old friends was saying some very nasty things about him. Roosevelt said, "Is that so? When did this happen?" His secretary said, "Oh, the past few weeks." Roosevelt leaned back in his chair, took a puff from that long cigarette holder which he always carried, blew out a thoughtful ring or two, and said, "That's strange. I don't recall ever doing him any favor."

Message to Moscow

This was in the days of the great friendship between the United States and the USSR. The following telephone conversation is reputed to have taken place between Franklin D. Roosevelt and Joseph Stalin. Franklin D. Roosevelt calls up and gets the chief operator of Minsk, and he says, "Chief Operator of Minsk?" "Ya-ah!" "Connect me with the chief operator of Pinsk." And the call went from Minsk to Pinsk to Stalingrad, and finally it got through to the great hall in Moscow where Stalin was. Then Franklin D. Roosevelt got on the wire and he says, "Hello, Joe? Frank! Giants three, Dodgers nothing."

Roosevelt's Greatness

A hillman told me the other day that Roosevelt was the greatest man that ever lived. "Greater'n Jesus Christ," he said solemnly. "Christ said, 'Follow me and ye shall not want.' Roosevelt says, 'Set down, boys, and I'll bring hit to ye.' "

Politics in Westchester County

The true politician thoroughly enjoys and appreciates the *mot juste*, even when it is at his own expense and sometimes, indeed, particularly when it is at his own expense. It is an indication that he's still important enough to be hated. President Roosevelt's favorite story was about the commuter from Westchester County, a Republican stronghold, who always walked into his station, handed the newspaper boy a quarter, picked up the *New York Herald Tribune*, glanced at the front page, and then handed it back as he rushed out to catch his train. Finally the newsboy, unable to control his curiosity any longer, asked his customer why he only glanced at the front page.

"I'm interested in the obituary notices," said the customer.

"But they're way over on page twenty-four, and you never look at them," the boy objected.

"Boy, the son of a bitch I'm interested in will be on page one."

☞ **10** ☜

Spellbinders and Bureaucrats

An Illinois lawyer, in defending a thief, said to
the jury: "True, he was rude, so air our bars.
True, he was rough, so air our buffaloes. But he
was a child of freedom, and his answer to the
despot and tyrant was that his home was on the
bright setting sun."

San Francisco Call
December 3, 1856

Introduction

The traveling anecdote in America has profited greatly from the traveling men who have helped to collect and disseminate as well as create anecdotal humor. Thus the storytellers' grapevine telegraph is supplemented by the story carriers—the peddler, the itinerant actor and showman, the traveling salesman, the circuit-riding lawyer, judge and preacher, and the stump-speaking politician. Because the last two like to pride themselves on being more or less "oneddicated" men of the people, they are especially close to the oral and traditional sources.

There are two kinds of political storytellers. The first is the spellbinder and demagogue who uses the story simply as a vote-getting expedient or as a smokescreen for ignorance and prejudice. Davy Crockett learned early that both the treat and the funny story relieve a dry subject, and make a candidate popular. On a higher level, a storyteller like Lincoln is the voice of the people rather than merely the people's choice or the mouthpiece of party bosses. With him the story and storytelling are more than politics; they are life itself.

The late Alben W. Barkley, "Washington's greatest storyteller," was particularly successful in retelling old stories so that they were transformed and transplanted—"revivified and refertilized," writes Beverly Smith, "in . . . the rich soil of Old Kentucky."

Because the rural political gathering is a social gathering, seeking entertainment even more than enlightenment, the good stump-speaker raconteur must be an actor, a mimic, and a showman, and, above all, one of the folks, just a big old country boy, like "The same old Delmar" in the latter's East Texas political speaking.

"Well, I come out here to help on this graveyard workin', and you all know that's all I done. I didn't go around these farms and stop a man at work to 'lectioneer. When I see a man puttin' in a honest day at the plow, and I want to ask his vote, I walk right down the row with him, and maybe take a hand at the plow—while I haven't plowed none since I been in office. . . . Now you all know that the present Gov'ner of our state is tryin' to git the County Sup'intender's office made appointive insteada lettin' you all elect who you want. . . . Well, when that happens you won't see spittoons in the County Sup'intender's office any more. . . . But you all know me—I always liked my cut o' Star Navy. It always seemed to me that when you can slap a man on the back and git a chew o' tobacco outa him, that he's a feller you understand. Well, maybe Ah'll chew myself outa office, but if I do I sure haven't forgot how to plow."

Bounding the United States

Among the legends of [the] Civil War there is a story of a dinner-party, given by the Americans residing in Paris, at which were propounded sundry toasts concerning not so much the past and present as the expected glories of the American nation. In the general character of these toasts, geographical considerations were very prominent, and the principal fact which seemed to occupy the minds of the speakers was the unprecedented bigness of our country.

"Here's to the United States!" said the first speaker. "Bounded on the north by British America, on the south by the Gulf of Mexico, on the east by the Atlantic Ocean, and on the west by the Pacific Ocean!"

"But," said the second speaker, "this is far too limited a view of the subject, and, in assigning our boundaries, we must look to the great and glorious future, which is prescribed for us by the manifest destiny of the Anglo-Saxon race. Here's to the United States!—Bounded on the north by the North Pole, on the south by the South Pole, on the east by the rising sun, and on the west by the setting sun!"

Emphatic applause greeted the aspiring prophecy. But here arose the third speaker, a very serious gentleman, from the far West. "If we are going," said this truly patriotic gentleman, "to lessen the historic past and present, and take our manifest destiny into account, why restrict ourselves within the narrow limits assigned by our fellow countryman who has just sat down? I give you the United States!— Bounded on the north by the Aurora Borealis, on the south by the procession of the equinoxes, on the east by the primeval chaos, and on the west by the Day of Judgment!"

Lincoln's Jackass Story

Once there was a king, who hired him a prophet to prophet him the royal weather. One day, the king notioned to go fishin' but the best fishin' place was nigh unto where his best sweetie-pie lived. So he aimed to wear him his best clothes. He called in his imperial prophet and said, "Prophet, is hit a-comin' on to rain?" And the prophet says, "No, yo' Highness, hit hain't a-comin' on to rain, not even a sizzle-sozzle."

So the king he put on his best clothes and he got his fishin' tackle, and he started down the road toward the fishin' place and he met a farmer with an umbrella over his head and ridin' a jackass.

The king drewed himself up and he says, "Farmer, I hired me a high-wage prophet to prophet me my weather and he 'lows how hit hain't a-comin' on to rain, not even a frog-duster." So the king he went a-fishin' and hit come on to rain, a clod-buster and chunk-mover.

And the king's clothes was wetted and they shrunk on him, and the king's best gal she seen and laughed and the king was wroth and he went home and he throwed out his prophet. And he called to the farmer and says, "Farmer, I throwed out my prophet and I aim to hire you to prophet me my weather from now on'ards."

And the farmer says, "King, I hain't no prophet. All I done this evenin' was to look at my jackass' ears. For if hit's a-comin' on to rain, his ears lop down and the harder hit's comin' on the lower they lays, and this evenin' they was a-layin' and a-loppin'."

And the king says, "Go home, farmer, I'll hire me the jackass." (And that's how it happened. And the jackasses have been holding down all the high-wage government jobs ever since.)

Burying the Jackass

It seems that an old fellow one day was driving his cart, pulled by a jackass, through the best residential section of the town, and in front of the home of the leading citizen the jackass dropped dead. The poor old fellow, after an appropriate mourning period, unhitched the cart and drew it away, but he left the body of the jackass in front of the prominent citizen's house.

When the leading citizen arrived home and saw the jackass, he went to the telephone and called his congressman at Washington. The said legislator was known for his lack of courtesy, and when he heard the story of the jackass over the phone, he went up in the air and demanded that his constituent bury the animal and stop bothering the congressman. "That's all right, Congressman," the citizen said. "I'll be glad to bury the jackass." "Well," said the legislator, still annoyed, "why in heck did you call me up about it?" "Congressman," replied the constituent, "I intended to bury the jackass. But before I did, I wanted to let his relatives know he was dead."

The Great Man

I have lived long enough to have known many such: senators who have filled the galleries when they rose to speak; House heroes living while they could on borrowed money, then hanging about the hotels begging for money to buy drink.

There was a famous statesman and orator who came to this at last, of whom the typical and characteristic story was told that the holder of a claim against the government, who dared not approach so great a man with so much as the intimation of a bribe, undertook by argument to interest him in the merit of the case.

The great man listened and replied, "I have noticed you scattering your means round here pretty freely, but you haven't said 'turkey' to me."

Surprised but glad and unabashed, the claimant said, "I was coming to that," produced a thousand-dollar bank roll and entered into an understanding as to what was to be done next day, when the bill was due on the calendar.

The great man took the money, repaired to a gambling house, had an extraordinary run of luck, won heavily, and playing all night, forgetting about his engagement, went to bed at daylight, not appearing in the House at all. The bill was called, and there being nobody to represent it, under the rule it went over and to the bottom of the calendar, killed for that session at least.

The day after, the claimant met his recreant attorney on the avenue face to face and took him to task for his delinquency.

"Ah, yes," said the great man, "you are the little rascal who tried to bribe me the other day. Here is your dirty money. Take it and be off with you. I was just seeing how far you would go."

The comment made by those who best knew the great man was that if instead of winning in the gambling house he had lost, he would have been up betimes at his place in the House, and doing his utmost to pass the claimant's bill and obtain a second fee.

Washington "Nut" Story

Two businessmen, John and Jim . . . came to the capital on an urgent business project to plead for Federal assistance:

They worked for days in the capital, frantically seeing agency officials and assorted flunkies—clerks and receptionists who really made them sweat.

At last their mission was crowned with success. They retired to their hotel for a night of relaxation and imbibing. Late that night, Jim was awakened from a snooze by a noise in the bathroom. He found John lying in the bathtub, his arms outflung with only his hat, shorts and shoes on, yelling, "There ain't no lions in here, there ain't no lions in here."

Jim looked around him and proceeded to try to rouse John from this condition. He met with no success, so he ran to the phone, leafed through a directory and called a doctor. "Doc," he pleaded when he at last made contact with a medico, "you've got to come over here fast. My partner and I have been knocked around in circles in this nutty town for days, and I'm afraid it's gone to his head. He's lying in the bathtub shouting that the room isn't full of lions. But I tell you, Doc, he's crazy. The place is full of 'em."

"Arsenal of Bureaucracy"

[During World War II] a Japanese spy . . . had been sent to Washington to spot targets for a Japanese raid. Reporting to his superiors, the spy said, "It is useless to bomb Washington. The American government has been very forehanded. If you completely destroy one building and everyone in it, you accomplish nothing. For they already have two other buildings completely staffed with people doing exactly the same thing."

The Deaf Anti-New Dealer

There was an old gentleman who hated Roosevelt. He hated anything that had to do with the New Deal. Once, visiting his nephew in a New Jersey town that was notoriously New Dealish, he attended church. The old man had an ear trumpet—he was kinda deaf. The preacher was new. At the conclusion of the sermon the old man shouted to his nephew, "Who's the new preacher?" Upon which the nephew shouted into his uncle's ear trumpet, "Uncle, he's the son of a bishop." The uncle then shouted back, "Ain't they all?"

Progress

The Southern congressman . . . , interviewed on his sixtieth birthday, was asked by a reporter, "You've been in Congress for a long time, haven't you, sir?"

The representative replied, "Ah shuah have. Just about twenty-fahv yeahs."

The reporter continued, "Then you've seen some mighty big changes, haven't you?"

And the answer came: "Yeah, and Ah've been against them all."

Top Knot Come Down

[Senator Samuel J. Ervin's] gift for the illustrative yarn first drew attention in the debate over the censure of Senator Joseph R. Mc-

Carthy. The Wisconsin Republican had attacked Mr. Ervin before the latter took the floor. The attack was based on a quotation taken out of context and attributed to Senator Ervin.

Mr. McCarthy's habit of lifting statements out of context, Senator Ervin said, reminded him of the nineteenth-century Carolina preacher who became enraged at the female habit of wearing the hair in gaudy top knots. The preacher decided to invoke the gospel against this vice. Gathering all the ladies to church, he delivered a mighty sermon on the text, "Top Knot Come Down."

After the sermon, an angry woman declared the sermon a fraud and challenged the preacher to find any such text in the Bible. The preacher opened the book and pointed to the seventeenth verse of the twenty-fourth chapter of Matthew. It read:

"Let him which is on the housetop not come down to take anything out of his house."

The Successful Candidate

An uncle of mine tells of a Smoky Mountain candidate he heard on one occasion. Two other speakers preceded him to the stand, both giving long harangues about the problem of taxes. The audience was obviously exhausted. When the third candidate arose, he shifted his eating tobacco from one side of his mouth to the other and said simply, "Folks, there's jist two things about these here taxes that I want to say: if they're too high, we'll lower 'em; if they're too low, we'll hist 'em."

He sat down. He was elected.

The Eloquent Candidate

Extensions of the local Saturday courthouse lawn sessions are the all-day barbecues and dinners-on-the-ground. In spite of radio and television, the local folks still like personal appearances by a political speaker, especially when he has a hillbilly band and is a good spellbinder himself. This too has been carried to extremes, as in the case of the host-candidate who arose after a succulent repast and read to the large crowd a speech which had been written for him. He got along all right until the end, when in his eloquent onrush to the climax he capped the finale with the words: "March forward with me into the dawn of a new day! Pause for applause."

"Pitchfork" Ben Tillman

"Pitchfork" Ben [Tillman] was never in better form. He would shout, flourish his arms, grind out his words between set teeth, and run all the gamut of impassioned oratory and invective. Occasionally he would spin around like a toe dancer, the proof sheets of his speech waving in the air. . . .

During his speech a page boy placed a glass of water before him, but he waved the boy away.

"I never wet my whistle when I am talking," he said. "I can't run a windmill on water."

A Born Orator

One Kentucky gentleman meets another Kentucky gentleman, and they address one another with that solemn earnestness which is characteristic of Southern high life:

"Good mohning, sah. Hope you are well, sah. Whar have you been this mohning?" "I have just come f'om the coat-house, sah. Sen'toh Blackbuhn has been making a speech—the finest speech I have heard since the wah. He is a bawn awter, sah—a bawn awter!" "Excuse me, sah, but what do you mean by 'a bawn awter?'" "A bawn awter! Don't you know what a bawn awter is? Why, sah, you and I would say, 'two and two make fo',' but a bawn awter would say, 'When, in the coase of human events, it becomes nec'sa' or expedient to coalesce two intergers and two other intergers, the result—I declah it boldly and without feah or favor—the result, by a simple arithmetical calculation termed addition, is fo'!' That's a bawn awter, sah!"

The County Attorney Defends the Judge

A lawyer from the "Settlemints" was representing a corporation at a session of the county court in Breathitt County, [Kentucky]. Judge

Jim Hargis, of feud fame, was in the chair. The county attorney, somewhat weak in jurisprudence and grammar, but not lacking in eloquence, took up the cudgels for the judge, and thus unburdened himself:

"May it please the court: The gentleman representing the corporation is a man who has pretensions at larnin'. He hails from the county of Henry, where the limpid waters ripple over limestone pebbles. From thar he hailed to the city of Louisville, where he rubbed his withers against college walls. From thar he hailed to the county of Lee, where the sarvice blossoms and the honeysuckle mingle, and from thar he hailed to this good county where the lilies grow. But with all his larnin' he cain't change the mind of this court, for his honor on the bench is a man who knows the law, and is an honest, upright, biased, partial and unchaste gentleman."

Testing the Whisky

Many years ago Senator Beck and Senator Blackburn, the latter then a member of the lower house of Congress, were asked by a Kentucky friend to go with him to his room and sample a jug of McBrayer whisky.

The invitation was accepted, and after they had each taken a drink, Senator Beck said, "That is splendid whisky, but has a strong taste of iron in it."

"Impossible," said his friend, "there is no iron in the water of Anderson County, and the contents of this jug were taken from a barrel. What do you say, Blackburn?"

"Well," said Blackburn, "I do not care so much about the iron taste as I do about the taste of leather in the whisky."

The friend again exclaimed, "It is impossible that there should be any taste of leather in that barrel of whisky."

On his return to Kentucky the mutual friend went to Mr. McBrayer and insisted that all the whisky should be taken out of the barrel and a critical examination made of its contents. To his astonishment he found one small piece of leather attached to a carpet tack.

The Candidate's Qualification

[In Vice-President Alben W. Barkley's] childhood days in Graves County . . . a man could hardly aspire to public office unless he was a disabled Civil War veteran. One day in a brush arbor at Wingo four candidates were making their appeal to the voters.

The first candidate had crutches, and an empty trouser leg pinned ostentatiously to his rotunda. "I heared the call of duty," he said, "and I fit enduring the war. I lost my leg at Shiloh, and I therefore appeal for your suffrage." The second candidate told how he had lost his arm at the battle of Cynthiana. The third pointed proudly to the patch over the eye he lost in Vicksburg.

Now the fourth candidate hobbled forth. "I never fit in the war," he said, "and I never got wounded. But, my fellow citizens, if physical disability is a qualification for office, I can tell you this: I am the doggonedest most ruptured son-of-a-gun you ever saw."

Riding Slow

[A] Republican I had heard about . . . thought he would get himself a state job when Kentucky elected its first Republican governor in 1895.

This hungry Republican . . . got on his mule and rode all the way from Somerset to the state capital, Frankfort, a distance of about a hundred miles. He hung around for about six months. Finally all his money was gone and he still had no job, so he saddled up Old Nell and started for home.

On the outskirts of Frankfort he met a friend, who asked him why he was in such a hurry to go home.

"Hurry!" exclaimed the disappointed job seeker. "All my life I've heard that the office should seek the man. Well, I've been here six months and haven't seen an office seeking a man yet. If you happen to run across one after I've gone, will you please tell it that I'm a-ridin' out Somerset Pike, and ridin' damned slow!"

Private John Allen in New York

[Private John] Allen was invited to New York to address the American Bankers Association. He said, "I don't know why they invited me to address such an august body, but I put $80.00 in my pocket and got on the train and went to New York. They told me before I left home to come to the Waldorf-Astoria Hotel, so I did. I walked up to the clerk and told him who I was and he said, 'Mr. Allen, we have a nice suite of rooms reserved for you, the bell boy will show you to them.'

"Well, I went up to my rooms and after a while I decided I would go down in the lobby and look around awhile. I walked up to the clerk and said, 'Sir, you have a mighty nice place here, all this fine furniture, rugs, drapery, chandeliers, etc. I would like to look around a little.' He said, 'I'll be glad to show you our place.' We came to a suite of rooms that was about equal to the one that I had and I said, 'My friend, if I am not too inquisitive, how much do you get for a suite of rooms like this?' The clerk said: 'One hundred dollars a day.' Well, I didn't say anything but I thought, 'My God, I can't stand that, my $80.00 will be gone before tonight.'

"When we got back to the lobby I went immediately to the Western Union telegraph office and sent myself a telegram in care of the Waldorf-Astoria. I went back and sat down to wait. In a few minutes I was paged, 'Telegram for Mr. Allen, telegram for Mr. Allen.' I answered the boy and he gave me the telegram. I opened it and read as if I was surprised. I went to the clerk and handed him the telegram and told him I was awfully sorry that I had to leave and that I would not be able to stay with them, but my Aunt Sally had found out that I was in New York and that I simply must come out and stay with her while I was there. The clerk read the telegram and it said, 'John I will be angry with you if you do not stay at my house. Signed, Aunt Sally.'

"I said to the clerk, 'How much do I owe you for the short time I've been here?' To which he replied, 'Not a thing, sir, the American Bankers Association has already paid for your suite of rooms for three days.' You can imagine how I felt at hearing this."

Private John Allen and Bilbo

Uncle John [Allen] had once made the rash promise that he'd leave Mississippi if [Theodore G.] Bilbo was re-elected Governor. When he was re-elected, Bilbo sent Uncle John a wire reminding him of his promise and received this answer: "Mississippi has gone to hell and I'm going to St. Louis." Uncle John came back to Mississippi, but never again acknowledged that he was a Mississippian. He always signed himself: "Private John Allen, Tupelo, U.S.A."

Alfalfa Bill in Heaven

"Alfalfa Bill" had such a big voice and so much confidence in his ability to use it that they told this story on him while he was Governor of Oklahoma.

It seemed that Saint Peter came down and asked him to reorganize the heavenly choir. Bill Murray said, "All right, get me ten thousand sopranos, ten thousand contraltos, and ten thousand first tenors. Hurry now, be off!"

Saint Peter started off at a trot, then hesitated and said, "But, Governor, what about bass."

"Bass, hell!" roared Bill. "I'll sing it myself."

Quanah's Two Wives

Almost the last of the colorful Indian chiefs who used to file into Washington and tell the troubles of their tribes to the committees of Congress was Quanah Buller, of Oklahoma. One of the problems that troubled the administrators of Indian groups was the fact that they were a little loose in the matter of marriage. Many braves, it was reported, had more than one wife. The representatives of the White Father admonished their leaders against this. The chairman of the Senate Committee on Indian Affairs was particularly disturbed when he was told that Quanah Buller himself had two wives. He told Buller that he must go back to Oklahoma and get rid of one of those wives. The next year when the chief appeared the chairman questioned him.

"Did you get rid of one of those wives?" the chairman asked. "No," said Quanah.

"This will never do," the chairman thundered. "You go back home and tell one of those women that she will have to go back to her people."

"You tell 'um," said Quanah.

"Louder!"

While speaking at an open-air meeting, [a Texan] was interrupted by a man in the crowd who shouted, "Louder!" The speaker raised his voice. In less than a minute the same man again called, "Louder!" Again the speaker raised his voice, until its volume reached away out beyond the edge of the crowd. When the man for the third time called, "Louder!" the orator paused for a second, and then continued, "Fellow citizens, the period will at last arrive when the vast machinery of this universe must stop, and all its wheels be motionless; when the spheres shall cease to roll, and all the defined periods of time be lost in eternity. In that awful hour, when the mighty Gabriel shall descend from the battlements of heaven, and, placing one foot on the sea and one on the land, shall force a blast from his trumpet that shall reverberate throughout the remotest corners of the universe, *some doggoned fool will holler, 'Louder! Louder!'* "

Coeducation in Texas

The Texas legislature was in session at Austin. One of its members (let us call him Doak) was more or less illiterate. A bill asking for an appropriation for the University of Texas was up for debate. The opposition group had a caucus with Doak for the purpose of winning his support against the bill. Their spokesman opened up on Doak: "Look here, Doak, did you know they 've got coeds over there on that campus?" Doak looked puzzled. "Did you know they use the same curriculum?" Doak looked pained. "And listen: the boys and girls over there even matriculate together!" "Well, that settles it!" said Doak. "I'm ag'in that bill!"

The Most Orderly Lynching in Years

It seems that a Texas governor was elected on an anti-lynching plat-form. And he heard, a few months after he was elected, that there was a danger of a lynching at Longview, that a notorious criminal had been caught, and the populace was aroused. So he sent one of his chief deputies up there, and he said, "Now, if there's any trouble there I want you to report to me immediately and I'll call out the militia. I don't want to have any trouble."

Well, about three days later he went down to breakfast and found the governor's mansion invaded by reporters, and all of them wanted a statement from him on the lynching at Longview.

He said, "What lynching at Longview? I sent my chief deputy up there to make sure there wouldn't be any trouble."

So he got on the telephone and called up there and said, "Sam, what's this about a lynching?"

"Well, he's dead all right."

"Why, you sonuvabitch, didn't I tell you to call me up and let me know if there was a sign of any trouble?"

"Now take it easy, Governor, there wasn't no trouble at all. It was the most orderly lynching in years."

Jim Ferguson's Defense

[Texas Governor James E. Ferguson] was [once] charged with filing exorbitant expenses on an allegedly official journey he made to New York. "Gentlemen," Jim replied, "when I, as a farm boy, went in to Temple to spend the night, I slept in the wagon yard. Then I was representing Jim Ferguson. In New York I was representing the great state of Texas. And I thought nothing those Yankees had was too good for the Governor of Texas."

Politics in Wyoming

Senator Robert B. Howell, of Nebraska . . . was quite a hunter and was invited by a member of Congress from a neighboring state to accompany him on a hunting trip near Yellowstone Park and the adjacent mountains.

They were enjoying the trip and became quite friendly. Late one evening when too far from camp to return, they had to look around for shelter. They sighted a light and on making their way to the door of the cabin were invited in and given a hot dinner and quarters for the night. Reminiscing over the supper table and feeling in good spirits as we all do after an enjoyable meal, Howell's companion turned to him and said, "This is one of my camping grounds and the people here are very fond of me. At the last election you will be surprised to know that I received all the votes in this precinct except three." Just at that moment he was called away and the woman who had prepared the supper came up close to Howell and whispered, "What he said is true, Mr. Howell, but he forgot to tell you there are only five votes in this precinct."

The Farmer Is the Goat

This young snort from the agricultural school came out there to North Dakota to look over my land and my stock. He said he was goin' to appraise everything on my farm for the government. He said he was goin' to make a report on everything there and help me pull out of the red.

Well, he looked over everything, wrote it all down on the record neat as a pin; stuck his nose into everything there.

He thought he just about had everything when he saw an animal looking around the house. We keep the old goat because we had him so long. "What's he," the young squirt said, "and what's he for?"

I said, "You're the expert here. You tell me. I ain't supposed to tell you."

"Well," he said, "I don't know what it is. I'll have to wire back and find out what it is so I can put it down on my report."

"All right," I says, laughing, "you do that."

So he wired clean to Washington to Secretary Wallace, I guess, and he said, "There's an object here and I don't know what it is. It's long and lean with a bald head, chin whiskers, empty lean stomach, a long sad face, and sad cadaverous eyes. What is it?"

And Wallace wired back: "You wet-behind-the-ears, mewling baby jackass! That's the farmer!"

Winning Statehood for New Mexico

All New Mexico's most efficacious leaders of politics and business had done their best to get Congress to admit the territory as a state. Arguments against were that half the population did not speak English, that thousands were Indians, that almost everybody was illiterate. William Randolph Hearst, however, favored statehood for both New Mexico and Arizona and, at his own expense, he brought out a private carload of congressmen to see for themselves.

Colonel Sellers, asked to prepare a reception for the honorable statesmen, had a grandstand erected in the vacant lot at the corner of Fourth and Central. The band had practiced up, the fire company had new uniforms, the National Guard was ready to act as escort, the mayor and the president of the Commercial Club had prepared speeches. Colonel Sellers had made some private plans.

A Navajo was on hand, a stunning Indian about six feet six in height and with a profile that had served the Breece Lumber Company well as an advertising feature. He might have been a chief just as well as anybody. He knew no English. Colonel Sellers knew little Navajo. But José Platero knew both. Colonel Sellers gave orders via José.

"When I step on Hosteen's foot he is to talk. I don't care what he says; just talk. When I take my foot off he is to stop. See? Does he understand that? Good."

When the time came, Colonel Sellers, looking his best in soft shirt, flowing tie, cowboy boots, and Navajo jewelry, took the stand. Introducing the Navajo he explained that this noble redman too favored statehood for New Mexico. He did not mention that this redman favored nothing the government did, and was altogether out of favor with the government for refusing to send his children to school. But Hosteen's looks were beyond cavil, his voice organ-like, his dramatic delivery brought tears to the hardiest.

Colonel Sellers' foot came down. The Indian spoke, his resonant voice booming in bass, his incomprehensible syllables rolling like swift water over hard stones. Colonel Sellers removed his foot and the Navajo stopped, looking at the white man.

Colonel Sellers then improvised a moving oration about how the Indian loved the land, revered these great white men from Washington whence came all blessings, was grateful for the government's gifts of schools, agents. . . . When Colonel Sellers ran down he replaced his foot on the Navajo's toe and again the primitive language flowed out in a stream of Wagnerian magnitude.

It took only about three acts. The Navajo's peroration was fine, as delivered by Colonel Sellers. The applause was deafening. Even congressmen applauded with vigor, convinced by this noble example of the First American. Colonel Sellers is satisfied to this day that he and the Navajo really won statehood that day. The actual date of admission is 1912; still perhaps those congressmen had never forgotten the telling arguments of the Navajo.

Man-Eating Packer

A party of men from Utah . . . set out on a gold-prospecting expedition in December, 1873, in the San Juan mountains. After suffering hardship and privation, they reached the camp of Chief Ouray of the Ute Indians, who told them, in effect, that they were silly to travel in winter and might as well remain with him until spring. Most of them, being reasonable men and already very cold, thought Chief Ouray's idea fundamentally sound. But six of the band—Packer, Bell, Humphrey, Swan, Noon, and Miller—were still full of American enterprise and said they'd press on to the gold fields without further waste of precious time.

Six weeks later Packer turned up alone at the Los Pinos agency, seventy-five miles from Lake City, complaining that he had gone lame and been deserted by his no-account, though still enterprising, companions. He had been subsisting, he said, on roots and small game. But apparently roots and small game had agreed with him remarkably because he was bursting with health and his first request was for whisky rather than food. The agency people told each other that this Packer was quite a man, yes, sir, quite a man, and were sorry when his restless spirit urged him on to Saguache, a community some distance away.

Although Packer had claimed to be broke while in Los Pinos, he seemed to have come by some drinking and gambling money by the time he arrived in Saguache.

Meanwhile an Indian had arrived at the agency with strips of flesh he said he'd picked up along Packer's trail. And that spring, after the snows had melted, a photographer for *Harper's Weekly*, crossing the plateau, stumbled upon the remains of five men whose skulls had been crushed and whose bodies had been partially stripped of their flesh. Packer was in trouble, but had an explanation. He said he had been forced to kill Bell, who went insane, in self-defense, and later found that Bell had killed the other four men. The whole episode had been so distasteful, Packer explained, that he couldn't bring himself to talk about it when he first arrived back in civilization.

The Los Pinos agency people wanted to believe Packer, but found it so difficult that they arrested him instead. But not having a jail, they chained him to a rock, from which he soon escaped. He was not recaptured until ten years later in Wyoming. Then he was returned to Lake City for trial. By that time, the two-party system was established in Lake City and law and order were rearing their pretty heads. Packer was given an efficient trial and sentenced to be hanged. His trial and sentencing were strictly bipartisan. All jurymen were Republicans, but the judge, M. B. Gerry, was of the Democratic and minority persuasion.

Bringing the trial to a close he shouted, "Alfred Packer, you man-eating son of a bitch, stand up." When Packer obeyed, the Judge went on, "Alfred Packer, you depraved Republican cannibal, I hereby sentence you to hang by the neck until you are dead. There were only six Democrats in Hinsdale County, and, by God, you've et five of them."

"Melancholy" McCullon

A turgid orator, so noted for his verbosity and heaviness that he had been dubbed "Melancholy" McCullon, was assigned to speak at a mining camp in the mountains. There were about fifty miners present when he began. But when at the end of a couple of hours he gave no sign of finishing, his listeners dropped away. Some went back to work, but the majority sought wherewith to quench their thirst, which had been immensely aggravated by the dryness of the discourse.

Finally there was but one auditor left, a dilapidated, weary-looking old fellow. Fixing his gaze on him, McCullon pulled out a man's size six-shooter and laid it on the table. The old fellow rose slowly and drawled out, "Be you goin' to shoot, ef I go?"

"You bet I am," responded McCullon. "I'm bound to finish my speech, even if I have to shoot to keep an audience."

The old fellow sighed in a tired manner, edged off slowly, saying as he did so, "Well, shoot, ef you want to. I may jest as well be shot as talked to death."

☞ **11** ☜

Fable and Foible

"Suppose you had a large cattleyard full of all sorts of cattle—cows, oxen, bulls—and you kept killing and selling and disposing of your cows and oxen, in one way and another—taking good care of your bulls. By-and-by you would find that you had nothing but a yard full of old bulls, good for nothing under heaven. Now, it will be just so with the army, if I don't stop making brigadier-generals."

ABRAHAM LINCOLN

Introduction

The fabulist, as W. H. Herndon wrote of Lincoln, sees "philosophy in a story and a schoolmaster in a joke." In giving life to inanimate objects and the power of speech to animals, the fabulist harks back to the time when men believed that everything has a soul, and so failed to distinguish carefully between nature and human nature.

Before the animal fable, satirizing human behavior, there was the animal tale, concerned with animal characteristics. Even though animal characters and the moral may drop out, the allegory and the philosophy remain constant.

The close connection between the fable and the proverb is seen not only in the proverbial moral tag but also in the fact that both the fable and the proverb involve a metaphorical or symbolic use of an incident. Thus the fable may arise out of or give rise to a proverb, folk saying, or byword, and the proverb may be an incipient or residual fable, as in Poor Richard's saying, beginning "A little neglect may breed great mischief; for want of a nail the shoe was lost."

Here is a modern shaggy-dog fable involving a switch on the proverbial comparison, "packed in like sardines." Two sardines were swimming about in New York Harbor when one of them suggested that they go up to the Bronx for the week end. "I'd rather not," objected the other, "it's too long a swim." "Then how about going by subway?" "What! And be packed in like people!"

In America the moralized fable has become the vehicle of hero worship, patriotism, and the ethics of success. Perhaps the most familiar example is Parson M. L. Weems' story of George Washington and the cherry tree, which combines fable with apocryphal biography. The following story from *Room at the Top* illustrates the use of fable in books of edification and self-help.

"An old farmer [called] his three idle sons around him when on his deathbed, to impart to them an important secret. 'My sons,' said he, 'a great treasure lies hid in the estate which I am about to leave to you.' The old man gasped. 'Where is it hid?' exclaimed the sons in a breath. 'I am about to tell you,' said the old man; 'you will have to dig for it . . .' but his breath failed him before he could impart the weighty secret; and he died. Forthwith the sons set to work with spade and mattock upon the long-neglected fields, and they turned up every sod and clod upon the estate. They discovered no treasure, but they learned to work; and when the fields were sown, and the harvests came, lo! the yield was prodigious in consequence of the thorough tillage which they had undergone. Then it was that they discovered the treasure concealed in the estate, of which their wise old father had advised them."

The Two Travelers and the Oyster

As two men were walking by the seaside at low water, they saw an oyster, and they both stooped at the same time to pick it up. One pushed the other away, and a dispute ensued. A third traveler coming along at the time, they determined to refer the matter to him which of the two had the better right to the oyster. While they were each telling his story, the arbitrator gravely took out his knife, opened the shell, and loosened the oyster. When they had finished, and were listening for his decision, he just as gravely swallowed the oyster, and gave them each a shell. "The Court," said he, "awards you each a shell. The oyster will cover the costs."

Franklin's Fable of the Speckled Ax

A man . . . in buying an ax of a smith, my neighbor, desired to have the whole of its surface as bright as the edge. The smith consented to grind it bright for him if he would turn the wheel; he turned, while the smith pressed the broad face of the ax hard and heavily on the stone, which made the turning of it very fatiguing. The man came every now and then from the wheel to see how the work went on, and at length would take his ax as it was, without further grinding. "No," said the smith; "turn on; turn on; we shall have it bright by and by; as yet, it is only speckled." "Yes," says the man, *"but I think I like a speckled ax best!"*

And I believe this may have been the case with many, who, having, for want of some such means [of self-examination and discipline] as I employed, found the difficulty of obtaining good and breaking bad habits in other points of vice and virtue, have given up the struggle, and concluded that "a speckled ax was best."

The Captain's Rule

When men are employed they are best contented; for on the days [the militia men] worked they were good-natured and cheerful, and, with the consciousness of having done a good day's work, they spent the evening jollily; but on our idle days they were mutinous and quarrelsome, finding fault with their pork, the bread, etc., and in continual ill humor, which put me in mind of a sea-captain whose rule it was to keep his men constantly at work; and when his mate once told him that they had done everything, and there was nothing further to employ them about, *"Oh,"* says he, *"make them scour the anchor."*

The Yankee and the Quaker

Some years ago, a young New Englander found himself in the back parts of Pennsylvania, ashore as to the means of living. In this strait he applied to a wealthy Quaker in the neighborhood for help.

"I will furnish thee with work, and pay thee for it, friend," said the Quaker, "but it is not my custom to give alms to one able to labor, like thee."

"Well, that's all I want," said the Yankee. "Of course I am willing to work."

"What can thee do, friend?"

"Anything. I will do anything to get a little money, to help me out of my difficulties."

"Well—there is a log yonder; and there is an ax. Thee may pound on the log with the head of the ax, and if thee is diligent and faithful, I will pay thee a dollar a day."

"Agreed. I'd as soon do that as anything else."

And so the youth went to work, and pounded lustily with the head of the ax upon the log. After a time he paused to take breath; then he began again. But after an hour he stopped, threw down the ax impatiently, and walked away, saying, "I'll be hanged if I'll cut wood without seeing the chips fly!"

The Quaker's Coat

[A] Quaker . . . ship owner, being disturbed by the profanity of one of his workmen, said to him one day, "Jack, I think if thee should wear my coat for a week, thee might cure thyself of thy habit of swearing." Jack agreed to try it, and on returning the coat at the end of the week, the Quaker asked, "Well, Friend Jack, did thee have any inclination to swear while thee was wearing my coat?" "No," said Jack, "but I did have a terrible hankerin' to lie."

An Indian's Parable

When General [Benjamin] Lincoln went to make peace with the Creek Indians, one of the chiefs asked him to sit down on a log. He was then desired to move, and in a few minutes to move still further. The request was repeated till the general got to the end of the log. The Indian said, "Move further." To which the general replied, "I can move no further." "Just so it is with us," said the chief, "you moved us back to the waters, and then ask us to move further."

"Don't Swap Horses in Midstream"

The setting up and the bowling over of the generals commanding the army defending Washington from McDowell at Bull Run to Meade at Gettysburg resembles a grim game at tenpins. The President, who tried to find a professional captain to relieve him of his responsibility as nominally war-chief of the national forces, therefore smiled sarcastically when the ninety-ninth deputation came to suggest still another aspirant to be the new Napoleon, and said to it:

"Gentlemen, your request and proposition remind me of two gentlemen in Kentucky.

"The flat lands there bordering on the rivers are subject to inundations, so the fordable creek becomes in an instant a broad lake, deep and rapidly running. These two riders were talking the common topic—in that famous Blue Grass region where fillies and *fill-es*, as the *voyageur* from Canada said in his broken English, are unsurpassable for grace and beauty. Each fell to expatiating upon the good qualities of his steed, and this dialogue was so animated and engrossing they approached a ford without being conscious of outer matters. There was heavy rain in the highlands and an ominous sound in the dampening air. They entered the water still arguing. Then, at midway, while they came to the agreement to exchange horses, with no 'boot,' since each conceded the value of the animals, the river rose. In a twinkling the two horses were floundering, and the riders, taken for once off their balance, lost stirrup and seat, and the four creatures, separated, were struggling for a footing in the boiling stream. Away streaked the horses, buried in foam, three or four miles down, while the men scrambled out upon the new edge.

"Gentlemen," concluded the President, drawing his moral with his provoking imperturbability, "those men looked at each other, as they dripped, and said with the one voice, 'Ain't this a lesson? Don't swap horses crossing a stream!' "

The Eagle and the Owl

An eagle and an owl having entered into a league of mutual amity, one of the articles of their treaty was that the former should not prey upon the younglings of the latter. "But tell me," said the owl, "should you know my little ones if you were to see them?" "Indeed I should not," replied the eagle; "but if you describe them to me, it will be sufficient." "You are to observe then," returned the owl, "in the first place, that the charming creatures are perfectly well shaped; in the next, that there is a remarkable sweetness and vivacity in their countenances; and then there is something in their voices so peculiarly melodious." " 'Tis enough," interrupted the eagle; "by these marks I cannot fail to distinguish them; and you may depend upon their never receiving any injury from me."

It happened not long afterward, as the eagle was on the wing in quest of his prey, that he discovered amidst the ruins of an old castle a nest of grim-faced, ugly birds, with gloomy countenances, and voices like those of the Furies. "These, undoubtedly," said he, "cannot be the offspring of my friend, and so I shall venture to make free with them."

The Ox and the Mule

An ox and a mule worked for a farmer; they were hitched side by side to a plow and, day after day, pulled it across the fields.

One night the two came wearily back to their stable where they were fed and their stalls bedded down. The following conversation ensued.

"Mule," said the ox, "we've been working too hard recently. I'll tell you how we can get out of so much work."

"How?" asked the mule, naturally.

"It is very simple. We will play off sick and then we can lie here in our stalls all day and enjoy ourselves."

The mule, being an exceedingly intelligent creature, said, "You can do that if you choose, but I prefer to work. That is what we were meant for."

The next morning, when the farmer came out, the ox played sick. The farmer bedded him down with clean straw, gave him fresh hay, a bucket of oats and oil meal, and left him alone for the day and went forth and plowed with the mule alone.

All day the ox lay in his stall, chewing his cud and enjoying himself thoroughly. That night when the mule came in, the ox asked him how things had gone.

"It was hard and we did not get much done," said the mule.

"Did the farmer ask about me?"

"No," replied the mule. "He did not speak of you."

"Well, then," said the ox, pleased with his cleverness, "I think I'll play sick again tomorrow. It's exceedingly pleasant to lie here and rest and have my food brought to me. I don't know why I didn't think of this long ago."

"I think," said the mule, "I'll go back to work tomorrow as usual."

So the ox played off again and lay in his stall and lived on choice food.

That night, when the mule came in, the ox again inquired how things had gone.

"About the same as yesterday," answered the mule.

"Did the farmer say anything about me?" asked the ox.

"Yes, he did," said the mule. "It chanced, as we came to the end of the plow row, a butcher drove by and stopped and asked the farmer if he had an animal he would sell. 'Yes, I have,' said the farmer. 'I have an ox I would like to dispose of.' The butcher agreed and drove on and that was the end of the conversation," said the mule, beginning to eat his oats.

"Snail, Snail"—

A snail was crossin' de road for seben years. Just as he got across, a tree fell and barely missed him 'bout a inch or two. If he had a been where he was six months before it would er kilt him. De snail looked back at de tree and tole de people, "See, it pays to be fast."

The Animals' Convention

A convention [was] once held by all the animals of the world. In this convention they all agreed to live in peace and harmony—they would not fight and prey on each other. The fox and the chickens would live together, the dog and fox, the lions and lambs, etc.

Next morning after the convention the fox went down to the water hole to get a drink of good clean cold water. When he walked down and bent over to drink, reflected in the clear water was the image of a nice big fat hen perched on a limb above the water hole. The fox looked up and said, "Good morning, Mrs. Hen. Come on down and get a fresh drink of this good water." "Oh, no," said the hen, "I'm afraid of you." "Why," said the fox, "don't be afraid of me. I won't hurt you. Don't you know at the convention we agreed not to bother each other?"

About that time, off in the distance a dog barked. The fox perked up his ears and listened. The dog barked again and the fox began to lope off. The hen cried out to him and said, "Mr. Fox, why are you running away? Don't you know the dog won't hurt you?" "Yes, but that damn dog might not have been at the convention," said the fox.

Einstein Explains the Theory of Relativity

I was once walking in the country on a hot day with a blind friend and I said I could do with a drink of milk.

"Milk?" said my friend. "Drink I know, but what is milk?"

"A white liquid," I replied.

"Liquid I know," said the blind man, "but what is white?"

"The color of a swan's feathers."

"Feathers I know, but what is a swan?"

"A bird with a crooked neck."

"Neck I know—but what is crooked?"

I took his arm and straightened it. "That's straight," I said. Then I bent it at the elbow. "And that is crooked."

"Ah!" cried the blind man. "Now I know what you mean by milk!"

What Sweetens the Tea

Two Talmudic students were having a scientific chat.

"What is it that sweetens a glass of tea," inquired one, "is it the sugar or the stirring?"

"Certainly the sugar," declared the other. "For without sugar you cannot make it sweet."

"And I say it is the stirring that makes it sweet. For it will never get sweet unless you stir it."

"Then what do you need the sugar for, if the stirring does the whole thing?"

"Just to know how long to stir."

Justice

A poor man was complaining to his grocer. "There is no justice in this world," he wailed. "The rich, who have the money, can buy all they want on credit, while the poor must pay for everything in cash. If there were any justice on earth, the rich should pay cash, and the poor should buy on credit."

"It all sounds very well in theory," was the grocer's retort, "but if I were to extend credit to all the *shleppers* in this neighborhood, I'd soon be poor myself."

"Why, then, you would have nothing to worry about," beamed the poor man. "You'd be able to get everything on credit!"

Chinese Philosopher in the Subway

[Said] the Chinese diplomat and philosopher, Li Hung-chang, [on his visit to New York in 1896], when his official guide hurried him off one subway train into another a few feet away, "Why do we change?"

"Oh, that train was a local."

"And what is this?"

"This is an express. It makes no stops till we reach Grand Central. We save six minutes."

A pause.

"And what," asked Ambassador Li, "are we going to do with that six minutes?"

The Honest Lawyer

It is said there is a chapel in Rome dedicated to one St. Evona, a lawyer. He came to Rome to entreat the Pope to give the lawyers of Brittany a patron. The Pope replied that he knew of no saint but what was disposed of to other professions, and he had none to spare for the lawyers, at which Evona was very sad, and begged so earnestly that at last the Pope proposed to him that he should go around the church blindfolded, and after he had said so many prayers, that the first saint in the group which he might lay hold of while blindfolded should be the patron of lawyers.

The good old lawyer started in his round, and at the end of his prayers he stopped at an altar, reached out his hand and laid hold of the image of the devil which lay at the feet of St. Michael, and cried out in his blindness, "This is our Saint; let him be the patron of my profession—the law."

Upon the removal of his blindfold, and observing what a patron he had chosen, he was shocked to death, and coming to Heaven's gate, he knocked hard, whereupon St. Peter asked who it was that knocked so loudly; he replied that it was "Evona the advocate." "Away, away," said St. Peter, "there is but one advocate in Heaven; there is no room for you lawyers." "O! But," said Evona, "I am that honest lawyer who never took fees on both sides, or ever pleaded in a bad cause, nor did I ever set my neighbor by the ears, or live by the sins of the people." "Well then," said St. Peter, "come in," and thereupon St. Peter sent an angel to the earth to inscribe upon the tombstone of St. Evona:

God works wonders now and then.
Here lies a lawyer, an honest man.

Lawyers in Hell

Going into a barroom one cold night, [Lorenzo] Dow found a number of men, among whom were several lawyers, grouped about the stove. As a joke they made no place for the newcomer, while one of the lawyers asked, "Where are you bound for, Dominie?"

"Heaven," was the quick reply.

"Where have you come from?" was the next question.

"Hell," was the answer.

"How did you find it there?" one of the lawyers asked.

"All the lawyers in the hottest place, just the same as here."

With that sally he secured a place by the stove.

The Fox Hunter in Heaven

St. Peter grew tired of guarding the Pearly Gates and left a fox hunter temporarily in charge.

"Now don't let anybody in unless his name is in this big book," said St. Peter as he left.

The fox hunter took up his stand at the entrance, determined to do just as he was told.

Presently a man walked up to the entrance and gave his name. The fox hunter looked in the big book carefully before answering. He cast a forbidding glare toward the newcomer. "Sorry, buddy. Your name ain't in here, so you'll just have to go down below."

The newcomer, looking very sad, tried a sympathetic appeal. "I've always been a pretty decent person. Can't you figure out some way you can get me in?"

"Nope."

Just then several beautiful foxhounds trotted up to the gateman and began rearing up on him affectionately.

"Those your foxhounds?" the newcomer asked.

"Yep. We've been havin' some mighty good chases lately, too." Then a sad look went over the gateman's face. "I ain't complainin' about the place here, y'understand, but they's one thing that makes things mighty lonesome. They ain't any fox hunters here to chew the rag around the campfire with me." He sighed. "It's mighty tough, huntin' by myself."

"I'm an old fox hunter. Why, I've got a dog back home that's the fastest one in the county," the newcomer said hopefully.

The gateman's eyes sparkled with delight. He grasped the newcomer's hand with a strong grip. "An old fox hunter, did you say? Come right in, buddy, come right in! The whole place is yours!"

The Admiral in Heaven

A bishop and an admiral died and presented themselves for entry through the Pearly Gates. St. Peter sized them up, pulled the admiral inside and closed the gate in the bishop's face. A long time elapsed, during which the bishop heard great activity inside—trumpets blowing, angels' voices singing and all other indications of a big party.

After a long time, the gate opened again and the bishop saw the end of the admiral's reception—velvet carpets over the gold paving, flowers scattered everywhere, and a rain of rose petals in the air. There were many garlands on the admiral, who was being escorted by a large bevy of the most beautiful angels. While the bishop watched, they rolled up the carpet, brushed all the flowers away and made preparations for a common garden reception. The bishop got sore and wanted to know why so much preferment was shown for the admiral and so little for himself.

"We are all the time bringing bishops through the Pearly Gates," was the reply, "but this is the first time within anyone's recollection that we have had an admiral!"

The Archangel Michael Visits New Mexico

At one time it is said that the Archangel Michael, because he had a great affection for that country, made a *visita* to New Mexico. He appeared first to the archbishop, a much overworked man who fretted, polishing his glasses with his handkerchief. "Dear, dear!" said the archbishop. "I grow old faster than I thought. I must really get me a new pair of spectacles."

Then the Archangel appeared to a *rico* [a rich man] who was also very charitable and a devoted son of the Church. The rico sent for his wife. "Wife," he said, "I think you must discharge that new governess that you have for the children. I am sure she is telling them too many fairy tales."

So Michael wandered about until he found a poor sheepherder tending his flock on the hillside under Truchas, and he appeared to him also. The herder fell on his knees in the midst of his sheep. "Great Lord," he said, "will it please you to bless me before you go?"

The Globe

I was asking an old man of seventy-four if he was a believer, and he said, "Well, they's things so deep we can't understand 'em. It's like a teacher told the children: 'There wasn't no creation—the world was always here.' So one day he went out of the room. A kid made a globe out of cardboard or somethin' and set it on the teacher's desk. So when he come back he said, 'Where'd that thing come from?' And the kid said, 'Why, it was always here.' And the teacher said, 'I know a dang sight better.' And the kid he said, 'Well, that's what you been a-tellin' us.'"

God and the Devil

"Yes," said the harness-maker philosophically. "They's always two points of view.

"They's them as likes hosses and them as don't; they's them as want liquor sold here in Wallingford and them as don't; and they's them as think Miz Small oughta get a deevorce from Emanuel and them as don't.

"They's always been two points of view, and I s'pose always will be.

"My ma's granddaddy use t' tell that when God set out t' make the world the Devil come an' set on th' fence watchin' him.

"'What y' cal'c'latin' t' build, God?' says the Devil.

"'I'm makin' a world an' a firmament,' says God, standin' off, kinda proud, lookin' over his handiwork.

"'Yes,' says the Devil, 'I might know y' would. Y' wouldn't be satisfied ontil y'd spoiled my nice chaos.'"

Why Folks Ain't Got Tails

Long time ago—long before the War, the good Lawd made the world, and then He rested a day. The next mornin He decided to plant a garden in the world He'd done made, so He set out the Garden of Eden. Then He say to Heself that a garden such as that needed somebody to live in it, so He made Adam, the first man. Adam, he was kinda lonesome, so the good Lawd took pity on him and made him a wife—Eve was her name, and she was the first woman. She and Adam was just like folks is today, except they had big long tails like cows.

The Lawd, He says to Adam and Eve, says He, "Adam, this here garden is for you and Eve. Stay here, keep good care of it, eat any of these fruits and berries and yarbs, all 'cept this one tree with the yaller fruits on it. Yeah, that's the one. Don't you touch that fruit. That there's my tree, and you mustn't touch it." Then God left the garden. Adam knowed He was gone, cause he heard the gate click.

Adam walked around awhile, and pretty soon he found hisself lookin at that forbidden fruit. He couldn't seem to take his eyes off it. It looked bettern all the other fruit in the garden. When he couldn't stand it no longer he whirled in and ate every fruit-thing on that tree. That night he slept hard, right on through till late the next mornin.

When the day break, the Lawd come back to have a look around His garden. When He seen what Adam had done He didn't even take time to open the garden gate—He put His hand on top of the fence and jumped right over it. Such a sight He never saw—where last night had been a tree full of ripe fruit, this mornin there wasn't a scrap left—it had all been et. He looked thisaway, and He looked thataway, but Adam and Eve was clear out of sight.

The Lawd called, "Adam!" But there wasn't no answer. "Adam!" the Lawd called agin. Still Adam lay low and didn't say nothin. Then the Lawd called a third time, "Hey, Adam—you come here right now!" And so Adam come a-inchin up to God to take his chastisin.

"How come you to eat up all my fruits after I done told you not to?" asked the Lawd.

"It musta been Eve done it," said Adam.

"That won't do, Adam," said the Lawd. "Just look at them big footprints around that tree. Eve ain't got no sucha foot as that."

Then Adam got scared and took out for the bushes, with the Lawd right in behind him. Adam couldn't run so fast on account of havin eaten so many of them 'simmon things, and also because of havin to drag that big long tail of his. He run and he run, but he couldn't outrun God. After they had made two or three turns around the garden, God caught up with Adam enough to grab hold of that tail of his. He set His heels in the ground, and fetched up. *Zook!* Out come Adam's tail, clear by the roots! And ever since then folks ain't had no tails.

Why Women Talk So Much

When God made Adam and Eve, Eve was plumb dumb. So Adam said to God, "God, this here woman is dumb as they make em. She can't talk none. I can't get no pleasure out of bein with her, cause she got no tongue."

Just then a rabbit come hoppin by. God reached down and snatched off the rabbit's tail and stuck it in Eve's mouth. The hair on the tail made her spit, and ever since then women been waggin their tongues tryin to spit the hair out.

Why We Say "Unh-Hunh"

Ole Devil looked around hell one day and seen his place was short of help, so he thought he'd run up to Heben and kidnap some angels to keep things runnin' tell he got reinforcements from Miami.

Well, he slipped up on a great crowd of angels on de outskirts of Heben and stuffed a couple of thousand in his mouth, a few hundred under each arm, and wrapped his tail round another thousand and darted off towards hell.

When he was flyin' low over de earth lookin' for a place to land, a man looked up and seen de Devil and ast 'im, "Ole Devil, Ah see you got a load of angels. Is you goin' back for mo'?"

Devil opened his mouth and tole 'im, "Yeah," and all de li'l angels flew out his mouf and went on back to Heben. While he was tryin' to ketch 'em he lost all de others. So he went back after another load.

He was flyin' low agin and de same man seen him and says, "Old Devil, Ah see you got another load uh angels."

Devil nodded his head and said, "Unh-hunh," and dat's why we say it today.

Bible and Swimming

Preacher had to go to work. So he got to the ferry and the ferryboat had started, so he hollered and hollered at the ferryman. So the ferryman came over. The water was pretty high. The preacher said, "What about crossin'?" The ferryman said, "All right, you can come, water's pretty high though." So the preacher got in the boat and the ferryman commenced to rowin'. So the ferryman was a powerful wicked fellow; he never went to church in his life. So the preacher said, "Brother, do you belong to any church?" The ferryman kept on rowin'. He said, "Nope, I don't belong to any church." The preacher said, "One quarter your life's gone if you don't belong to church." Then he said, "Do you ever read the Bible?" The ferryman kept on rowin'. He said, "Nope, I never read the Bible." The preacher said, "That's a pity. Two fourths of your life is gone." So the ferryman kept on rowin'. The preacher said, "Do you know anything about istronomy?" The ferryman kept on rowin'. He said, "Nope, I don't know anything about istronomy." Preacher said, "Too bad, three fourths of your life is gone." Almost that time they done sprung a leak in the boat. The ferryman saw the boat was sinking and got him ready to jump. He said to the preacher, "Reverend, do you know anything about swimmin'?" The preacher said, "No, I don't know anything about swimmin'." The ferryman said, "Damn if the whole of your life ain't gone!"

Organized

One day Ananias, tall coachman of the Kaufmans, was driving his master down a long lane on the way to a neighboring plantation when a horsefly alighted on the mane of one of the horses. "Massa," said Ananias, "you see dat hossfly on dat hoss's mane? Watch me git 'im." Ananias had the reputation of being the most exact wielder of the coachwhip in the county, and his master always enjoyed watching him wield it. Ananias raised his whip and split the horsefly into small pieces.

A little farther down the lane Ananias looked over and spied a bumblebee on a sunflower. "Massa," said Ananias, "you see dat bumblebee on dat sunflowah? Watch me git 'im." Ananias raised his whip again, and the bumblebee was torn into shreds by the snapper on the end of it.

After a little while the master noticed a hornets' nest hanging from the limb of a tree by the side of the road. "Look, Ananias," said he. "You see that hornets' nest hanging from the limb of that tree by the side of the road? You are such an expert with the coachwhip, let me see you cut that hornets' nest off the limb."

"No, sah, Massa," said Ananias, "Ah ain't gwine bothah dem hornets, 'case dey's auganized."

Ten-Cent Cotton

Yonder come Brother Zeke. He ain't much on preachin', but he's the out-prayin'est parson that ever went to town on Sat'day. He can ask fo' mo' things in less time than airy farmer that ever flung buckshot mud off'n his boots. When he steps out to the edge of the pulpit an' stretches his arms out front of him an' rolls his eyes up to the skies an' starts prayin', it looks jes like he's expecting the good Lord to start drappin' the blessin's in his arms then an' there. Like the time back in 1932. Brother Zeke walked out to the edge of the pulpit, an' rolled his eyes to the sky an' stretched his arms straight out in front of him an' started prayin':

"Oh-o-o, Marster, Thou hath know'd me from the day of my birth even unto this day an' time. Thou knowest me in the days of prosperity when the manna was plentiful hereabouts; an' Thou seeth me in them days. Oh-o-o, Marster, Thou seeth me in them days goin' round sowin' seeds of righteousness 'mongst the thorns of iniquity, an' Thou said, 'Let it be so.' An', oh-o-o, Marster, it was so.

"Now, oh-o-o, Marster, Thou seeth me in these days of adversity, oh-o-o, Marster, Thou seeth me goin' up'n down the cotton fiel', tryin', oh-o-o, Marster, tryin' by the sweat of my brow to feed six children with some four-cent cotton. Thou seeth me on Sunday mornin' goin' down the Big Road with my elbows out an' the bottoms of my foots reachin' the groun' through the soles of my shoes. Thou hast hear'd the Bossman say that the cotton us done raise won't compensate him for the meat us done et. Now, oh-o-o, Marster, even as Thou knoweth all things that's possible, Thou knoweth also that feedin' six children on four-cent cotton ain't one of 'em; and I beseech Thee, oh-o-o, Marster, I beseech Thee to look down deep in the bottom of my heart, an' make search roundabout an' if you find airy hoe, airy gee-whiz, airy go-devil, airy mule or airy cotton-planter, pluck them, oh-o-o, Marster, pluck them an' cast 'em into the sea of everlastin' forgetfulness; for as long as cotton ain't worth but four cents, I ain't goin' need them no mo'. Amen."

Folks, you know that prayer it got answered, yessir, it sho was answered; for it weren't long before the good Lord took an' drapped this here Mister Roosevelt right down in Brother Zeke's arms, an' said, "Give that Negro ten cents for his cotton!"

A Still Tongue Makes a Wise Head

There was once a Negro farmer who was a hard worker, stood well with everybody, and owned his own home in the post oaks on the edge of the Brazos bottom. He was a man of considerable intelligence and raised his three oldest daughters to be school teachers. His youngest child was a boy, and by the time he had reached the age of seventeen it dawned upon the father that his son was a fool. The son also began to understand he was a fool. But the father did not give up hope. He took great pains in trying to train the boy so that he would not act so foolishly.

One day he said to him: "Son, you talks too much. Dat's how people knows dat you am silly. Hain't yer never heard dat er still tongue makes er wise haid? Efen you'd keep yer mouf shet, folks wouldn't fine out what er fool you is."

The boy took the lesson in good faith and agreed to do his best to keep people from finding out.

Not long after this the old man and his son took a load of stovewood to town. They drove the wagon up on the square and the old man got down, went into a store, and left the boy sitting on the load of wood.

A merchant across the square saw the wood and hurried over to buy it. Coming up to the wagon, he looked at the boy and called out, "Hello, boy, do you want to sell that wood?"

The boy rolled his eyes but kept his mouth shut.

Again the merchant asked, "How much will you take for that wood?"

Still the boy looked wise and never said a word.

Exasperated and disgusted, the merchant turned on his heel remarking, "Humph, you must be a fool."

Soon afterwards the old man came out of the store and climbed up on the wagon. The boy looked at him sadly and said, "Pappy, dey's done found hit out, en I hain't opened my mouf."

The Greatest Pleasures

A wealthy Kentucky breeder was entertaining a member of the British nobility, also a horseman, at his farm. It was a bland spring afternoon, and instead of taking his visitor from stall to stall, or field to field, the Kentuckian ordered the grooms to lead the brood mares and yearlings past the front porch where they could be inspected from the comfort of a chair. If you've ever been in Kentucky, you know what happened next. A man in white coat appeared, bearing two juleps, with straws and mint sticking out of them.

"You know, sir," said the host as he settled back to sip, "the greatest pleasures in life are thoroughbred horses and good whisky."

A very sound thought," said the visitor, "though I imagine that in England the preference would be for a high tea and a good fast cricket match."

Out on the lawn a groom holding a brood mare turned, wondering, to another.

"Do you suppose," he said slowly, "that neither of them gentlemens has heard of women and watermelon?"

The Hog Dealer's Consolation

There was a man in Indiana who had a way of taking his own advice, though he generally had to do things afterward to get even with himself. He was a hog dealer, and one season he drove a lot of hogs to Indianapolis, about a hundred miles distant, though he could get nearly as good a price at a town much nearer home. Arrived at Indianapolis, he learned that prices had gone down, so he held on for a rise, but when offered a good price he stood out for more, and insisted that if he did not get it he would drive the hogs back home, which he finally did, and sold them for less than was offered him in the city. When one of his friends asked him why he had acted so unwisely, he replied, "I wanted to get even with them city hog-buyers."

"But did you?"

"Well, they didn't get my hogs."

"But what did you get out of the transaction?"

"Get? Why, bless your thick skull, I got the society of the hogs all the way back home."

Secret of a Happy Life

[Texan] John Messenger . . . for a long time lived alone in a hut and kept rattlesnakes in an improvised cage in his fireplace. . . . James L. Abney, a lawyer, . . . asked him one day to divulge his secret of a happy life.

"The secret," said Mr. Messenger, tossing his Whitmanesque beard and fingering the red bandanna he wore around his neck, "is really quite simple. It consists not in doing certain things but in avoiding certain things, things which are bound to cause a man grief. There are four things I have avoided all my life and that is why I'm a happy man."

"Well, what are they?" asked Abney.

"A hay baler, a stud horse, a chippy, and a celluloid collar."

The Wisdom of a Lifetime

Jesse O. Wells was a sage of the hill country of Pulaski County, [Kentucky]. He lay dying one day in 1912. He had been a mighty man in his time, but he now lay on his deathbed at the ripe old age of eighty-five. The friends of Mr. Wells, his children, grandchildren, and great-grandchildren had gathered at the little mountain home where the patriarch was about to make his peace with God. The old man's breathing grew harder, and he knew the hour of his death was at hand. He announced he wanted all his friends and kinsmen to gather in the room where he lay.

Everybody gathered around the bed. The old man raised himself from the pillow and looked into their faces.

"I want to tell you," he said, "the wisdom I have learned in my lifetime. I want to leave you the experience I have gained in eighty-five years."

The silent crowd around the bed leaned forward to catch the last words from the old man's tired lips.

"This is what I have learned," he said. "First, when you are out carrying a gun, never let your dog travel the road ahead of you. Second, always bring your maul and wedges in at night."

And then the old man sank back to his pillow and passed to the Great Beyond.

"Help Yourself to the Mustard"

More than one Texas youngster who pouted at the food set before him was met with the parental injunction to "help yourself to the mustard." The injunction was derived from a tale common enough in stagecoach days. As the tale went, a traveler from the East alighted from the stage one day to get dinner at some remote stand. He was confronted by the rough and ready fare of Mexican *frijoles* boiled with "sow belly," a pone of cold bread, and, to one side, a pot of mustard. The Easterner shoved the dish of *frijoles* and salt pork aside with something like contempt and did not even look at the bread. "I want something to eat," he announced.

"Well, just help yourself to the mustard," the stage driver cordially replied, and the phrase became a byword of the ranges.

A Mortgage on Hell

As farmers and tenants were arranging their affairs for the coming year about this time, they frequently had to borrow money, mortgaging their land or other property. There was one old gentleman who was a good hand at taking mortgages on the stock and implements of the farmers to whom he sold goods. Whenever the debt came due, he would immediately foreclose and take the mortgaged property.

One day a number of men were standing around in his store. Suddenly one of them said, "Fellers, I had a quare dream last night. I dreampt I died and went to Hell. I got ter looken aroun' over Hell fur to see what I could see, an' run acrost a big iron kettle. Says I, 'I'll jest turn it over and disciver what's under thar.'

"I started to turn it over, when the Devil seed me, and yelled, 'Hey, thar, don't turn over that pot!'

"Says I, 'Why not?'

"Says he, 'Wal, it's thisaway. I've got Hiram Smith under thar. You let him out and he'll have a mortgage on Hell inside er fifteen minutes.' "

"Keep Your Seat, Mr. Greeley"

Horace Greeley had taken the stage from Genoa, Nevada, for Sacramento [or, according to some versions, Placerville]. The Kingsbury grade out of Genoa is very steep and the progress of the four-horse stage was very slow. Mr. Greeley had an appointment in Sacramento and became quite agitated on account of the long, slow ride to the summit. He frequently rose to his feet and tapped the driver on the back and asked him if there was something that could be done to speed things a bit. Needless to say, this annoyed the driver almost beyond human endurance. Finally the summit was reached and the horses were changed. The trip down from the summit was quite a different matter. The horses moved along fast around the corners and very, very frequently Mr. Greeley was forcefully moved from his seat, to the great elation of the driver who would intermittently turn his head around and yell, "Keep your seat, Mr. Greeley, I'll get you there on time."

[The remark later became famous and has been used countless times in speaking to one who is getting excited.]

A Little Leather

We were driving the cows away from Deep Wells, where we had left their calves to be weaned. One old cow, remembering her calf, would keep breaking back, causing no end of trouble. Don Francisco told one of the younger boys to double his *reata* and bring it down over her back a few times, which the boy did, and the cow entered the herd and went along without giving us any more trouble.

Don Francisco chuckled. "A little leather, laid on now and then, fixes things wonderfully." He went on to tell me the story of the meek man, his shrewish wife and the stubborn mule.

The husband was hard at work in the corral. Feeling thirsty, he called to his wife to bring him a drink of water. She not only would not bring him water, but began a severe scolding; and to escape her tongue and find peace, he walked off along the *camino* to a grove of trees where he sat down facing the road.

After a time an *arriero* (packer) with his train of mules drove up. There was a log across the road and each mule passed over in good order until the last one came up. This animal snorted at the log and turned back down the road. The *arriero* drove it back and made two or three attempts to drive it over, but the mule proved too obstinate. Finally the *arriero* lost his patience and untied the *tapa ojos* (blinds) he used to cover the mules' eyes with when he loaded them, and carried attached to the saddle. He gave the mule a good tanning, and when he was through, it was glad to jump over the obstruction and go on with the others. The husband watched the whole performance, and approaching the *arriero* he said, "Señor, do me a great favor and sell me that leather you used on the mule. It seems to have a special virtue." The packer answered, "I can't sell it because without it I could never hope to handle my mules."

But the husband persisted, saying, "If that strap can make twenty mules behave, perhaps with it I might tame one woman."

The *arriero* was a married man and in the end he sold the *tapa ojos* to the husband, who went home with his purchase and back to work in the corral. In a little while he called for water, and receiving none, he went into the house, put a bench in the middle of the room, then catching hold of his wife, he unlimbered the leather and began using it exactly as the *arriero* had done.

At each blow he would say, "Jump the log, you stubborn beast." After a few hearty whacks his wife jumped the bench at his command. Laying the leather where it would be ready to hand in the future, he went out to work again. Eager to test the effectiveness of the leather in inducing obedience, he called for water. His wife came running out with the gourd and when he drank, she said, "Dearest, how many times do you want me to jump the bench?"

The Non-Union Calf's Head

You say you don't believe in unions. Well, that's what the boss likes to hear. He wished no worker would believe in unions and we'd run around as individuals. And so, fellow workers, now you put me in mind of an old woman that come in the butcher shop and she wanted to buy meat and she had no money to amount to anything, because her husband was a wage slave and working for small wages.

And so she looked around in the shop for something cheap, and while she's looking around for something cheap, you know, she spied a union house card in the shop.

And she thought, "Well, that calf's head is about the cheapest thing I see in here. There ain't much to eat on it, but it will make us good soup." So she says to the butcher, "I'll take the calf's head."

Then again she looked at the union house card and she said, "Butcher, is this a union shop?"

And he said, "Yes, ma'am."

"Well, then this must be a union calf's head."

"Yes, ma'am, this is a union calf's head."

"Well, I don't want it, because me and my husband we have no use for these labor unions. They're nothing else but trouble makers. And if this is a union shop, then that must be a union calf's head. And I don't want no union meat. I want unorganized meat."

"All right," the butcher said. "Lady, just wait a minute and I'll give you some unorganized meat."

So he takes the calf's head out in the back yard and he comes back with the same calf's head and proceeds to wrap it up.

And she says, "Now, butcher, is that non-union meat?"

He says, "Yes."

"Well, it looks like the same calf's head you had here a while ago and told me it was a union calf's head.

"Yes, ma'am, it's the same calf's head, but I had it out in the yard and I knocked its brains out, and now it's a non-union calf's head."

☞ **12** ☜

Spun Yarn

An old man in Vermont was notorious for retailing village news; and he was always angry when anything happened without his being the first to tell it. A couple of wags met him one day, and said to him, "Do you know, Uncle Tom, they have caught a famous great whale up in the creek yonder?" (A whale, by the way, could not have been crowded into the creek.) "Ha! have they *cotched* him?" said the old man; "I *haard* they *was arter* him."

FREEMAN HUNT

Introduction

In his essay on "How to Tell a Story," Mark Twain distinguishes three types of funny story: "The humorous story is American, the comic story is English, the witty story is French. . . . The humorous story may be spun out to great length, and may wander around as much as it pleases, and arrive nowhere in particular; but the comic and witty stories must be brief and end with a point. . . ." There is still a fourth type, as Mark Twain realized when he added: "Very often, of course, the rambling and disjointed humorous story finishes with a nub, point, snapper, [dropped] in a carefully casual and indifferent way."

The modern taste for the shorter, snappier forms of humor has more or less ruled out the long-winded, rambling, pointless yarn. It has not, however, eliminated the longish story which has both a nub and a build-up, such as the shaggy dog story of *Wit's End* or the bizarre story of *Spun Yarn*. The bizarre or queer story is a story of improbable incidents or odd characters, involving mystery, magic, apparitions, coincidences, and the like. Unlike the yarn, bizarre stories end somewhere, but like the yarn they may take a long time getting there. Part of this leisureliness is due to the necessity of establishing and sustaining a mood—fantastic, romantic, ironic, grim, grotesque, macabre. Part of it is due to the necessity of making the unfamiliar familiar and the improbable probable through circumstantial detail.

Although most of these stories are traveling or migratory stories, they are told in local or localized versions. Many of them are local legends. Still others are human interest stories, whose "deceptive freshness" conceals considerable age and enables them to get past the editor into the newspapers and periodicals as "original" and "true" stories that happened, say, to "Aunt Mabel's housekeeper." Once in print, they take on the character of the "twice-told" and edited tale—a certain self-consciousness as well as polish—the earmarks of the story written to be read rather than told to be heard.

Spun Yarn runs the gamut of local legend, witch and ghost story, human-interest story, personal reminiscence, traveler's and old-timer's tale. More clearly than any other anecdotal type, the "spun yarn"—home-spun or fine-spun—mirrors the world-in-flux of the traveling or floating story, which shifts back and forth between oral tradition and print, between anecdote and yarn, between the improbable story told and believed as true and the true story that sounds delightfully improbable.

Settling a Village Quarrel

The people in a certain town in New England got into a quarrel among [themselves], and many efforts were made to reconcile them, but all failed. At last they agreed firmly among themselves to submit their difficulties to the judgment of a certain godly minister in a distant town. So they appointed two men, one of each party, to wait on the minister, and relate the cause each party had for dissatisfaction; and the minister was to write his judgment of the case; then the people would all meet on the day he was to send them his pastoral letter, and have it read by the clerk of the town, and they would all abide by his judgment and counsel. So after the good minister heard the story of the quarrel from the two delegates, and had written his opinion and counsel to them, he had occasion also (it being in the spring of the year) to write a few lines to a farmer, on one of his farms at a small distance.

It so happened that the messengers that were to carry the letters both came up at the same time, and being in a hurry, the good man made a mistake; he folded the letters without superscriptions, and gave the letter intended for the farmer to the messenger that came from the town, and sent that for the town to the farmer. The people of the town were all assembled, waiting, when the messenger came, and the clerk read the hasty written scroll as follows: "You had better see that your fences are put up well in the first place. Plough your ground deep; and sort your seed; be careful not to sow foul seed; and take care of that great ugly bull. I think you had better poke him. The rest I will tell you when I come."

The people, on hearing this, were all astonished, and sat for a while in amazement. Some said they could not understand it. At last one arose, and he understood it—that the meaning was all revealed to him. First, he said the putting up the fences that were down, signifies the discipline of the church. We have neglected those good rules of discipline: they serve to protect and guard us against evil passions; and, when neglected, like a fence thrown down, leave the field open to wild beasts. Secondly, the ploughing the ground deep, signifies the breaking up the fallow ground of the heart, that everyone should search his own heart, and prepare it for the good seed. Thirdly, the sorting of seed, signifies that we should be careful not to believe every story that is told us; but examine faithfully into everything, and receive nothing but the truth. We have not done this, but we have been guilty of evil-speaking, and of backbiting one another; and we have all done wrong. And fourthly, as to the great ugly bull, by that he means the devil; he has done us much harm, and we have not resisted him as we ought to have done; therefore we ought all to unite and resist and poke the devil.

This explanation was satisfactory. They all took it as good counsel, and it laid open the true cause of all their troubles. They began to confess their faults one to another; and pray one for another, and soon all their difficulties subsided, and the great wound in the peace of the town was healed.

Salmon or Cod?

One day . . . Smith caught a fine salmon, which he took into his house and showed to his wife, saying, "What shall we do with this salmon?" Said his wife, "You're going down to —— tomorrow, aren't you?" "Yes," said Smith. "Take it and on your way stop at Parson Jones's and make him a present of it." He said he would. His wife packed it in a cloth and sewed it up very neatly, and the next morning he put it in the box of his vehicle and started off. He stopped to dine at a tavern on the way, and told the landlord what he was going to do with it. The landlord went out and got the salmon, brought it into the house, took it out of the cloth, put in a lot of dried codfish, hay, and stone, sewed up the cloth neatly, and put it back into the vehicle. Smith went on, stopped at Parson Jones's, and told him that he and his wife thought that they would make him a present of a salmon. He took out the bundle, left it there, and then went on to the next town. After having transacted his business, he started for home the next morning, stopping at the parson's on the way to inquire how they liked the salmon. They began laughing, and when he asked what they were laughing about they told him that he didn't bring any salmon, and showed him what he had brought. He was somewhat amazed, but thought that they had better sew up the material he had brought and he would take it back. So it was sewed up, and he put it in his box. Again he stopped at the same tavern to dine, and when he saw the landlord he told him what had happened. The landlord went out, got the bundle, took out the stuff, replaced the salmon, and sewed up the bundle. Then Mr. Smith went home, and after having unharnessed his horse he went into the house and sat down. His wife said: "Why, Smith, you seem to be in a quandary; what's the matter?" He said: "I thought I carried a good salmon down to Parson Jones, but it turned out to be nothing but a lot of dried salt fish, hay, and stones." "Pooh!" said his wife; "didn't I sew him up and don't I know? Where is it?" "In the box in the vehicle in the barn." "Get it, and bring it in here," said his wife. He brought it in, opened it, and there was the salmon. "Ah," said Smith, shaking his fist at the salmon, "you're a dashed good salmon on the Kennebec, but down on the Penobscot you're nothing but a cod."

The Woman Who Sold Winds

There was a woman who lived in Taniscot, [Maine], about the middle of the last century when it was a center of shipping and exported the oak and pine of its woods, the ice of its lakes, and the red brick made in the yards along its river banks to most of the world. She kept a sailors' boarding house, ostensibly, but she had a good trade on the side in selling winds.

Although one thinks of a witch, particularly a seaport witch, as a rather cosmopolitan person, this woman seems to have retained a good deal of local pride. So one evening when she heard two captains in her boarding house boasting of their respective vessels, which were waiting ready-laden for Boston, and of their general handiness and remarkable speed, she naturally took the side of the Taniscot captain—the other was an outsider from Bath maybe, or maybe Bangor. Anyway the woman made some excuse to call the Taniscot captain out of the room, where he sat arguing with the other man.

When she had him in the darkness of the hall, she whispered to him fiercely, "Bet him all you have, and I'll give and I'll give and I'll give you a wind, and you'll be in Boston by morning."

That sounded pretty impossible even to the Taniscot captain, but when a witch told you to do something in those days you did it, and asked no questions. So he went back and laid the bet with the other man and then roused up his crew and went down to his vessel and hauled up anchor in the dark—or what dark there was, for the moon was rising. There was a downriver wind rising too, of which there'd been no hint earlier in the evening, so they made good time with an outgoing tide. When they sailed into the ocean a strange thing happened: the following wind veered into the east—it was still a following wind. There was no tacking, no feeling about to keep the sheets filled, nothing at all for the captain and crew to do but set all sail and dance down the coast while the cook put the coffee to boil on the galley stove. Hour after hour went by, and the wind never faltered nor shifted again. Like a big broom sweeping a ball of paper before it, that breeze carried the Taniscot vessel straight to the entrance of Boston Harbor and then, with a sidewise flick, it tossed her in.

The moon was gone and the morning star was just beginning to pale and there was light on the eastern horizon when the ship came in to its usual berth at T Wharf after such a voyage as no Maine vessel ever has had before or since.

"Got in kind of early, didn't you, Captain?" asked the watchman, holding his lantern for the captain to step ashore.

The captain nodded.

"Had a fair wind," he said laconically.

Thar She Blows!

Eight and fahrty weeks at sea and never a drop o' oil in the casks. 'Twas in the early fifties when I was fust mate on the whaler *Sassy Sal,* aout o' New Bedford. We was a-sailin' down the Mosambique Channel when the man on the lookout says, "Thar she spaouts!" And I comes aft and I says, "Cap'n Simmons," says I, "thar she spaouts!" Cap'n Simmons gazes aout over the side an' he sees one little cloud a-scuddin' along the horizon. "Mr. Sims," says he, "it's a-blowin' quite too peart. I don't see fitten for to lower."

An' I goes for'ard; an' the man on the lookout shaouts, "Thar she spaouts and *blo-ow-ows!*" And I comes aft and I says, "Cap'n Simmons," says I, "thar she spaouts an' *blo-ow-ows.* Shall I lower?" "Mister Sims," says he, "she may spaout an' she may blow, but as I have told you once before it is a-blowin' quite too peart. I don't see fitten for to lower."

An' I goes for'ard; an' the man on the lookout sings aout, "Thar she spaouts an' *blo-ow-ows* an' BREACHES!" An' I comes aft an' I says, "Cap'n Simmons," says I, "thar she spaouts an' *blo-ow-ows* an' BREACHES! Shall I lower?" "Mister Sims," says he, "as I have told you twice before it is a-blowin' quite too peart. I don't see fitten for to lower."

An' I goes for'ard; an' the man on the lookout says, "Thar she spaouts an' *blo-ow-ows* an' BREACHES an' BELCHES!" An' I comes aft an' I says, "Cap'n Simmons," says I, "thar she spaouts an' *blo-ow-ows* an' BREACHES an' BELCHES! Shall I lower?" "Mister Sims," says he, "she may spaout an' she may blow, an' she may breach an' she may belch, but as I have told you four times before, it is a-blowin' quite too peart. I don't see fitten for to lower."

An' I goes for'ard; an' the man on the lookout shaouts, "Thar she spaouts an' *blo-ow-ows* an' BREACHES an' BELCHES an' *sparm at that!*" An' I comes aft an' I says, "Cap'n Simmons," says I, "thar she spaouts an' *blo-ow-ows* an' BREACHES an' BELCHES an' *sparm at that!* May I lower?" "Mister Sims," says he, "as I have told you seven times before it is a-blowin' quite too peart. *I* don't see fitten for to lower. But Mister Sims," says he, "if *you* see fitten for to lower, you may lower, Mister Sims, an' be good goddammed to you!"

So I goes for'ard an' I sings aout for volunteers. An' the boys just tumbled over each other a-droppin' into the boat. An' I did lower. "Shove off," says I, an' they shoved off. Well, we chased that critter the main part of the fore watch an' hove along side o' her abaout eight bells.

"Boys," says I, "I am the best man with the long dart as ever sailed aout o' New Bedford. Shall I sock it to her?" "Sock it to her!" says they. An' I socked it to her. An' it tuk!

Well, that night, as I come alongside the lee gangway, thar stood Cap'n Simmons, the tears in his eyes as big as fish balls! "Mister Sims," says he, "you are the best fust mate as ever sailed with me on the *Sassy Sal*. In the starboard till o' my locker you will find some prime Havana seegars, the best o' whisky, gin, an' some fine aould Medford New England Rum. Them is yourn," says he, "all as you may want o' them is yourn for the remainder of the voyage."

"Cap'n Simmons," says I, "I am a man what sees his duty an' does it. You may take your prime Havana seegars an' stick 'em! An' you may take your best o' whisky, gin, an' fine aould Medford New England Rum an' stick *them* too. All I want on this voyage is *seevility*, an' that of the goddammest cheapest sort!"

An' I goes for'ard.

The Music-Chair

All up and down the Cape one hears yarns. . . . Many of them are worthwhile and practically all of them fit the locality and the people. And, in so many cases, the yarn spinner claims to know or have known the person or persons concerned in the happening. Just where and when the hero of the tale said this or that and why he said it.

But one learns, after a time, to take the story for the story's sake and to reserve a certain amount of skepticism where its localization is concerned. . . .

[The friend who tells me a story] had, in all probability, heard it from a friend of his, who had heard it from somebody else, who, in turn, had heard it from another somebody, who, in order to make his yarn a trifle more appealing, transferred names and localities to those nearer home. . . .

Once I was planning to write the story of a little girl adopted by two old retired sea captains. I needed an incident to introduce my little heroine, and a relative of ours, who happened also to be the president of the firm publishing my books, told me a story which I thought would be just what I needed. He said it was absolute fact and the event took place at the funeral of his wife's aunt in a Vermont town.

The old lady, the aunt, had been an important personage in that town and her funeral was largely attended. The parlor was crowded, every chair occupied. The minister was on the point of rising to begin the ceremony when up the aisle came a dignified and wealthy spinster who had been a close friend of the deceased. Behind her came the local undertaker, carrying a chair which he had taken from one of the rooms on the floor above. That chair was an importation from abroad and was peculiar to itself. Under its seat was a music box and when one sat in the chair the box began to play.

The undertaker placed the chair for the late comer, the minister rose and opened his prayer book, the dignified spinster sat down, and the box struck up "The Campbells Are Coming. Hurrah! Hurrah!"

I liked that story and asked permission to incorporate it in my first chapter, which permission was granted. The novel had been on sale for a few months when, on the steps of the post office in the Cape town where I spend one half of the year, I was introduced to a portly person who seemed to have a grievance against me.

"Tell me," he demanded, rather hotly, I thought, "how did you get hold of that music-chair story you put into that latest book of yours?"

"Oh," I replied serenely, "that is a true story. The incident happened in Vermont at the funeral of the aunt of the wife of a good friend of mine."

His florid face grew redder. "It did not!" he snorted. "It happened at the funeral of my own grandfather in New Hampshire. That story, sir, is an heirloom in our family. You tell it well enough, except that you are wrong when you say the chair played 'The Campbells Are Coming.' That chair, sir, was brought from Germany and it played 'Ach, Mein Liebe Augustine.' "

Which was bad enough, but, after I returned to our winter home near New York, I received a letter written by an inmate of an old ladies' home near Augusta, Georgia.

"Dear Sir": the letter began. "We have been reading your novel aloud here at the Home and it occurred to me that you might be interested to know where the incident of the 'music-chair' which you describe in your book actually took place. One of the ladies here was born and reared in a little town not far from Augusta, and the chair played at the funeral of her grandmother there. You have it exactly right, except for the tune which the chair played. It was not 'The Campbells Are Coming,' but 'Comin' Through the Rye.'"

And since then I have been informed, with dates and particulars, of two other funerals, in places remotely distant from each other, where that chair played.

. . . Do you wonder I am skeptical as to the localization of a good story?

A Simple Family

There was going to be a hanging in the Schoharie jail yard, and Zadig Lape and his boy Sam counted on going. Zadig's woman wanted to go too, but Zadig told her that it was no kind of a thing for a woman to see. Then she said it couldn't be decent for a boy to see, and Sam couldn't go. Zadig didn't care if he couldn't. But Sam, who was kinda simple anyway, wanted to go because he had never seen a hanging. So he just let out an awful beller and hollered and bawled until his ma told him he could go to the hanging if he'd tell her when he got back just how 'twas. He give his word he would, and away he and his pa went in the big bobsleigh, for it was wintertime, behind Zadig's spanking team of sorrels. Horses was Zadig's "speciality" when there wa'n't no hanging to take his attention.

Well, the hanging went off all right, and Zadig and Sam started for home. When they got there, Zadig went to the barn to fodder the stock, and Sam went into the house to tell his ma how things had gone. He told her all about the way the prisoner was led out, the praying for him and all. Then when it come time to show how the job was done, Sam went and got a rope and fastened one end of it to a big iron hook in the ceiling and made a slip noose in the other end. When he got the noose all fixed about ten foot from the floor, he told his ma that, if she would stand on a chair that he set for her and let him slip the noose over her head, he'd show her just how the hanging was done.

She was so simple that she done just as Sam told her, and when he got everything fixed just right, he said, "And now they kicked the block out from in under the feller like this." And with that he kicked the chair right out from in under his ma's feet. He never thought to kill his ma, because she'd been awful good to him. But he was that simple he didn't realize what he was a-doing. No more did his ma, because she was simple, too.

When he saw his ma a-hanging there looking so kinda strange with her eyes a-popping out of her head, he was scared and shoved the chair back in under her feet. But of course it didn't do no good because her neck was busted plum in two. Sam got the butcher knife and cut the rope, and when he seen how his ma just fell outa the chair onto the floor in a heap, he most lost all the few wits he'd ever owned. But he had sense enough to know that he'd killed his ma and would likely be hung for murder like the feller he'd seen hung at Schoharie. Not knowing what to do, but hoping to save his hide, he drug his ma over to her rocking chair by the windy and somehow propped her up in the chair with her knitting in her hands naturaler than life.

When Zadig come from the barn, he seen her a-setting there as he'd seen her hundreds of times before—only not noticing him—and he thought to have a little fun with her. He was great on jokes, surprising folks when they wa'n't expecting nothing and the like of that. So he made a snowball—what he thought was a soft one—and trun it agin the windy. But by Jocks, it went right through the glass and hit his woman on the temple, or at least so it appeared. Sam hadn't fixed her to stand snowballing, so she just toppled out of her chair onto the floor. Zadig felt awful because he hadn't counted on scaring her into a fainting fit. He rushed into the house, threw snow into her face, and done everything he'd ever hearn tell of and made up some, to bring folks out of a fainting spell. But nothing worked. He called to Sam, but Sam was out of hearing. After a spell he made up his mind that his woman was dead and that he had killed her. He knew that when the neighbors found out, he would be tried for murder and most likely hung like that feller at Schoharie. Yet in a way he was innercent. He had liked his woman and been good to her.

All at once he thought of a plan to save himself from being hung. He went and got Sarah's bunnit and blanket shawl and wrapped her up for a ride. Then he went to the barn and hitched the horses to a sleigh that was loaded with straw that he had pitched down from the mow for bedding the stock when it come chore time. He druv up to the back door that nobody could see from the road and somehow got Sarah a-top of the load. Her body sagged over so she 'peared to be half laying down. But she looked quite natural and Zadig didn't lose no time in jumping onto the seat and driving off like the Old Boy hisself was after him. Up hill, down dale he went, lickety-split, plying the gad at every jump until he come to a steep pitch with a sharp turn at the foot. As the horses came near the turn, he lashed them to top speed, the sleigh slewed as he had calculated, and over she went into a gully. The horses was so scared that they tore themselves loose and legged it for home and left Sarah and Zadig with the hull load of straw a-top of them.

"Horse-Car Poetry"

Great as was [Isaac H.] Bromley's success as an editorial writer [on *The Tribune*] his most widespread triumph was achieved by a bit of doggerel which was published with no suspicion of its nearly unlimited possibilities of popularity. In the summer of 1875 one of the streetcar lines in New York City posted the following notice in its cars:

> The conductor, when he receives a fare, will punch, in the presence of the passenger,
> A blue trip-slip for an eight-cent fare,
> A buff trip-slip for a six-cent fare,
> A pink trip-slip for a three-cent fare.

This had been posted for several weeks and had attracted no attention as containing lyrical qualities. Sitting in one of the cars on an evening journey downtown with his friend, Noah Brooks, formerly of *The Tribune* staff but then on the staff of *The Times*, Bromley said suddenly, "It's poetry, by George! Brooks, it's poetry!" Brooks, who had been dozing, asked what was poetry. Pointing to the notice Bromley said, "Why, don't you see? The lines are all of the same length and all begin with a capital letter. Doesn't that make poetry?"

Reaching *The Tribune* office, he wrote out the "poetry" as follows:

> *The conductor when he receives a fare,*
> *Will punch in the presence of the passinjare,*
> *A blue trip-slip for an eight-cent fare,*

A *buff trip-slip for a six-cent fare,*
A *pink trip-slip for a three-cent fare,*
All *in the presence of the passinjare.*

CHORUS:
   Punch, brothers, punch with care, &c.

In the work of composing, Bromley was aided by members of *The Tribune* staff but the inspiration was all his own. The "poem" was published inconspicuously on one of the inside pages of *The Tribune,* without signature, but its merits were so extraordinary that it could not remain hidden. It was copied instantly by newspapers in all parts of the country. It not only caught the popular fancy but seized upon it like a nightmare. Once fixed in memory, it stayed there in spite of all efforts to be rid of it. In my journeys in the cars where the notice was displayed, I saw passenger after passenger get in, seat himself, and as soon as his eyes fell upon the notice, he would begin mumbling, as his lips showed, the tantalizing lines. From that moment, he was doomed. He could only take his eyes away by leaving the car. I saw a serene Quaker couple, in the beautiful garb of their faith, fall captive in this way. They sat down opposite the notice, and their eyes fell upon it simultaneously. With a slight start, they looked inquiringly at each other, then back to the notice, and then the mumbling of the lips began.

Everybody fell a victim to the jingle. It was set to music, parodied, and quoted everywhere and on all occasions. Mark Twain caught the infection and wrote an amusing account of his sufferings, which was published in the *Atlantic Monthly,* in February, 1876, under the title of "A Literary Nightmare," in which he maintained that the only way by which he could rid himself of it was to give it to somebody else. This publication gave rise to a quite general belief that Mark Twain was himself the author of it, and that belief persists to the present day. In *Scribner's Monthly,* of April, 1876, Bromley himself, under the fictitious name of "Winkelried Wolfgang Brown," published a true account of the authorship, claiming for himself the honor of founding a new school of verse to be known for all times as "Horse-car Poetry."

Its fame spread to other lands and it was translated into other tongues. *The Western,* a St. Louis magazine, found relief in a Latin anthem, with the chorus:

Pungite, fratres, pungite,
Pungite cum amore,
Pungite pro victore
Diligentissime pungite.

It reached Paris and appeared as follows in the *Revue des Deux Mondes:*

LE CHANT DU CONDUCTEUR
  Ayant été payé, le conducteur
  Percera en pleine vue du voyageur,
  Quand il reçoit trois sous un coupon vert,
  Un coupon jaune pour six sous c'est l'affaire.
  Et pour huit sous un coupon couleur
  De rose, en pleine vue du voyageur.

  CHOEUR:
    Donc, percez soigneusement, mes frères,
    Tout en pleine vue des voyageurs, &c.

On the City Desk

Over the ticker comes a story from the City News Association about a traffic accident. The city editor calls to one of the desk men: "Hey, Murphy, do a rewrite on this yarn about a little girl killed by a hit-and-run driver up in the Bronx."

Murphy takes down the details: A young girl, on her way home from school, while crossing the street, hit and run over by a speeding driver who didn't stop to ascertain the damage done. Name and address. Only child of so and so. Student at P.S. 68.

Murphy finishes the story, walks to the editor's desk, lays the copy in the basket, and says, "Chief, may I go home now? That little girl was my daughter."

The Mattress

There is a servant girl who, for many years, has kept her earnings under a mattress. She has never said anything about it to her employers, who are a devoted man and wife. . . . They finally give her a well-earned vacation. And when she returns, the maid finds that her employers have sold her old mattress and given her a brand-new one.

She squawks bitterly, and tells them of the money that was hidden in the old mattress. After much trouble, they repurchase the old mattress and find the money intact. They return it to the maid, but they make her promise that, from now on, she will keep her earnings in the local savings bank. She promises that she will do so.

Two weeks later, the bank fails. Her employers feel terrible about the situation because they have given their poor servant a bad steer.

But the girl isn't a bit worried. Force of habit had been strong within her. A few days after depositing it, the girl had withdrawn her money from the bank. And it now reposes upstairs under the new mattress.

The Ghost Rider

This is a favorite story after a flood, a big fire, an earthquake, or a disaster of any sort. You can almost count upon its arrival.

Two men are driving along in their car. As they ride through a lonesome neighborhood, an elderly woman steps to the center of the road and hails them. They stop—and the woman tells them that she is desperately in need of a lift to her home. Her daughter is awaiting her, she says, and the last trolley has already left.

They agree to take her to her destination, since they are going in that direction. She sits, alone, in the back seat of the car—and gives them her address. They proceed.

After a few miles, one of the men looks around. To his amazement, the elderly passenger has vanished! She has either jumped or fallen from the car. The two men argue. One is in favor of going back and looking for the woman. The other feels differently. He says the passenger looked queer to him, and he is in favor of going to the address she gave and asking for the daughter she mentioned. Since he is driving the car, he wins the argument.

Arriving at the house in question, they leave the car and ring the bell. The door is opened by a young woman who, by her resemblance, is obviously the daughter in the case. The men attempt to tell her what has taken place, but she places a finger on her lips and motions them forward.

They advance into a room that holds a casket in the center. And in the casket, a victim of the previous day's disaster, is the woman who had vanished from their car only a few minutes earlier.

The Mink Coat

A businessman in Peoria (I think in this instance, at least, it was Peoria) had an extravagant wife who fancied that her delicate person ought to be encased in a mink coat. She had brought the matter tentatively into conversations with her husband and had been made aware that he thought more of three or four thousand dollars than he did of her necessity. But she was a smart woman with a few hundred dollars of idle capital in her own bank account, so she evolved an ingenious plan to force him to co-operate.

She bought the coat on a charge account. But she didn't wear it. Instead she carried it around to Uncle Moe's pawnshop where she put it in what I believe is called "hock" for about three-quarters of its value. This estimate of what she got may be wrong. It presupposes a talent for salesmanship that seems a little incongruous in an extravagant housewife. But for the purposes of the narrative we may let it stand.

At any rate, with the cash that Uncle Moe so generously allowed her, plus the bulk of her bank balance, she paid her account at the store and forestalled the possibility that such an item as "mink coat" might appear on any bill presented to the gruff old husband.

Having completed these transactions she went home, told her husband that she had found the pawn ticket in the street and gave it to him.

"I am all atwitter to know what this represents," she told him. "From what I hear of pawnshops I gather that they are very stingy with their advances. So if you'd run around tomorrow and pay this ticket it may be that we can get something very beautiful for a small portion of its true worth."

The husband who was just as dishonest as he was crusty said that he'd see about it. The next night he returned home in an unusually cheery mood.

"That pawn ticket called for a nice piece of fur," he told her as he laid a cardboard suit box on the table. "I'll not tell you how much it cost. But that doesn't make any difference. I think we got a real bargain."

She opened the box and disclosed a scrawny skunk neckpiece of a type that hadn't been worn by anybody but other people's cooks for many a long year.

She didn't have a word to say—not then or even the next day when she went to the gruff old husband's office and saw the lovely blonde stenographer emerging for lunch in her new mink coat.

The Guilty Hotel Guest

A New York clergyman . . . staying at the [Washington] Mayflower said that he found on his return to New York that he had inadvertently slipped into his bag a shoehorn marked with the name of the hotel. He promptly wrote a note to the manager confessing his theft and enclosing fifteen cents to cover the value. "I am," he wrote, "not accustomed to pilfering."

Back came the reply, "Don't do such a thing again. The shock is too great. Never in the history of the Mayflower has anything like this happened before. Come again, Doctor, and you may carry off anything that isn't nailed down."

The Blanket

There is a story of a German clerk attached to one of the American Military Government headquarters. Somehow he got hold of an all-wool army blanket and suggested to his wife that maybe he could exchange it for a carton of cigarettes. "Don't be foolish," his wife counseled him, "who wants a blanket? Come, let's unravel the blanket and I'll knit all-wool socks. Then you'll have something to barter with."

For the next four weeks, the couple devoted all their time to painstakingly unraveling the blanket, thread by thread. Then the hausfrau knitted her first pair of socks.

Visiting the barter exchange, the clerk auctioned off the socks and finally accepted two packs of American cigarettes in return for the all-wool hose.

His wife continued to knit and knit and knit . . . and the husband continued to exchange the laboriously made socks for two packs of cigarettes.

Finally came the day when the thread was gone. "Fritz, my man," the wife said, "with all my stretching, all I could knit from what's left of the blanket is this one sock. Go and see what you can get for it."

Filled with doubts, Fritz went to the exchange again and looked up his customer. "Here," he said. "I've only one sock today. How many cigarettes will you give me for it?"

The black-market cigarette dealer's face lit up with joy. Grabbing the sock, he dropped an entire carton of cigarettes into Fritz's hands.

Fritz stared in amazement. "I don't understand. For weeks I've given you pairs of all-wool socks and you gave me only two packs. Now for one sock you give me a carton. Why?"

His friend looked up and patted him on the cheek. "This sock," he said triumphantly, "is the most precious of all—it's all my wife needs to finish the blanket she's knitting."

Mountain Hospitality

[A] Mr. Ogilvie, formerly so well known in Virginia as a supporter of the Godwinian philosophy, conceiving a vehement desire to see the western country, set off from Richmond, for Lexington, in Kentucky. It was in the month of October, after a most lonely and wearisome day's ride, that a little before sunset, he came to a small cabin on the road, and fearing he should find no other opportunity of procuring refreshment for himself and his jaded horse, he stopped and inquired if he could be accommodated for the night. An old woman, the only person he saw, civilly answering him in the affirmative, he gladly alighted, and going in to a tolerable fire, enjoyed the luxury of rest, while his hostess was discharging the duties of hostler and cook. In no long time, she set before him a supper of comfortable but homely fare, of which, having liberally partaken, and given divers significant nods, the old woman remarked she "expected" he "chose bed," and, pointing to one which stood in a corner of the room, immediately went into the yard awhile, to give him an opportunity of undressing.

Before he had been long in bed, and while he was congratulating himself on his good fortune, the latch of the door was drawn, and there entered a dark-looking man of gigantic stature and form, with stiff black hair, eyebrows and beard. He was apparently about eight and twenty, was dressed in a brown hunting shirt, which partly concealed a pair of dirty buckskin overalls, and he wore moccasins of the same material. Mr. O. thought he had never seen anything half so ferocious. As soon as this man entered the room, his mother, for so she proved to be, pointing to the bed, motioned him to make no noise; on which, with inaudible steps, he walked to the chimney, put his gun upon a rude rack provided for that and other arms, and sat softly down at the fire, then throwing a bright blaze round the room.

Our traveler, not liking the looks of the newcomer, and not caring to be teased by conversation, drew his head under the bedclothes, so that he could see what was passing, without leaving his own face visible. The two soon entered into conversation, but in so low a voice, that Mr. O. could not distinguish what was said. His powers of attention were wrought up to the most painful pitch of intensity. At length, the man, looking toward the bed, made some remark to his mother, to which Mr. O. heard her reply, "No, I hardly think he's asleep yet"—and they again conversed in a low voice, as before. After a short interval, while the man sat with his feet stretched out toward the fire, on which he was intently gazing, "Don't you think he's asleep now?" he was heard to say.

"Stop," says she, "I'll go and see"; and moving near the bed, under the pretext of taking something from a small table, she approached so near as to see the face of our traveler, whose eyes were indeed closed, but who was anything but asleep. On her return to the fireplace, she said, "Yes, he's fast asleep now."

On this the mountaineer, rising from his stool, reached up to the rack, and taking down with his right hand an old greasy cutlass, walked with the same noiseless step toward the traveler's bed, and stretching out the other hand, at the moment that Mr. O. was about to implore his pity, took down a venison ham which hung on the wall near the head of the bed, walked softly back to the fire, and began to slice some pieces for his supper, and Mr. O., who lay, more dead than alive, and whose romantic fancy heightened the terrors of all he saw, had the unspeakable gratification to find that these kind-hearted children of the forest had been talking low, and that the hungry hunter, who had eaten nothing since the morning, had forbore making a noise, lest they should interrupt the slumbers of their wayworn guest.

The Settin' Up

Dere was a fellow that went to one of he fren's settin'-up, and dis fren' was laid out dead on de coolin' board, and in some shape he wanted to go an' relieve him, an' he got down to prayer. Had a crowd of people there, too. He was prayin' dere wid he eyes shut, and he say, "Lord, be wid dis deceased brother, he gone, he is dead; if it be Thy will raise him; if it is not Thy will, God, save his soul. God, he leaves all he sisters, he brothers, he companions here behind him. God, be wid him, have mercy on him, save his soul. Father, it is within Thy power to raise him, it is within Thy power to save him. Lord, go with his bereaved family he leff behin'."

An' as he was down dere prayin', wid he eye shut, de man on de coolin' board raise up, an' set up, an' de people saw him an' slipped out an' sneaked out, an' he still prayin' an' he raise up an' open he eyes an' sawed no people but de dead man in front of him, an' he backed off de dead man an' grabbed up a ax, an' he say, "If you don't wait till I git out of here I'll finish killin' you."

An' ever since den mens has been more perticular 'bout what dey ax God to do.

Waiting for Henry

A house that was supposed to be haunted . . . had not been lived in for years, and the owners, anxious to sell it, decided to hire an old Negro to spend the night in it, in order to disprove the troublesome legend for the benefit of would-be purchasers.

The old man built himself a fire on the second floor, and, with his Bible in his lap, settled down in front of it for the night. Around eleven o'clock the door creaked and opened. He looked over his shoulder. There was no one there. He began reading his Bible with great fervor.

Then he heard footsteps and a little dog walked in the room, walked right up to the fire, licked out his tongue, took a few hot coals in his mouth, and chewed them up. Then the dog turned to the old man

and said, "Is Henry here yet?" The old man said not a word; he just
read that Bible harder than ever.

In a little while the door opened again, and in came another dog,
a larger one. It went to the fire, swallowed a whole mouthful of coals,
and, in a louder voice, asked, "Is Henry here yet?" The old man, shaking like he had been dipped in the pond in December, still said
nothing. The only sound was the chattering of his teeth as he steadily
applied himself to the Scripture.

Then another dog came in, and another and another, each a little
larger than the one before. Each one refreshed himself at the fireplace,
and each one asked the question, "Is Henry here yet?"

Finally, an enormous dog, about the size of a small lion, stalked in,
sauntered up to the fire, licked out a whole burning log, chewed it up
and swallowed it, and, in a terrible, deep voice, demanded of the old
man, "Is Henry here yet?"

This was more than the old man could stand. He grabbed up his
Bible and headed for the door. As he left, he shouted back over his
shoulder, "No, Henry ain't here yet—but if he comes here, you tell
him I've been here, but I'm gone!"

Hoosier Hot Bed

A preacher and his wife traveling through the backwoods . . . were
overtaken by nightfall near a one-room cabin whose tenants were
strangers to them, but who received them hospitably and asked them
to stay for the night. The housewife, as always, eagerly set about
doing her best for the guests. Chickens were killed and every pot,
skillet and pan set to work in the fireplace, for there were few cooking
stoves in rural Indiana even as late as 1840. After supper, guests and
entertainers sat about the fire and talked about the Bible, the crops
and thrilling, faraway places which the strangers had recently visited,
perhaps even such metropolises as Indianapolis and Fort Wayne.

One by one the six or seven children toppled over, drunk with
sleep, and were put to bed on pallets on the floor. At last the hostess
suggested that perhaps the guests might like to retire. She indicated
the only bed in the room as their sleeping place, and she and her
husband stepped out into the cold while the clergyman and his wife
hastily disrobed and got into bed.

"I'm afraid we're putting you folks to a right smart inconvenience," said the minister, when the others came in. "I hate to make you sleep on the floor."

"Oh, don't you worry about that, Parson," exclaimed the host, heartily. "We're used to it. Matter of fact, we've slept on the ground out o' doors more'n once."

The visitors, tired with their long day's ride, fell asleep within five minutes. Some hours later, the preacher's wife awoke with the vague impression that the bed was harder and rougher than she had thought it was. She turned over and her hand struck palpable wood. She felt it in amazement—rough puncheon surface—then lifted her head and looked about her. By the faint glow from the last dying coals in the fire she saw that she and her husband were lying, not in the bed, but on a quilt on the floor, while their host and hostess appeared to be occupying the bed.

Quietly she lay down again, drew the covers about her neck and fell asleep, but with the resolve to awaken as early as possible and see what the next move would be. As the story goes, the man and woman of the house arose before dawn, hastily and silently dressed, smoothed the bed a bit, lifted the supposedly sleeping guests—one of whom had much ado to keep up the pretense of unconsciousness—back into bed and covered them up, then set about reviving the fire and doing the morning chores.

The Bridge That Wasn't There

While [William H.] Raper was traveling a circuit in southeastern Indiana, he lost his way in the woods one dark night and wandered about for several hours. At last, in his wanderings he came to the banks of a stream. The rain had been falling steadily for several days, and he knew the water must be very high. He felt that to remain out all night in his exhausted condition meant death, and determined to cross the stream, if possible, and seek shelter on the other side. He dismounted and groped along in the darkness as best he could, until he came to what he supposed to be a bridge, and carefully led his horse onto it. As he proceeded, he felt it giving under him, step by step, but kept on until finally he reached the other side in safety. At a short distance he discovered a house, and, after arousing the inmates, obtained permission to stay all night. They asked him how he had been able to cross the creek; he said by the bridge; they were confounded, and told him there was no bridge there. In the morning they went to the place and discovered that in the darkness he had crossed on floating driftwood that had become jammed.

The Rose and the Baldwin

Up in the state, out my way, . . . there was a farmer [who] kep' an orchard. . . . He was just another kind of "Johnny Appleseed," for he doted on apples and used to beg slips and seeds of any new variety, until he had one hundred and eighty-two trees in his big orchard. . . . He fit off the bug and the blight and the worm like a wizard. If there was any one thing save his orchard he doted upon it was a daughter o' his'n, her name being Rose . . . An' yet he hankered much on the latest addition to his garden—a New York State [Baldwin] apple as he sent for and 'tended to at great outlay of time, anyway. "This here daughter" and "that there apple-tree" were his delights. You might say the Rose and the Baldwin, that were the brand of the fruit, were the apples of his two eyes!

Well, there were two men around there, who cast sheep's eyes, not to say wolfish ones, at the fruit and the girl. They both expected to have the other by getting the one. Well, one of those days the pair of young fellers lounged along and kinder propped up the old man's fence around the orchard. They was looking out of the tail of the eye more for the Rose than the other thing in the garden. But they could not help spying the Baldwin. It was the off year, anyhow, for apples, and this here one being first in fruiting had been spared in but one blossom, and so the old man cared for it with prodigious love. As mostly comes to pass with special fruit, this one, being petted, throve—well, you have no idea how an apple tended to can thrive. It was big and red-meller! Well, one of the fellers, being the cutest, he saw the other had his cane with him and was spearing a windfall every now and then, and seeing how close he could come to flipping the ears of a hog wallering down the lane, or mayhap a horse looking over the paddock fence. Then a notion struck him.

"Lem," said he, . . . "Lem," he says, "I bet you a dollar you can't fire at that lone apple and knock it off the stem—a dollar coin!"

For they were talking in coonskins them times. So Lem he takes the bet, and, sticking an apple on the switch, sends it kiting with such accuracy of aim that it plumps the Baldwin, ker-chung! in the plum center, and away fly both apples. Then, while he grabbed the dollar —the girl and the old soul come out, and the old soul see the pet apple rolling half-dented at his feet, and the girl ran between him and the two men. But the feller who was such a good shot, he sees a leetle too late what he had lost for a dollar and he scooted, with the old man invoking all the cusses of Herod agin' him.

The other feller he opened the gate as bold as a brazen calf, and said, anticipating the old man, "Oh, *I* don't come for apples—I want to spark your darter!"

The Rattlesnake-Bit Boot

A man killed a rattlesnake that had struck at his boot. He finished his day's work, went home, ate his supper, did the chores, read the newspaper, wound the clock, put out the cat, and prepared for bed. Soon after he had taken off his boots he became violently ill, and died before a doctor could be called. His son inherited the boots and put them on for his day's work. Late in the afternoon he finished his work, went home, ate his supper, did the chores, read the newspaper, wound the clock, put out the cat, and prepared for bed. Soon after he had taken off his boots he became violently ill, and died before a doctor could be called. A second son inherited the boots and put them on for his day's work. Late in the afternoon he finished his work, went home, ate his supper, did the chores, read the newspaper, wound the clock, put out the cat, and prepared for bed. Soon after he had taken off his boots he became violently ill, and died before a doctor could be called. One relative after another inherited the boots, put them on for his day's work, finished his work late in the afternoon, went home, ate his supper, did the chores, read the newspaper, wound the clock, put out the cat, prepared for bed, became violently ill, and died before a doctor could be called. Finally somebody cut up the boots with a razor and found the rattlesnake's fang, as small as a hair, embedded in the leather and projecting at a downward angle on the inside just enough to make a slight scratch when the boots were taken off.

An Ear for Music

Uncle Worthy was past eighty in 1905, but he was still a "fiddlin' fool," and when he received compliments on his rendition of "Over the Waves," which was the hit tune of that decade, he acknowledged the compliments with a gleam in his eye and gave most of the credit to his violin, which he held up for inspection. He said he had had it for "nigh onto fifty years." As he turned the instrument for all to see, there came a faint thump, thump, as if a small piece of leather or a little chip was loose inside and free to roll around.

"Got something in it you can't get out?" asked one of the young fellows.

"Nope. Got something in it I don't want out," came laconically from Uncle Worthy, who turned his left ear toward the group, as he glanced up with a tall-tale look in his eye. "It come out once or twice, and I punched it back. If you young bucks don't mind restin' a bit, I'll tell you how it all come about.

"I was company cook in G Company when we was sent out from San Antonio to help the Rangers run those damn Indians out of the Big Bend and the Devil's River country. We spent fourteen months on duty amongst that many million prickly pear and enough Indians to keep the Cap'n and the boys busy. But fixin' three meals wasn't enough to occupy my time, so I rode a pack mule over to a settlement, and bought, from a down-and-out sheepherder, this ole fiddle, which was shiny bright then, havin' just been bought at ole Indianola the year before.

"Well, the Injuns was plenty bothersome. Runnin' fights would take place and there would be a few less Injuns; and then sometimes we'd have to trim up a mesquite slab fer one of the boys. But never could the fellows get a shot at the chief, who kept up his depredations, but powerful secretive like. He must have been brave or else he'd have left there. But he didn't. And because he didn't is why you hear that noise in this fiddle.

"Long toward night of about the last day we spent in that thorn-incubatin' region, I was roastin' some venison and musin' over the reasons the good Lord must 'a had for inventin' Injuns when, all of a sudden, somethin' zipped by my head and I felt a stingin' feelin' along the right side of my face and, in the same instant, I heard a shot to my rear. I reached up and felt a round hole in my right ear, which ain't been none too good since. In less than another minute I heard another shot and the Cap'n come ridin' down the side of the arroyo with his Springfield a-smokin'.

" 'One shot got the old chief,' snapped the Cap'n. 'He's lyin' where he fell. Don't touch him.'

"An hour later, the Cap'n explained and commanded—most of his explanations was commands—that the chief's body would serve as a warnin' to the rest of the Indians, which warnin', the Cap'n prophesied, would mean their leavin' fer good.

" 'I ferbid any man from botherin' the chief's body, on pain of reprimand or court-martial, or both.' With which injunction and snap of his jaw the Cap'n went to bed.

"Well, I turned in, too, after gettin' my bad ear turpentined and wrapped up a bit; but I didn't sleep fer thinkin' of my ear, which wasn't none too easy to fergit, and fer wishin' that the old chief had been a poorer marksman.

"Next mornin' we pulled out fer San Antone and the trail led right by the body of that old Indian chief. The Cap'n permitted us to stop and look at the old cuss's carcass. I reached down and made like I was straightenin' his head out, which had sort of got crooked as he fell. Then we filed out, makin' the trip with no mishap, savin' stops fer sore-footed animals.

There was, however, some wonderment amongst that bunch of troops as to the reason fer a certain mysterious and unpleasant odor that seemed to be constantly comin' from my riggin'. The Cap'n inquired of me what the matter was, and even looked at me with his blue Irish eyes in such a way as to offer the accusation that I hadn't gotten my share of baths. Now I hated to be thought a slacker in the matter of personal cleanliness—being the cook as I was—more than I hated the Cap'n's displeasure or even a reprimand. And I didn't believe he'd care much anyway, so I decided to come clean about the cause of that buzzard-bait odor.

" 'Cap'n,' I said, 'what you smell is that old Indian chief. You see, sir, when we passed his body the mornin' we left, I reached down to straighten his head out. But what I really done was to let my desires get the most of my soldier trainin' and cause me to whack off the old gent's right ear, which I deemed rightly due me in place of mine, which he injured fer what I feel to be the rest of my days. When I collected the compensation fer my ruined ear, I had no place to hide it; so I just slipped it into my fiddle.' "

The thump, thump, of Uncle Worthy's bit of retribution could be heard again as the fiddle, with a swinging flourish, was adjusted under the shaggy chin, and he settled back in his chair with an air of perfect harmony with the situation.

The Pie-Biter

[The] Pie-Biter . . . was very fond of sweet potato pie and would consume several pies at one sitting. His favorite manner of eating them was to stack them one above the other and bite through them all at once. From biting through two pies at a time, he advanced with practice to biting through three at once. Like most talented persons, he strove to further improve himself and before long was biting through four pies.

His exploits became known far and wide, and folks would travel many miles to see him eat pie.

There is something about fame and success, I am told, that gets into a man's blood. He is not content to rest upon his laurels but obeys that higher law which demands that he press onward and upward to new and grander heights. And so it was with the Pie-Biter. There came a day when he felt the urge to bite through five pies. He made known his ambition, and there was a great gathering of the yeomanry to see him make the attempt. Someone offered to bet him that he could not perform the feat. He at once accepted and the money was put up.

In the presence of a great multitude he stepped bravely forward for the test. The pies were stacked before him, one, two, three, four, five. Women wept and strong men shuddered as the moment drew near. When the Pie-Biter, opening his cavernous mouth to its fullest reach, encompassed with his jaws all five of the pies, a mighty cheer arose from the throng. Suddenly a look of dismay and then of anguish spread over Pie-Biter's features as his teeth sank inexorably into the pie. He could not make his teeth meet. Try as he might, he was unable to bite through the stacked pastry.

In a moment he abandoned the attempt, bursting into the bitter, scalding tears of disappointment. And not until then did he discover that somebody had failed to remove the tin plate from under one of the pies.

Oil versus Water

Water in a place like [Texas], and in times such as we have had, transcends almost everything else—politics, morality, and the international tension. Water is our life.

While we were drilling our second well, Ross Smart, the driller, called me over one day and said, "Feel this stuff on the drill, and smell it. It's slippery and smells oily." Another time, his drill pulled up some sparkling sand. "Looks like gold," he said hopefully. "Hell," I told him, "I don't want oil and I don't want gold. I only want water." So he went on for another hundred feet and got water.

Molasses

[Anthony Arnett] remained on his farm until the spring of 1859, when the news came of the rich gold strikes in the Pike's Peak country. This excitement was a welcome relief to the reckless spirits of the country, who were beginning to chafe at the quietude. The land seethed with the news of this new discovery, following as it did so closely upon the heels of the Forty-niner strike. It was "Pike's Peak or Bust."

Arnett outfitted three wagons with enough supplies to start a store. This time he took his wife and son, Willamette. A young man, John Topping, accompanied the party. They reached Denver without any trouble, stopped one night, and proceeded to Golden City, ten miles west, which was at that time more important than Denver.

It was in Denver that an event occurred which the family had reason to remember in after years.

Arnett camped near a small log grocery store and saloon. The storekeeper came out to talk with him about his trip. Finding that he had a supply of provisions, the businessman was ready to drive a bargain.

"What's that in the barrel?" he asked, pointing to a barrel in one of the wagons. "Ain't whisky, is it?"

"No," was the answer. "That's molasses."

"Molasses!" exclaimed the other. "You don't mean it. Why these Missourians have been runnin' me fair crazy askin' for molasses. What'll ye take for it?"

Arnett was informed as to prices in the new country. "She's worth three hundred dollars just as she sits."

The storekeeper looked thoughtful. "Would ye trade it?" he finally asked.

"Don't know. What for?"

"See that land right over there?" queried the merchant, pointing to a strip of prairie land on their left. "I'll trade you the whole hundred and sixty for the barrel."

Arnett looked the land over—it was raw prairie—and then at the little cluster of cabins. No, he decided, she was no good. He could take that molasses and peddle it out for five hundred dollars.

"Nothing doing," he told the storekeeper, and that closed the [discussion].

That hundred and sixty acres of land is the heart of the downtown district of Denver.

Going on to Golden City, Arnett established a store in a tent. The precious molasses barrel was rolled in. The young man, John Topping, slept in the tent. During the first night he kicked open the spigot on the barrel and let all the molasses flow out on the ground. The queer part about it was that he did not awaken until the next morning, but spent the night in a welter of stickiness.

A Run on Castor Oil

Some years ago a railway was being built near Butte, Montana, and it was arranged that each of the numerous laborers employed should pay one penny per week to a medical practitioner, so that they might have his services in the event of accident, or medicine in the case of illness.

During the summer and autumn neither illness nor accident occurred.

But when a severe winter followed, all at once the "navigators" began to call on the doctor for castor oil.

Each brought his bottle, into which an ounce was poured, until

the oil was exhausted, and the doctor was forced to send to Butte
for a further supply.

When that, too, was getting done, the doctor one day quietly asked
a decent-looking fellow what was wrong with the men, that they
required so much castor oil.

"Nothing wrong at all, Doctor," he replied, "but we grease our
big boots with it!"

The "Jerky" Trial

Plenty of Joneses here in the Siskiyous. . . . I remember a few years
back when you'd a thought ever' other man in the county was named
Jones. You know it's agin the law in Oregon to kill deer out of season,
but most of the mountain folks don't pay much attention to it. One
day Sampson Jones came into Gold Beach with three mules loaded to
their hocks with jerky (that's dried venison) and started peddling it.

He was arrested and brought before the J.P. and a jury em-
paneled. Fact is, seven of the jury was named Jones, and, believe it or
not, even his honor hisself was named Jones. Witnesses were called
and the jerky put in evidence. One man took the stand, chawed a
hunk of the dried meat, and solemnly pronounced it sturgeon. He
swore he had dried thousands of pounds of sturgeon and nobody
could fool him. Another as positively swore it was mutton; another
said it was calf; another shark; another goat; and another mule or
maybe burro.

The case was presented and the jury deliberated as long as any
of them could eat jerky and then announced their verdict. It read:

"We the jury find the defendant not guilty, but recommend that
next time he do not bring in so much at one load."

☞ **13** ☜

Barnyard and Barroom

A traveler spent the night in a backwoods cabin. They had green beans for supper, but the stranger didn't get as many beans as he wanted. He watched regretfully as the half-emptied platter was put back in the cupboard. There was only one bed, so the visitor slept with his host and hostess, the host occupying the middle of the bed. Late in the night all three were awakened by a commotion among the poultry. The hillman sprang out of bed, snatched his shotgun, and rushed out, shouting something about chicken thieves. The wife whispered, "Stranger, now's your chance!" So the traveler got up, went out into the kitchen, and ate the rest of the green beans!

VANCE RANDOLPH

Introduction

From his picaresque predecessor, the Yankee peddler, the Traveling Sales-man inherited a way with the ladies and a ribald tongue. On the railroad and hotel circuit, the sleeping car and the double-bedded room ("How Did He Find Out?") provide opportunities for the bedroom humor of travelers. But in the horseback and horse-and-buggy age the exigencies of hospitality in the one-room, often one-bed cabin and other backwoods sleeping arrangements gave rise to many a comedy of errors.

In the 1833 campaign for Congress, Davy Crockett played a cracker-barrel bedroom joke on his opponent "Peg-Leg" Adam Huntsman, which resulted in the latter's defeat. While canvassing together, they were put up in the same room of a farmhouse. During the night Crockett got up and pretended to try to force the door of the room in which the farmer's daughter was asleep. Then, holding a chair in front of him, with his foot on the bottom round, he stumped back to his room. The angry farmer, awakened by his daughter's scream, accused Huntsman: "I . . . heard that damned old peg leg of yourn too plain," and caused his friends to change their votes, swinging the election to Crockett.

In addition to the bedroom comedy of the backwoods cabin, the cracker barrel has its comic barnyard mythology. Here belong the erotic fables of bulls, heifers, and sows, and privy pranks and japes. The outhouse has produced two nostalgic classics of American *sub rosa* literature, James Whitcomb Riley's poem, "The Passing of the Backhouse" and Charles ("Chic") Sale's *The Specialist*. Recently, as Burges Johnson has pointed out, proprietary advertising in the newspapers and on the radio has helped to break down the taboos against lavatory humor.

In urban anecdotal humor, the slapstick of amatory pranks, mistakes and misunderstandings is supplemented with the ironic, frustrating shaggy-dog tricks and mysteries of fate (as in "The Mink Coat" and "What Was on the Card?"). Here, too, belongs the spicy double entendre of topical humor, as in the Mae West story. When asked by an inter-viewer if she were "an evil influence on young America" Mae West quipped, "No more than young America is an evil influence on me."

Increasing frankness regarding sex has restored the "improper" story to the place in print which it occupied in an earlier and coarser age. But the great bulk of bawdy stories that violate linguistic and/or situational taboos is still largely restricted to *sub rosa* circulation as the oral or sup-pressed literature of sophisticated society and perhaps its only genuine folklore.

A Good Short Story

"There are four requisites to a good short story," explained the teacher of journalism to the aspirants. "They are brevity, a reference to religion, some association with society, and an illustration of modesty. Now, with these four points in mind, write a short story in thirty minutes or less."

In five minutes Solly announced that he'd finished.

"That's fine," said the teacher. "Now read out your story to the class."

Solly read: " 'My Gawd!' said the duchess. 'Take your hand off my knee!' "

The Biter Bit

The cow belonging to a certain parson was stolen, and he did not fail to remind his congregation of the misfortune in all his sermons—as he continually exclaimed, "O my cow, my cow!" in imitation of the lamentation of David for his son Absalom. One day as he passed by the habitation of a poor man a little ragged boy sung out:

"Since my father stole the parson's cow,
We have had milk and puddings enow."

The parson concluded that the father of this boy must have stolen his cow, and he thought to turn this circumstance to his own advantage; and make his congregation believe that he had received an express revelation from heaven concerning his cow. For this purpose he clothed the boy, gave him money, and directed him to place himself in the gallery on the ensuing Sabbath, where he was, when called on, to sing the above couplet. On that day when the sermon was concluded the parson informed his congregation it had been revealed to him that a lad in the gallery would give him some information concerning his cow; and he did believe that such a lad would appear there and give them some information on the subject, which was as true as the gospel he had been preaching to them. He then called for the lad to come forward and say what he knew of the matter. The boy stood up and sung as follows:

"As through the parson's yard I stray'd,
I saw the parson a-kissing his maid.
He gave me a shilling that I should not tell
And these new clothes which fit me well!"

A Careless Cuss

Job Nickerson was called upon by his neighbor, Caleb Tilton. (The call was made in the very early morning, not that it matters.)

Said Caleb, "Job, your son Nathan has been calling pretty regularly on my daughter Debbie. He's done her wrong, and if something isn't done mighty sudden there's going to be a bastard in my family!"

"By Godfrey!" ejaculated Job. "Nathan is the most careless cuss that ever drew the breath of life! Just this morning he busted a hoe-handle for me!"

Plowing with the Bulls

A farmer was plowing his field with a pair of bulls when another farmer came back and said, "Jim, why are you plowing the field with your bulls. Why don't you use the oxen?"

"Don't want to use the oxen. Want to use the bulls."

"Well, if you don't want to use your oxen, why don't you use your horses?"

"Don't want to use the horses. Want to use the bulls."

"Well, if you don't want to use your horses, why don't you use that newfangled tractor your son just bought?"

"Don't want to use the tractor. Want to use the bulls."

"Well, just why do you want to use the bulls?"

"Don't want them to think that life is all romance."

"Boney" Quillan Gets Even

One rainy, sour day a drummer from Binghamton walked into one of Hancock's leading hotels, as was his custom when in town, and said, rather confidently, to the landlord, "I've got something new!"

"All right, what is it?" asked the hotelman, intrigued by the other's manner.

For answer the traveling man drew a pencil from one of his numerous pockets and proceeded to draw the picture of an outhouse on the wall of the room, during which time the loiterers watched with kindling interest. The landlord . . . remarked, "There goes 'Bone,' boys, we'll see if we can work it on him," and walking to the door he hailed "Boney." ["Boney"] Quillan walked into the barroom looking questioningly around as the landlord said, "See that picture there, 'Boney'?"

"Yes-s-s," wondering what it was all about.

"There's a man in that picture, 'Bone,' see if you can find him," the proprietor returned, leading Quillan closer to the object.

After gazing intently at the picture from all angles while the crowd in the barroom looked eagerly on, "Boney" finally exclaimed, "I don't see anything to it, I can't find any man there, where is he?"

"Why, he's inside that woodhouse cuttin' wood," the landlord laughingly responded, thoroughly convinced that he had worsted the redoubtable riverman at last.

"All right, boys, that's one on me. Step up! Step up! And none of your beer or thin liquors, give us the good old red-eye."

The gang in the barroom boisterously gathered around the bar and drank thirstily to Quillan's downfall on the best liquor in the house.

After finishing his drink with great satisfaction, "Boney" started for the door as unconcerned as you please.

"Hey there, 'Bone,' wait a minute, wait a minute, who's goin' to pay for them drinks?" the landlord demanded in no uncertain tones as Quillan was reaching for the doorknob.

"Why, that man in the woodhouse when he gets through!" replied the smiling waterdog as he closed the door behind him.

Why the Old Farmer Wouldn't Tell the Drummer the Time of Day

"It's an old, old story," Mr. Flood said. "I've heard it told sixteen different ways. I even heard a mixed-up version one night years ago in a vaudeville show. I'll tell it the way my daddy used to tell it.

"There was an old farmer lived beside a little branch-line railroad in South Jersey, and every so often he'd get on the train and go over to Trenton and buy himself a crock of applejack. He'd buy it right at the distillery door, the old Bossert & Stockton Apple Brandy Distillery, and save himself a penny or two. One morning he went to Trenton and bought his crock, and that afternoon he got on the train for the trip home. Just as the train pulled out, he took his watch from his vest pocket, a fine gold watch in a fancy hunting case, and he looked at it, and then he snapped it shut and put it back in his pocket. And there was a drummer sitting across the aisle. This drummer leaned over and said, 'Friend, what time is it?' The farmer took a look at him and said, 'Won't tell you.' The drummer thought he was hard of hearing and spoke louder. 'Friend,' he shouted out, 'what time is it?' 'Won't tell you,' said the famer. The drummer thought a moment and then he said, 'Friend, all I asked was the time of day. It don't cost anything to tell the time of day.' 'Won't tell you,' said the farmer. 'Well, look here, for the Lord's sake,' said the drummer, 'why won't you tell me the time of day?'

" 'If I was to tell you the time of day,' the farmer said, 'we'd get into a conversation, and I got a crock of spirits down on the floor between my feet, and in a minute I'm going to take a drink, and if we were having a conversation I'd ask you to take a drink with me, and you would, and presently I'd take another, and I'd ask you to do the same, and you would, and we'd get to drinking, and by and by the train'd pull up to the stop where I get off, and I'd ask you why don't you get off and spend the afternoon with me, and you would, and we'd walk up to my house and sit on the front porch and drink and sing, and along about dark my old lady would come out and ask you to take supper with us, and you would, and after supper I'd ask if you'd care to drink some more, and you would, and it'd get to be real late and I'd ask you to spend the night in the spare room, and you would, and along about two o'clock in the morning I'd get up to go to the pump, and I'd pass my daughter's room, and there you'd be, in there with my daughter, and I'd have to turn the bureau upside down and get out my pistol, and my old lady would have to get dressed and hitch up the horse and go down the road and get the preacher, and I don't want no God-damned son-in-law who don't own a watch.' "

How Did He Find Out?

A weary traveling man arrived late one night in a town where he had trouble in getting a room on account of a convention being held there.

After a fruitless search he arrived at a small hostelry on the out-skirts and stated his plight. At first the clerk refused, but finally told him they had a suite of two rooms, with connecting doors, one of them being occupied by a young lady.

"But," the clerk told him, "if you will sneak in very quietly and go to bed she'll never know you're there."

The traveler promised to be careful, was shown the room, and disappeared within.

Ten minutes later a frightened guest returned to the office very hurriedly—in his nightshirt.

"My goodness, man," he yelled, dashing in, "She's dead!"

Balm in Gideon

At the Congress [Hotel in Chicago] I once found a Gideon Bible containing a thoughtful marginal note. It was one of the Bibles that told guests in a pasted-in foreword what chapters were recommended for despondency, loneliness, and other such maladies afflicting the spirit of the weary traveler. For loneliness, the recommended cure was Psalm 23. This particular Bible bore a note in a neat feminine handwriting at the end of Psalm 23. It said: "If still lonely, call Greenwich 2384."

It Could Have Been Worse

There was once a man who had a very obnoxious trait. Whenever anyone said anything sad to him, his reply would be, "It could have been worse." So he comes home one night and finds his wife all excited. "Oh, darling," she says, "don't ask. I'm so upset and so nervous."

"What do you mean you're so upset and so nervous?"

"You know Johnny next door. Well, he came home tonight and he found his wife in bed with his best friend. So he pulled out his gun and he shot his best friend and he shot his wife and then he killed himself."

So he says, "So what! It could have been worse."

So she says, "What do you mean, 'It could have been worse'? For twenty-five years I've been married to you and any time anybody tells you anything serious or sad, you always say, 'It could have been worse.' How could this have been worse?"

He says, "That's simple. If it was last night, it would have been me."

The Exurbanite's Story

Once upon a time, an exurbanite will tell you, a man bound for the 5:12 got lost in the Commodore bar, missed the 5:12, ordered another drink, missed the 5:32 narrowly, ordered another drink, easily missed the 6:02, ordered another drink, and then missed the 7:02. By this time he had found a complaisant young lady who, fearful that he might catch cold, took him home and bundled him up tenderly, keeping him warm under a comforter. When he arrived home the next night he marched straight up to his wife, looked her straight in the eye, and announced, "Darling, I cannot tell a lie. Last night I got drunk and spent the night with a blonde." Frostily she glared at him. "Don't give me any of that," she snapped. "How much did you lose?"

Making Friends

A young man from the Midwest who had a good job in New York was asked by his employer how he liked living in the city. "Fine," he said, "except for one thing. In all the time I've been here I haven't been able to make friends. Why, I haven't even met a girl I could have a date with."

"I'll tell you what I would suggest," said his employer. "Go to Grand Central station and take a commuter train to one of the Westchester suburbs like Scarsdale. Get off at the station and you'll find the customary number of cars with wives sitting in them waiting for their husbands. Now there is always bound to be one husband who fails to arrive for some reason or other, and you can imagine the poor wife's disappointment. After all, it's no fun to be slaving all day over a hot stove preparing a fine dinner and then have to eat it alone. Women like that are generally very susceptible to sympathetic overtures. Talk to her kindly and the chances are that she will invite you to dinner and you'll become very good friends."

The Midwesterner did as he was told, and everything worked out exactly as predicted. After a splendid dinner and a pleasant conversation, he and the young wife became very friendly. After several hours the husband arrived, burst open the bedroom door, and began to berate his wife. Then noticing the Midwesterner, he said, "Hell! I told you Scarsdale, not Hartsdale!"

"The Frog Prince" Up-to-Date

Once upon a time there was a beautiful Princess. Playing on the green of her lovely castle, she was tossing a golden ball into the air and catching it. She missed it once, and the ball started to roll into the nearby brook. A frog, noticing it, grabbed it before it hit the water and returned it to the Princess.

So delighted was the Princess that she said to the frog, "Thank you, froggy. I want to reward you."

"No," answered the creature, "you have repaid me enough by allowing me to be in your presence."

But the Princess insisted. "But, froggy, I must reward you for saving my golden ball. What do you wish?"

"Since you insist," the frog replied, "then for my reward I should like to sleep in your golden bed."

"Granted," agreed the royal maiden. "Hop along with me." The two jumped into bed and went to sleep.

The next morning, when the Princess awoke, she noticed alongside her a handsome, blond Prince.

And would you believe it? To this day, her mother doesn't believe a word of this story.

Beulah's Babies

Miss Beulah Jones . . . once turned up at Columbia Hospital, a Washington institution that specializes in maternity cases. Although at Columbia for the usual reason, Beulah made a point of insisting that she was unmarried.

"That's a bit unusual," said the clerk who interviewed her. "What's the father's name?"

"Smith—Leonard Smith," Miss Jones replied.

She was admitted, and her baby was born in due course, no further questions asked. And in about a year she was back.

"Well, Beulah," said the same clerk, "back again. I suppose you're married now."

"No, not yet," said Beulah.

"Who's the father this time?"

"Leonard Smith."

Another year went by, and the same thing happened again.

"Why in the world don't you marry him?" the clerk asked this time.

"Well," said Beulah, "he just doesn't appeal to me."

Even Stephen

A [Rodanthe, North Carolina], fisherman named Black Luke had a wife that got tired of him and said she wanted to marry another fisherman named Charley. Well, she wasn't much good, so Black Luke said it was all right with him, and he'd let her go if Charley gave him something to trade for her. Charley said all right, he'd give two good fishing nets, and he brought 'em over to Black Luke that night. Black Luke took 'em, but he couldn't go to sleep worrying. And soon as it got daylight, he knocked on Charley's door. When Charley opened up, Luke handed him a net. "You give me two nets for her yesterday," he said. "I don't want to cheat you, so I brought this net back. She ain't worth but one."

The Parrot and the Priest

The priest was walking along, and he passed the pet shop and admired the very gorgeous bird in the window, and stepped inside and said to the proprietor, "I'd like the parrot." And the proprietor says, "Well, the parrot is $75, but I'd rather not sell it to you." "Why not?" And he says, "Well, the parrot is very profane, very profane. It would embarrass you and the parishioners and your children, and I decline to sell it to you." The priest said, "Well, I could convert the parrot as I do my flock." He said, "No, I decline. But I will get you a parrot. I have some coming from South America. And as soon as I have gotten it and trained it I'll call you." The Reverend said, "That's grand."

About two months later the shopkeeper called the priest and said, "I have your parrot, Father." And he rushed down immediately, and there, segregated from all the other birds, was this beautiful bird enclosed in a case of glass.

The shopkeeper said, "Now I want to show you about the bird before you take it."

And they went into the little room where the parrot was contained. And there were two strings tied to the bird, one on the left foot and one on the right foot. And the shopkeeper pulled the string on the left foot and the bird started reciting the Lord's Prayer, and went on through.

The priest said, "Oh, God, that is wonderful! That is wonderful!"

And then he pulled the string on the other foot, whereupon the parrot started reciting the Ave Maria, which was perfectly grand, perfectly grand. And the priest said, "It's wonderful. Now tell me, tell me. What would happen if I pulled both strings at the same time?"

Whereupon the parrot spoke up and said, "You damn fool! I'd be flat on my a—!"

The Stud

Jim the stud Negro . . . was chiefly responsible for the ratio of three Negroes to one white in the Black Belt. All the big slaveowners, so the legend goes, kept a big black buck at stud to produce more slaves— just as they kept a blooded bull to increase their herds. . . .

So Jim became famous. His master was so pleased with him that he didn't make him work at all, just kept him around to exercise his one talent. Other planters used to rent him from time to time to help replenish their depleted stock.

. . . The owner of the Louisiana estate had heard of Jim's value as a multiplier of property and, being in Alabama on business, approached the gifted black man's master with the proposal that he rent him. Jim's owner, a kindly man, said he had no objections so long as the slave would not be unhappy so far away from home. "If Jim wants to go," he said, "take him and welcome."

"How fur is it, boss," said Jim, "to down aroun' New Orleans?"

" 'Bout five hundred miles, Jim."

"An' how fur is it back?"

"Just about the same."

"An' how many gals you got down there on your plantation?"

" 'Bout two hundred."

"Well, boss," said Jim, "I'll go. But it seems a mighty fur piece for just a few days' work."

Honest, Impulsive Harry

This story was told at a convention of young businessmen in Memphis, Tennessee. No ladies were present. The chairman of the group was trying to get a charity donation of twenty-five dollars. Harry Jones, a newspaper man of Mayfield, Kentucky, jumped to his feet and said that he would take care of the matter. The chairman told this story about Harry Jones to explain his nature.

When Harry was a young boy living in Louisiana, he was a most impulsive youth. He had always had a longing to push a jake [privy] into the bayou. One morning he was waiting for a school bus. Just as the bus pulled up, Harry pushed the jake into the bayou and went right on to the bus as though nothing had happened.

That afternoon when Harry returned from school his father was waiting for him. "Son, did you push the jake into the bayou?"

"Yes, Father," Harry bravely stated, "I cannot tell a lie."

Harry's father got his belt off and sternly said, "All right, son, bend over. I'm going to have to whip you."

Harry tried to explain that George Washington's father didn't spank George when he chopped the cherry tree down.

"Yes, son, but George's father wasn't in the cherry tree."

"Black" Shade and the Chippy

"Black" Shade Combs (so-called from his black beard and mustache to distinguish him from other Shade Combses), along with other mountaineers, found himself in the "Settlemints" one day, in Frankfort. They all went to the elite Capitol Hotel for dinner. Opposite them at the table sat a great lady, appareled in her best. A waiter approached to take her order. "First, waituh, bring me a tiny piece of beefsteak as tender as a chicken's breast. Second, a modest portion of asparagus tips gently smothered with vinaigrette sauce. Third, a small bowl of potage seasoned with mushrooms and nightingale tongues. Fourth, a thimbleful of honeyed and spiced nectar as sweet and soothing as an infant's cordial. Finally, a soft, silken napkin to spread upon my bosom—and please inform me who the gentleman is that sits opposite me."

"Black" Shade laid no claim to education and culture, but he was blessed with native wit and intelligence. But now he was thinking, and thinking fast. He did not know that the woman was of easy morals and notorious reputation, but that made no difference. Finally, the waiter came Shade's way to take his order. "First, fetch me a quart of moonshine likker as strong as hell. Second, a big bowl of onion soup full of hog kidneys and mountain oysters. Third, a plate of hominy swimmin' in hog grease. Fourth, a hunk of beefsteak as tough as a saddle-skirt. Finally, a burlap sack to spread over my hairy breast, and"—pointing straight at the courtesan opposite him— "please make known to me the name of the chippy that sits opposite me."

Settling Paternity

A timid [Kentucky] Highlander was accused of being the father of an illegitimate child. The mother "laid" it to him, and he was summoned to the county seat to answer the charge in court. He returned home in the afternoon, and stood at the gate in front of the house in fear and trembling, while his wife stood at the door waiting for him. Wifie, sternly: "Well, out with it, what did they do about it?" Hubby, hesitatingly: "Why—er—that nasty-stinkin'-thing went and swore the brat to us."

Saved

A shiftless man showed up at the county relief agency to ask for help in supporting a numerous family, including a twelfth child just born.

The agent took him to task for creating responsibilities he could not handle. Texans think a man ought not to bite off more than he can chew. The man swore it would never happen again; said that if it did he would go and hang himself on the nearest cottonwood tree. Within a year he showed up again, needing help for a family including the inevitable new baby.

"I thought you were going to hang yourself if your wife had another baby," the agent said.

"Well, now, I did say that," the man explained. "And I remembered my promise. And when the baby was a-comin' I did go out and I took a piece of rope, and I went out to the old cottonwood tree and I pulled a wagon under a limb to stand on. And I threw the rope over the limb and took a hitch around my neck, and I started to step off, but just then a voice said to me, 'Sam, you may be hangin' an innocent man.' "

Verbal Taboo

A big spotted bull belonging to a Pike County, [Kentucky], farmer strayed away from home one morning. The farmer started down the road in search. Upon meeting a neighbor, or coming to a house, the farmer would ask, "Have you seen a big pied'ed bull pass this way?"

His friends all answered in the negative. At last he came to a house where a woman unexpectedly stepped to the door in response to his call. Not wanting to mention the subject of bulls in her presence, yet anxious to find trace of his fine specimen, the farmer amended his question and asked, "Ma'am, I don't reckon you saw a big pied'ed cow pass this way?"

"No," she replied, "but I saw a big pied'ed bull pass here a while ago."

"That's her, that's her!" exclaimed the farmer.

The Smart Sow

Two old maids set up farming in the country, although they knew nothing about it. They decided to raise pigs. A farmer up the road had a boar. They loaded the sow in a wheelbarrow and took it to the farmer. They brought it back but didn't see any sign of the sow having pigs. So they loaded the sow in the wheelbarrow again. Still no sign of the sow having any pigs. So one day they decided to cart the sow off again to the boar and when they went out to catch her, she was sitting in the wheelbarrow.

The Talking Heifer

A little old farm boy sent off for a course in ventriloquism. After he had studied in private for a while he thought he would try it out on the hired hand. He hid up in the hayloft and watched until the hired hand came out to milk the heifer. The hired hand squatted on the stool, and as he looked up, the heifer turned her head around and suddenly seemed to speak and say, "Hey, let go of my left tit." The old farm hand stared back in amazement.

"I mean it. Let go!"

The hired hand dropped the milk bucket and tripped over the stool. He ran up to the house and said to the farmer, "Give me my wages. I'm quittin'."

"Why, what's the matter, Zeke?" the farmer asked.

"I'm not saying what's the matter, but if that spotted heifer out there tells you anything about me, it's a damn lie!"

Grandpa and the Benzine

This family lived near the crossroads country store and they had a half-wit cousin living with them. And she had heard about the wonders of cleaning with benzine. She had always used soap and water and she was dying to clean with benzine. So one Saturday when the folks hitched the mules to the wagon to drive off to town, she said she didn't want to go. Just as soon as they had gone she hiked down to the crossroads country store with a couple of milk buckets and bought herself five gallons of benzine. She came back and poured it in a tin washtub and began cleaning. She cleaned the walls and the window sills and curtains and everything. After she had cleaned everything in sight, she was left with the washtub full of dirty benzine. She didn't know what to do with it. And she didn't want it around there when the folks got back from town, because she had been forbade to clean with benzine. So she had to get shut of it before the wagon came back. She thought awhile and then she went and built up a big roaring fire in the kitchen range. But just as she was about to pour it on the fire, she got a sudden inspiration. She carried the tub out to the privy and poured all the benzine down one of the privy holes.

Well, just about that time the family came driving up in the wagon and they all got out. Grandpa had a copy of the *Saturday Blade & Ledger* he'd bought in town. And, as was his custom, he took the *Saturday Blade & Ledger* to the privy to read about the goings-on in town during the past week. He hobbled out to the privy, sat down, got out his corncob pipe, lit a match, and threw it down the hole. There was a terrific explosion, the privy went up in the air, and Grandpa was blown out into the road. The whole family came running out, yelling, "Grandpa! Grandpa! What on earth happened?"

"I don't know," said Grandpa, sitting up and rubbing his forehead. "It musta been something I et in town."

A Morals Case

Old man Rhodes came stomping into town, into the J.P. court. Says to Judge Throgmorton, "Judge, I want to swear out a warrant for indecent exposure."

Judge says, "Where did this take place, Dusty?"

"Well, sir, I got five growing daughters out there on my place. They're getting up around marrying age and I gotta protect their morals. You know them high school boys is coming down there by the railroad trestle and going in swimming naked."

So Judge says to him, "Why, Dusty, that there swimming hole is three miles from your house. How can those boys going in swimming there imperil the morals of your daughters?"

"Well," Mr. Rhodes says, "Judge, my daughters got a spyglass."

Figuring Relationship

A hillbilly son was courting a girl named Esmeralda over in another holler. When his pappy heard about it he got worried and said, "Son, I'll have to tell you I was sparkin' Esmereldy's ma about nine months before she was born."

The poor hillbilly boy just moped and mooned about until his mother took him aside and said, "Son, don't pay your pa no mind about Esmereldy bein' yore sister cause—you ain't his'n either."

The Bolster Test

[Back in the old days] when cabins were small and crowded, . . . a boy and girl were put into the same bed, with a big bolster between them for propriety's sake. Next day the two were walking near the house, and came to a low wall. "I can git across all right," said the girl, "but I'm afeared *you* cain't make it." The young man was astounded. "What d'ye mean, I cain't?" he asked indignantly. "Well," said the girl, "a feller that cain't climb over a bolster ain't goin' to have much luck with a stone wall!"

The Hayloft

A hillbilly, on his son's thirty-seventh birthday, said, "Son, there's somethin' I oughta tell you about women."

The son says, "Aw, shucks, Paw. I ain't interested."

The old man says, "You don't know what you're missin'."

The son says, "Paw, I've got my old dog Bessie, my twenty-gauge shotgun, and you. That's all I want."

The old man says, "Son, you don't know what you're missin'. I'm goin' over the mountain tomorrow and get Lena and I'm gonna bring her here and you and she are goin' up in the hayloft and you'll find out what I'm tellin' you is true."

So the next day the old man brought Lena and sent her up in the hayloft with his son. The old man waited for about an hour. Then the little door up top opened and the son stuck his head out, and he says, "Paw, you know my dog Bessie. She's a mighty nice dog."

And the old man says, "She sure is."

The son says, "Paw, she's yourn." And he closed the door.

About an hour or so later the door opens again and the son sticks his head out and he says, "Paw, that shotgun of mine is a mighty fine gun, ain't it?"

The old man says, "It sure is."

The son says, "Paw, it's yourn."

The old man says, "Son, you don't know what you're talkin' about. You don't want to give everything away."

The son just closed the door.

A couple of hours later the door opens again and he says, "Paw." The old man looks up. "What is it, son?" he says.

"I want you to go inside my bedroom where there's a loose board. You open it up and there's my life's savings under there. It's $8.14, and it's all yourn."

And the old man says, "Son, you don't want to do that. You're just actin' fractious. You're gonna change your mind when you come down."

And the son says, "Paw, I ain't comin' down."

Upbrush Wedding

In the cavernous hallway of a county courthouse, a rural couple approached the janitor, who was incidentally justice of the peace, and asked to be married. The janitor-justice complied and pocketed the fee. On the way out the three of them stopped beside a baby buggy. The justice, knowing the rules of rural politics, pulled back the pink blanket and patted the infant's head.

"Purty baby—whose is hit?"

The rural swain answered with casual complacency, "Oh, it's ourn. You see, the roads was so blamed bad last winter that we couldn't very well get down to town."

The Shivaree

An old farmer in the backwoods of Michigan lost his wife, a most amiable and respectable woman. About a month later, notwithstanding the age of the widower, he married a young and giddy girl. The neighbors, who had great respect for his departed spouse, were very indignant. So the night of the wedding festivities a crowd gathered from all points—men, women and children. They carried tin pans, kettles, horns, and at a late hour began such a din as was never heard before. The old man stood it as long as he could, but finally threw the door open and, waving his hand for silence, said, "It is a shame for young folks to make such a racket round here so soon after a funeral!"

Howard Mace

Howard Mace . . . became the principal figure in a story which was regarded as a bit on the bawdy side, and which is still told by old-timers who want a belly laugh. Howard was not yet twenty-one years old when he decided to go into partnership with a friend of his in the operation of a small men's-furnishings store in Lampasas. To do this properly he had to go through a formal legal proceeding at the courthouse, by which he could have his disabilities as a minor removed. He was over at the courthouse when a well-known local dowager came into the store and asked for Howard.

"He's over at the courthouse," said Howard's partner, "having his disabilities removed."

"Oh," sighed the woman. "Isn't that just too bad! He was such a promising young man."

Indian Sign

As you know, the —— Hotel down in Houston, Texas, is supposed to be one of the finest hotels in the United States. The story goes that a big Indian from the Southwest went down there. The room clerk inadvertently just pushed him a card without looking to see who it was, and the Indian took the pen and very laboriously inscribed an X where his name should be.

When the clerk found out what he had done, he looked up and said, "Well, ex-excuse me, sir. I—must see about this."

So he went back to talk to the manager, and he said, "Look, sir, I've made a mistake here. It seems as though inadvertently I've given a card to an Indian to sign and that isn't exactly the kind of clientele we cater to."

The manager waved him away and said, "Go get rid of him. Do anything you want to. Tell him they're a thousand dollars a room, or anything, but get rid of him, by all means."

So the clerk went back and said, "Now, I'm very sorry, sir, but, you see, the only rooms we have left now are a thousand dollars apiece, you know, and, of course, that's a little more than you'd care to pay."

The Indian never budged. He simply reached under his blanket, and pulled out a thousand-dollar note, laid it down, and said, "Takum."

Well, that confused the clerk even more. So he went back to see the manager, and said, "Look, this man has paid me a thousand dollars. He *wants* a room."

"Oh, that can't be. A thousand dollars isn't enough to take a man of that type. No, no, no, no! You can't do that. Go back and get rid of him."

So the clerk went back and said, "I forgot to tell you, sir—we're very sorry—but the only rooms we have are the bridal suites, you know, and they are for five days, and, of course, they run a thousand dollars a night, you know, and that will be five thousand."

The Indian never budged at all. He just reached over, handed him the notes and said, "O.K. Takum."

"Well," said the clerk, "well, you see—you can't have a bridal suite," he says, "unless—you have—a—woman, and, of course, if you have a woman, why, you must also pay for her, and it will be another five thousand."

So the Indian reached in again and pulled out his notes, laid them down, and said, "Takum."

Well, when the clerk saw that much money on the counter he decided that it might be a good idea for him to keep it anyhow. So he said, "Oh, all right, that's fine. You'll take the bridal suite."

So he was about to put the card away when the Indian called him back and said, "Givum card."

And the clerk handed the card back to him. The Indian took out his pen and scribbled over the X, and very laboriously he drew a circle instead. He handed it back to the clerk. The clerk looked at the change in the signature and said, "Excuse me. I'm—a little curious. Why did you change from an X to a circle?"

The Indian looked at him and said, "Indian no givum right name in whorehouse."

☞ **14** ☜

Wit's End

A ventriloquist sold his performing dog as a "talking dog" to a man who wanted the animal to show off with. The dog looked up at his master and said reproachfully: "You mean, despicable man, to sell me for ten dollars after all I've done for you. So help me Moses, I'll never speak another word as long as I live." And he didn't.

Illinois Central Magazine, (1913)

Introduction

In the shaggy-dog story the humor of irrationality and nonsense reaches wit's end. Climaxing the raconteur's progress from rural cracker barrel to urban crackpot, this anecdotal genre to end all anecdotal genres is a catch-all of various types and devices of zany, screwball humor picked up along the way, from "pulling the rug out from under" to the trick or snap-of-the-whip ending.

According to Evan Esar, in *The Humor of Humor*, the shaggy-dog story is a development of the absurd or nonsensical drunk story popular in the 1920's. This so-called "shaggy story" (the dog came later) capital-ized on the amusing aberrations of intoxication, such as optical illusions, "alcohological" delusions, and the animal hallucinations of the d.t.'s. The talking animal, bird, fish, or insect of the shaggy-dog story is a borrowing from the animal fable.

In the same way that the shaggy dog is a culmination of several types, so Evan Esar sees it as diverging into several new types of absurdity, especially the "mad psychiatrist" story. The latest type to come along is a development of the "Little Audrey story" known along Madison Avenue as the "sick, sick, sick" or "nauseous" story. For example, a daughter con-soles her dying mother with the promise that her body will be cremated and the ashes placed in an urn on the mantel. "And every morning I'll take a spoonful of ashes, put it in a cup, add hot water, and have a cup of Instant Mother."

To Eric Partridge, in *The Shaggy Dog Story*, the genre is a develop-ment of the catch story, the tall tale (e.g., "Whispering Thompson and His Pet Trout") and the psychological (not logical) *non sequitur* story. For Max Eastman, in *Enjoyment of Laughter*, the story of "The Cake" is an example of the humor of "plausible nonsense," whose "pre-tense or claim to meaning" is distinct from the want of meaning in pure nonsense. The plausibility lies in the "suggestion of some approaching sense," creating an expectation that is frustrated by the abrupt "failure of the sense to arrive."

This combination of gradual expectation and sudden frustration is the key to the peculiar effectiveness and appeal of the shaggy-dog story. From it follow the structural devices named by Eric Partridge—the lead-in, the build up, and the letdown, with incidental "leg pullings" and "red herrings." Essentially the shaggy-dog story is a hoaxing story (sometimes called "spoof" story) with the reader himself being taken in by the trick ending. The sudden unexpectedness of the *non sequitur* or "inconsequent" conclusion belongs to the humor of what Eastman calls the "irony of fate," in which life itself follows the shaggy-dog pattern of lead-in, build up, and letdown, nothing turns out as expected, and in the end the joke is on us.

Meyer

Meyer is the by-product of the Yiddish literary and theatrical world [of New York]. He knows the great ones intimately, yet prefers to sit at the [Second Avenue] café table with the "boys." There is always a smile on his face and a story on his lips. In the telling of a story he becomes so convulsed with laughter that anyone listening must laugh along with him. I like Meyer's brand of humor.

Rumor has it that Maurice Schwartz, director of the Yiddish Theater, is wont to dominate the stage by taking the best roles for himself. Thus, it is argued, the younger actors in his company never have the chance to advance to stellar parts. Meyer happened to be a participant in one such discussion and quickly came to the defense of his distinguished friend.

"This is the most unfounded piece of gossip I have ever heard," Meyer fumed. "On occasion Mr. Schwartz has been very generous with the leading parts. Take, for example, his recent production of the *Brothers Ashkenazi*. Did he play both brothers?"

One afternoon I dropped into the café and found Meyer with several of his cronies in a heated discussion over the respective merits of the Yiddish press and radio. One of the group was particularly excited, and expressed the view that neither the radio nor the press was doing anything to uphold the dignity of the Yiddish word.

"Actually," he raged, "what is the difference between our radio and the press?"

"Well, for one thing," said Meyer, "you can't wrap a herring in a radio!"

Meyer was once asked what is talent. He frowned, wiped his glasses with a dollar bill, and spoke.

"Talent is difficult to define. Perhaps I can best answer the question by showing what is lack of talent. A person lacking talent would be an actor, who in everyday life stutters, but when given the part of a stutterer, begins to speak straight!"

Meyer's favorite gags are about himself. He relates an incident of the depression days when he was on relief and was starving regularly instead of at intervals, as he does now. One day at the café he walked over to a friend and quietly asked him for fifty cents with which to buy a meal. His friend slapped him on the back and howled, "Meyer with his jokes—always clowning!"

A Critic

A man bought a ticket to one of the Yiddish plays on the Lower East Side. Before the show was half over, he hurried out and stood at the box office asking for his money back.

"Why, didn't you like the show?" the ticket seller asked him.

"Oh, I liked it," he answered.

"Well, then, wasn't your seat a good one?"

"Yes, it was a good seat," he said.

"Well, then, what's the trouble?" the ticket seller asked.

"I'm scared to sit alone in the theater."

The Lost Theater Tickets

One of the real classic Broadway yarns is spun by John Shubert, who claims it actually happened to a Shubert employee.

A short, slightly stooped man wearing a well-pressed suit stepped up to the box office of one of the Broadway legitimate theaters about ten minutes before curtain time. "May I speak to the treasurer, please?" he asked the ticket taker.

"Jack, front and center," the busy man growled, "get Sam. A guy here wants to make with some words."

In a few moments a quizzical, shirt-sleeved gent peered from behind the "reservation" window. "Something you wanted, bud?" he asked.

"Yes, sir, if you don't mind. I'd like my four seats for tonight's show —seats D12, 14, 16 and 18. You see, I haven't got the tickets with me, but I did take down the locations."

"Look, mister, if you're careless, don't give me ulcers. Now trot along."

"Please, I'll make you a proposition. Send an usher down to prove that D12, 14, 16 and 18 are unoccupied. If they're empty, let my party use them. And what's more, to show my sincerity I'll give you fifty dollars to keep as security until the show is over."

The usher checked and reported the seats were unoccupied.

"Okay," the treasurer said, "I'll pass you in but I'm taking your fifty and if anyone shows up with the tickets not only will you be thrown out—but to show my sincerity I'll keep the fifty."

The party took their seats and during intermission filed into the lobby for a smoke. Graciously the treasurer beckoned the little man with the well-pressed suit to join him in his office.

"Mister," he smiled, "I've been in this racket a long time and I always thought I could spot a gate-crasher with half a sleepy eye open. You fooled me and I'm sorry if I was rough on you. It looks like you told a really legit story. We won't wait until the next act is over—here's your fifty bucks."

"That's mighty thoughtful of you and I appreciate it," was the reply. "It really wasn't my carelessness though; misplacing the tickets was my son's fault. I'm teaching the boy my business, and while we were working on a job this morning I ran across the tickets and told him to stick them into my vest pocket. Instead he got confused and slipped them into our client's vest pocket—now they're gone forever."

"What do you mean they're gone forever—say, what business are you in anyway?"

"Oh, I'm sorry. I thought I told you," the little man apologized,

"I'm an undertaker. Here, take my card, maybe I can do something for you sometime."

The Cake

A man went to a baker and asked him to bake a cake in the form of the letter S. The baker said he would need a week to prepare the necessary tins. The customer agreed, and returned a week later. Proudly the baker showed him the cake.

"Oh, but you misunderstood me," the customer said. "You have made it a block letter and I wanted script."

"Well," said the baker, "if you can wait another week I can bake one in script."

When the customer returned, he sorrowfully informed the baker that he had wanted the letter in pink icing and not in green.

"Sorry," said the baker, "but you'll have to give me another week to change it."

A week later the customer came back, and was delighted with the cake.

"Exactly what I wanted."

"Will you take it with you," asked the baker, "or shall I send it to your house?"

"Don't bother," said the customer. "I'll eat it right here."

The Accommodating Mortician

A bereaved widow stopped in at the mortuary to view her lately embalmed husband. "Oh, you have done a beautiful job!" she enthused. Then, pausing reflectively, she added a bit hesitantly. "There's one thing, though. I know I selected a blue suit, but I rather wish now I had chosen a brown one."

"Well, madam," said the kindly mortician, "if you prefer brown, we can easily make the exchange."

On her next visit, the widow expressed unqualified approval. "Brown is so much nicer," she said, "but I still feel guilty, putting you to so much trouble."

"Quite all right," assured the mortician. "As it turned out, we had a man in the next room dressed in brown; his widow preferred blue. So we made the exchange."

"Yes," said the apologetic widow, "but it was still a lot of trouble changing all those clothes."

"Oh," said the mortician, "we just changed the heads!"

Morris

Morris is walking along Seventh Avenue with his friend Abe, and they keep walking along the street and Morris calls, "Hello, Joe. Hello, Sam. Hello, Max. Hello, Jim. Hello, Bob. Hello, Garry. Hello, Frank."

And Abe asks, "Morris, what is this with you? What? You know all these people?"

He says, "Of course. They're all personal friends of mine. Look, my name is Morris. I know everybody."

Abe says, "Morris, don't give me that stuff. I'm a friend of yours. What do you tell me you know everybody? Maybe you know the Mayor?"

He says, "Bob? Bob is my best friend. I had lunch with him the other day."

Abe says, "I don't believe you."

"Come into the phone booth. I'll call him up and invite him to say hello to you."

So he gets on the phone.

"I'd like to speak to Bob Wagner."

"Who's calling?"

"Morris."

"Hello, Morris! How are you? What can I do for you?"

"I've got a friend of mine here. He doesn't believe I know you. Will you say hello to him?"

He says hello.

"Gee, Morris, that's amazing! Do you mean to tell me—I can't believe you know everybody. Maybe you know the—the—the Governor?"

He says, "The Governor? Ave? My bosom buddy! My wife and his wife went to the beauty parlor together the other day. Fact is, we've got dinner with them Friday night."

Abe says, "Don't give me that stuff!"

"I'll call him over the phone."

He gets Albany on the phone and he says, "I want you to say hello to a friend of mine."

Sure enough, Averell Harriman!

Abe says, "Maybe you're such a *knacker*—maybe you know the President?"

"Do I know the President? Ike? Ike's my bosom buddy. We're talking to each other four times a week."

Abe says, "Don't give me that stuff!"

"So, I'll call him up."

So he calls him up, and sure enough Morris knows Ike and Ike knows Morris. Ike says hello to Abe.

Abe says, "Look, Morris, don't give me that baloney you know everybody in the world. I know somebody you don't know."

"Please, this is Morris you're talking to. I know everybody."

So Abe says, "I'll tell you what. I'll make you a bet that you don't know the Pope."

So he says, "Look, my name's Morris. I know the Pope—guaranteed. I'll tell you what we'll do. We'll take a trip to Rome. If I don't know the Pope, I'll pay. If I know him, you'll pay for the trip."

"Fair enough."

So they go to Rome and sure enough they watch. The Pope comes out on the balcony every day at twelve o'clock, and he waves to the crowd in the piazza.

So Morris says, "You see, jerk. Tomorrow at twelve o'clock the Pope's going to come out there and I'm going to come out with him on the balcony, just to show you that I know him."

So Abe says, "Sure, sure."

So the next day comes around. Abe is waiting in the piazza and suddenly twelve o'clock rolls around and out comes the Pope. Morris got his arm around him and the Pope's got his arm around Morris. So Abe's looking up there and he's dumfounded. All of a sudden a little Italian kid comes by and he pulls him by the leg and he says, "Hey, mister, who's the guy up there with Morris?"

Asking Questions

Cohen meets Lapidus and says, "Lapidus, for so many years I know you and I always ask for your family. You never ask me once how things are with me?"

So Lapidus says, "All right, Cohen, how are things with you?"

"Don't ask!"

The Boy on the Bus

A little boy was riding on one of the old double-deck Fifth Avenue buses with his father. As they sat on the open upper deck, the little boy pointed to the Empire State Building and cried, "Daddy! Daddy! What is that tall building?"

The father looked up to the very top of the 102nd story and shrugged his shoulders. "I—I—I—don't know, sonny. I—I really don't know."

The bus went on and they passed the lions in front of the Forty-second Street Library. "Daddy! See those lions? See those two lions? What are they?"

The father looked at the lions, turned around, and said, "I'm sorry, son. I really don't know."

They went further uptown till they came to the statue of General Sherman at Fifty-ninth Street. The son was about to ask his father what it was, started to touch him, and said, "Daddy," then thought better of it.

The father turned around and said, "Go ahead, sonny, ask, ask! After all, if you don't ask, how will you *ever* find out?"

The Cab Driver's Story

Two men are in the cloak and suit business in New York. They're doing very well. All of a sudden they're getting bored and one of them says to the other, "Aw, let's go out to California. We'll go in the moving picture business and make some money."

So the two of them go out there and they make a big success with it. They're out there about ten or fifteen years. One day they're walking along Sunset Boulevard, bored, you know. And one of them says to the other, "Sam, what do you say? You got nerve?"

"What do you want—what?"

"Let's grab a cab and go to New York."

"Aw, you're crazy."

"What do you mean I'm crazy? You'd rather stay here alone in your room? Let's go!"

"All right. If you got nerve, I got nerve."

So they go up to a cab driver and they ask him, "Want to go to New York?"

He says, "I'll call up my boss. I'd like to go."

So he goes over and calls up his boss. He comes back and says he wants $1800.

"What are you worrying about eighteen hundred? I'll give you a few hundred besides. Let's go!"

So one of these fellers is getting in the cab, but he gets out again and says, "Sam, you get in. You know I get off first. I get off at Central Park West and Seventy-second Street."

Shaggy Scale Tale

A Port Chester man with time to spare before catching the 6:42 at Grand Central decided to weigh himself on a penny machine. The scales produced a card stating, "You are a white man, weight 159, and you will take the 6:42 train to Port Chester."

Incredulous, he went back, inserted another penny and was rewarded with a second card stating, "You are a white man, weight 159, and you will take the 6:42 train to Port Chester."

While he mulled that over, an Indian wearing a huge feather headdress walked by.

"Excuse me," the man said, stopping the Indian. "You would do me a great favor by helping me in an experiment. Here is a penny; please weigh yourself on these scales."

"Of course," said the Indian, stepping on the machine and inserting the penny. He received a card stating, "You are a full-blooded Cherokee Indian, weight 196, and you will take the 7:10 train to Boston."

"One more favor," pleaded the commuter. "Let me borrow your headdress a minute." He donned the feathers, stepped on the scales and inserted another penny. Out came a card stating, "You are a white man, weight 170, and you have fooled around with the Indian so long you have missed the 6:42 train to Port Chester."

Religion in Suburbia

An Englishman spent some time in the United States studying American life. On his return to England an American friend there asked him how he found the New York suburban area. "What impressed me most around such towns as Scarsdale," said the Englishman, "is the extreme religiousness of the women. Invariably when they drive their husbands to the station in the morning and say good-by, they cross themselves." The American smiled. "I am afraid you misinterpreted their gestures," he said. "They are only trying to remind their husbands about things they may have forgotten—tie, fly, handkerchief, wallet."

Pinochle in the Catskills

Three "weekend husbands," cloakmakers, sat playing pinochle in a Catskill "kochalein" (housekeeping apartment) one Sunday, on their weekly visit to wife and children. They sat playing in the living room, for several hours. Suddenly one of them raises his head from the cards and says, "Fellows, it's so nice out, let's move out and play on the porch." So they did. Several hours later, another raises his head from the cards and says, "Fellows, the sun is so lovely on the lawn, let's move out and play there." So they did. A few hours later, one happened to look up for a second and noticed a dandelion on the green lawn. "Joe," he asks the one on his left, "that flower on the lawn, what kind is it, do you know?" Joe looked up and answered, "Hmph, what are you asking me for? Am I a milliner?"

What He Found in the Fish

A group of East Siders were talking about the various objects found in fish. Said one of the group, "I must tell you of an interesting experience that I had about ten years ago.

"I fell in love with a beautiful girl. I proposed to her; she accepted me. Shortly afterward I had to leave on a business trip. I was away a few months, and before I returned home, I bought for my sweetheart a gorgeous diamond. I wanted to surprise her, and I was filled with the most pleasant anticipations.

"As I was reading a newspaper in the train, my eyes fell on a news item, describing the marriage of my girl to another man. I was enraged beyond words. As the train was crossing a bridge, I opened the window and tossed the precious stone into the river.

"A few months later, I walked into a restaurant and ordered a portion of fish. I took a bite and felt something hard. I took it out of my mouth and—guess what it was?"

"The diamond!" shouted the listeners.

"No, it was a fishbone," said the adventurer.

Betting on the Fish

The story . . . started with a poker game in Havana, in which our hero [W. T. (Fatty) Anderson], because of the mistaken assumption that three queens was the high hand, came out into the cold gray light of morning with several hundred miles of water and a five-dollar bill between him and his homeland.

On the way to his hotel he met a man carrying a large fish.

"What kind of fish is that?" he asked.

"Red snapper," said the fisherman.

"For five dollars it's not," said Anderson.

It developed that the fish was on the way to be sold, and it was agreed that the decision of the fishmonger would be final.

"What kind of fish is this?" said the fisherman, tossing it down on a block.

"No jokes in the morning," said the buyer. "You've been fishing these waters for years and you ought to know. Get on with you."

"Never mind that," said the fisherman. "To decide a bet, what kind of a fish is it?"

"It's a red snapper," said the merchant. "You know cursed well it is."

Anderson handed over the five-dollar bill.

"You win," he said, "but it was still a good bet. I had every other kind of fish in the ocean running for me."

The Smart Umpire

An umpire named Drubinka, working in the Alabama State League, was behind the plate in a game between Troy and Greenville when one of the batters began yelling and kicking dirt over a called strike. The batter kept up his bellowing longer than usual, and finally Umpire Drubinka took hold of him and said, "Now, just a minute, son. Take it easy. I want to show you something."

The umpire pulled a deck of playing cards out of his hip pocket. Fanning the cards out, he extended the deck toward the batter, told him to take one of the cards, look at it, and keep its face concealed. The player did so.

"You got the ten of diamonds," said Umpire Drubinka.

The batter, astonished at the call, had now forgotten his big beef about the called strike.

"How'd you ever figure that out?" he demanded.

"The same way I figured that last pitch was a strike," snapped the umpire. "Now let's play ball and leave smart matters to smart people."

Old Chris and the Third Baseman

Chris Von Der Ahe, fabulous president of the St. Louis Browns in the 1880's, walked into the clubhouse one day and discovered that some of the equipment had been badly damaged.

Chris summoned the members of the team and then demanded to know who had been damaging the property. No one answered. Chris surveyed the scene a moment, then announced, "I'll give one hundred dollars to find out who did it." Another long silence, during which Arlie Latham, the team's third baseman, pondered the possibilities.

Finally Arlie spoke. "I know who done it."

"Who?"

"Give me the hundred dollars first," Arlie insisted.

The money was handed over.

"I did it," said Latham.

Whereupon Chris let out a roar. "For that," he yelled, "I'm fining you fifty dollars!"

Then he stomped out of the room, bristling, satisfied that nobody could get away with anything on old Chris.

The Musical Mice

A fellow went into a bar and after he had a couple of drinks he said to the bartender, "Do you want to see something?"

The bartender said, "Sure."

So he took out a tiny piano and a stool and he laid them on the bar.

The bartender said, "That's cute."

Then the fellow said, "Wait, wait, you haven't seen anything yet." And he reached into his vest pocket and he took out a tiny mouse and he sat the mouse down on the stool and said, "Play." And the mouse started to beat out Rachmaninoff and Bach and Brahms and Beethoven.

The bartender said, "That's marvelous! I've never seen anything like it before."

And everyone in the bar started to come up and watch this.

The fellow said, "Aw, you haven't seen anything yet."

And he pulled out another little mouse and he put it next to the piano and said, "Sing." And while the pianist mouse was beating out the rhythm, the singing mouse sang arias from *La Traviata* and from *Tristan and Isolde,* and everybody in the bar was just thunderstruck.

One fellow said, "Do you know, that's the most wonderful thing I've ever seen in my life? I'll give you twenty thousand dollars for that, spot cash."

The bartender said, "Don't sell it. That thing's worth a million dollars on television."

The fellow said, "Aw, I'm going to sell it. I need the money."

So he took the twenty thousand dollars and the other fellow took the two mice and the piano and walked out.

The bartender said, "Boy! Are you crazy! You could have made a fortune with that."

"Aw, don't be silly! It's a phony!"

"What do you mean 'a phony'?"

"That mouse can't sing! The one at the piano is a ventriloquist!"

So What!

A man was coming home late one night—about three o'clock in the morning—when he saw a chap standing in front of a house with a horse. The man with the horse stopped him and said, "Brother, could you give me a hand here?"

"Well, what would you like me to do?" asked the passer-by.

"I want you to help me get this horse upstairs."

"Why?"

"Well, I can't tell you at the moment. I haven't got time to explain. Would you just mind helping me?"

Together they pushed the horse up the stoop and into the hallway, then up three flights of stairs and into the man's flat. When they got inside, the man with the horse said, "Now will you help me get the horse with his feet in the bathtub?"

Fearful that he might be dealing with a lunatic, the passer-by helped the man lift first one foreleg, then the second foreleg, then one hind leg, then the second hind leg, and there stood the horse in the bathtub.

"Now," said the passer-by, "would you mind telling me what this is all about?"

"Well," said the man with the horse, "I'll tell you. I've got a brother-in-law who lives here with me. He's a *very* smart fellow. I can't tell him anything. No matter what I tell him, he says, 'So what!' No matter what information I give him, he says, 'So what!' He's out late tonight. He'll be home about four o'clock. I want him to come upstairs, open the door, take off his clothes, put on his pajamas, go into the bathroom, then come running out yelling, 'Sol! Sol! There's a horse in the bathtub!' and I'll say, 'So what!'"

King of the Jungle

The day is bright. The jungle is green, overflowing with life and exuberance. A young lion in the jungle, very proud of himself, with his mane flowing, sniffs the fine air, looks at the beautiful sun, thinks how grand it is to be alive, in love with the jungle, in love with life, in love with the beautiful day, in love with himself. He beats himself on the breast, shakes his mane out of his eyes, opens his mouth like M-G-M Lion, and roars, "Gr-r-r-r-r-r-r! *King of the beasts!* KING OF THE JUNGLE! Gr-r-r-r-r-r!" And he thinks how beautiful it is to be a fine young lion like that. "Gr-r-r-r-r-r! *King of the beasts!* KING OF THE JUNGLE!" And he goes padding down the jungle lane, tail sticking up behind, throwing his mane out of his eyes. "Gr-r-r-r-r-r! *King of the beasts!*"

Around the bend in the jungle path he sees an elephant coming —swinging along, quiet, slow, heavy. He looks at the elephant and he lets out a roar of laughter. He says, "Look at you!" He says, "You're big." He says, "You're ungainly." He says, "You're funny-lookin'." He says, "You got a funny color." He says, "You ain't good for nothin' but totin' burdens in the heat of the day." He says, "Why don't you be like me? Gr-r-r-r-r-r! *King of the beasts!* KING OF THE JUNGLE!" He says, "You're made up wrong. You got your tail in front. You got your tail behind. You can't fight. You can't think. You can't do nothin'. Why don't you be like me? Gr-r-r-r-r-r! *King of the beasts!* KING OF THE JUNGLE!"

The old elephant just looked at him and w-a-g-g-ed o-n d-o-w-n the j-u-n-g-l-e p-a-t-h.

And the lion roared, "Gr-r-r-r-r-r! *King of the beasts!* KING OF THE JUNGLE!" and padded down the jungle path.

And suddenly he came upon another jungle animal. And this was a hyena. And he stopped and his laughter was ribald and shrill. And he says, "And look at you!" He says, "You ain't nothin' at all." He says, "You ain't even big like the elephant!" He says, "You're funny-lookin'!" He says, "You got on a mangy coat." He says, "The only thing about you that's outstandin' is your smell and that stands out too far." He says, "You smell bad. You can't fight. You can't think. You can't even tote burdens in the heat of the day." He says, "The only thing you can do is to smell bad, and you smell too bad, and to laugh, and I think you laugh at yourself. Why don't you be like me? Gr-r-r-r-r-r-r! *King of the beasts!* KING OF THE JUNGLE!"

And the old hyena looked at the lion and says, "Ha-ha-ha-a-a-a-a-a-a-!" and goes on down the jungle path.

And the lion says, "Gr-r-r-r-r-r-r! *King of the beasts!* KING OF THE JUNGLE!" And he went down the path.

And suddenly under a great big leaf he sees something slithering along and he looks there, and there is a jungle snake. And he walks around carefully and looks at him, and says, "And look at you! Down on your belly in the dust!" He says, "You are the depth of insignificance." He says, "You can't fight. You can't think. You can't work. You can't even tote burdens. You don't even smell bad." He says, "You're just nothin' way down there." He says, "You're funny-lookin'." He says, "You got on a funny coat. And when you change that you go somewhere and hide and then get the same coat all over again." He says, "You're cowardly. You won't fight. All you do is creep up on your enemy and bite him in the heel." He says, "Why don't you be like me? Gr-r-r-r-r-r-r! *King of the beasts!* KING OF THE JUNGLE!"

And the old snake looked up at him, and says, "Hs-s-s-s-s-s-s!" and is gone down the jungle path.

The lion beats himself on his chest and says, "Gr-r-r-r-r-r-r! *King of the beasts!* KING OF THE JUNGLE!" And his old tail goes straight up to the sky with the plume on it. And he throws the mane out of his eyes, beats his chest, and thinks how marvelous it is, how fine it is, to be young and beautiful and a lion, and the *King of the beasts!* and the KING OF THE JUNGLE! And he runs padding down the jungle path.

And suddenly under a huge jungle leaf he sees a tiny flicker. And he stops, and he walks around it, and he takes his paw and turns it over. And there under this huge green leaf is a little mouse. And the mouse looks up at him with his beady eyes staring, and the lion looks at the mouse, and the lion is taken aback. And then a roar fills the jungle as the lion looks at this tiny mouse. And he says, "And look at you!" He says, "You are just about nothin'! You are the last word in nothingness!" He says, "You're little. You're ungainly. You can't fight. You can't think. You can't work." He says, "The only thing about you that is big is your tail, and," he says, "that's all out of proportion." He says, "Why don't you be like me? Gr-r-r-r-r-r! *King of the beasts!* KING OF THE JUNGLE!"

And the little old mouse looks up at the lion, and puts those beady eyes on the lion, and says to the lion, "I been sick!"

The Educated Bulldog

[A] farmer had a son of whose ability he was very proud, and the son had a bulldog. When the boy was eighteen years old the farmer sent him way across the state to Earlham College to get an education. The boy took the bulldog along for company. After the boy and the dog had been at Earlham a month or so, the old man received a letter from his son.

This is what the boy wrote:

"Father, an astonishing thing has happened. The bulldog has begun to talk. Moreover, he seems to have a fairly good mind. I'd like to make a suggestion to you. If we educate the bulldog along with me here at Earlham, we'd have at the end of four years not only the one talking bulldog in the world, but the one and only talking bulldog with a college education. We could exhibit him then all over Indiana, charge admission, and make a lot of money. If you agree with me, Father, just send me double the usual amount of money for books, laboratory fees, incidentals, and miscellaneous. It will be a mighty good investment."

So for four years the farmer sent his son double the usual amount for the usual items, and finally the day came when his son and the remarkable bulldog were to return home with their college degrees. The boy wrote that the bulldog had made an outstanding record at Earlham and had taken honors in two subjects. He said that he and the dog would travel by train to Vincennes and then hire a boat to take them downriver to the farm.

The old man got very excited on the day they were due to arrive and he waited anxiously on the bank as the little boat approached. When the boy jumped ashore his father clasped him in his arms—and then he looked about him and said, "And where's our educated bulldog?"

"Well, Father," said the boy, "it was as I said. The bulldog graduated with honors and then we both took the train for Vincennes. When we got there, I hired a boat to bring us here. And on the way down, I said to the bulldog, 'Isn't it wonderful, in less than an hour, now, we'll be back with my father?'

" 'What, that stupid, uneducated old ignoramus?' said the bulldog, and, Father, it made me so angry to hear him speak so insultingly of you that I kicked him overboard. He couldn't swim a stroke and so he was drowned."

Grandpa Snazzy's Frog

Grandpa and Grandma Snazzy gave a big family party down in Van Buren, Arkansas, attended by all the [Bob] Burns aunts and uncles and cousins. A long table was set for supper, and when everybody was seated Grandma Snazzy went out to the springhouse and came back with a pail of milk. She began filling the guests' glasses. When she came to the host, Grandpa Snazzy, a small frog plopped into his glass with the milk and Grandpa just sat and stared at it without moving. Grandma proceeded along the table, and when she passed around to the other side she noticed her husband's trance. "Do you see something in your glass, Grandpa?" she asked. "Yes," said Grandpa, still staring transfixed, "and he sees me, too."

The Near-Sighted Texan

[There was a] near-sighted Texas oilman who couldn't see a foot ahead of him without his eyeglasses.

He bought himself a special de luxe Rolls Royce, flew it across from England in his own private plane, and took his four best friends out for a trial spin. Roaring along at 105, he suddenly removed his glasses—and a shriek of terror rose from four larynxes at once.

"You'll kill us all, Joe," they yelled in chorus. "Put your glasses back on, for Pete's sake."

"Take it easy, boys," Joe said calmly, stepping on the accelerator. "I had the windshield ground to my prescription."

The Talking Horse in the Oil Fields

A mule skinner was driving along a country road between two oil fields. Suddenly, as he came over a rise, one of his pneumatic tires picked up a nail. He got out of the car at once and set to work changing the tire, but it gave him considerable difficulty, for the tire was held onto the wooden spoke wheels with lugs and was on a split rim. As he worked he was startled to hear a voice say, "Mister, if you would loosen the top lug, that rim would come off easier." The mule skinner looked in the direction from which the voice came, but all he saw was an old gray horse standing nearby with his head across the fence. He set to work once more and soon he heard the voice again saying, "Why don't you use some common sense and loosen the lug at the top of the wheel and the rim will come off easier?"

"Bless my soul!" cried the mule skinner as he realized it was the horse that was talking to him.

"I beg your pardon," said the horse, calmly raising his head. "Do you mind if I ask why you are blessing your soul?"

"Great God!" said the mule skinner. "Can you really talk?"

"Talk?" said the horse. "Why, of course I can talk."

"Well, then, would you mind telling me why you are out on grass when you could be with Ringling Brothers Circus?"

"Certainly," said the horse. "I am in this pasture because I am resting up. I'm tired most of the time. Two years ago I ran in the Kentucky Derby and I've been tired ever since."

"Well, bless my soul," said the mule skinner again. "Who the hell owns you? Do you mind telling me?"

"Not at all," said the horse. "I belong to Farmer Jones, who lives on the hill."

The mule skinner repaired the tire to his car as quickly as possible and drove to the Jones farm as fast as he could step on the gas. He got out and knocked on the door. A lanky farmer came out, working his Adam's apple up and down, but the mule skinner thought that was just an eccentricity, for he had never seen a ventriloquist.

"See here, mister," said the mule skinner, "do you own that old gray horse down in the pasture along the road I just came over?"

"Sure," said the farmer. "I own that horse."

"I don't suppose you'd consider selling him, would you?"

"Maybe, if I got my price."

"Would you take a hundred dollars for that horse?" asked the mule skinner.

"He's yours," said the farmer.

The money was passed and the minute the mule skinner had shoved the bills into the farmer's hands he spoke out again.

"Now, Mister Jones, I want to tell you something about that horse you just sold me. He's a remarkable animal. Why, that horse talks."

The farmer slapped his sides and laughed. "Why, of course I know that horse talks. But now let me tell you something, mister. That horse never did run in the Kentucky Derby. He ain't never been out of Texas. That horse is the biggest damned liar you ever saw. He used to be owned by an oil field specialty salesman."

What Was on the Card?

One of his greatest ambitions was the "rope choker's" [cable tool driller's] desire to travel and see places; especially did he long to see France and the girls he had heard the returning soldiers from World War I tell about.

So the "rope choker" worked hard and saved his money, and one day announced to his friends that they wouldn't be seeing him around any more for a while; he was going to take a trip to France; he was going to travel; go places; do and see things.

He was naturally overjoyed at the prospect of a trip to Paris, especially in the spring, when Paris is at its best, with the trees coming out to bud on the boulevards, and the women, oo-la-la!

The "rope choker" was in high spirits when he arrived in Paris, along in the evening, and went to his hotel. On passing through the lobby, he saw a beautiful woman sitting there, a very beautiful woman indeed, who answered just about all the prayers of a "rope choker's" fraternity and also an American's dream of French women. In other words she was lovely. And to make it more perfect, she just as unmistakably gave him the "eye."

But since the lobby was crowded, and the bell boy had his bags, and he had to register, and he was dirty and tired, for all these reasons, he didn't speak to the woman just then, but he registered, and went up to his room, with the idea of hurrying back just as soon as he could.

The "rope choker" rushed back down with all possible speed, to see if he could find the woman. He looked all around the lobby; but she was nowhere to be seen; and finally he asked the clerk if he had seen her; and if so, where she had gone and could be found.

The clerk had not seen the woman, or at least pretended he had not seen her, but he said, "Monsieur, here is a card for you; perhaps the lady whom you saw left it for you." It was in his mailbox, of course.

The "rope choker" took the card, and though there was some writing on it, it was in French, and the "rope choker" couldn't read a word of French. He handed the card back to the clerk to read for him; and the clerk glanced at it and said, "Monsieur, this hotel is not for men like you. Please to pack your bags at once and get out."

The "rope choker" was dumfounded, and though he pleaded and pleaded with the clerk to tell him what was the trouble, the clerk would not tell him, but just repeated, "Monsieur, please to pack your bags and leave at once."

So the "rope choker" had to get out.

He spent a sad night in another hotel, and early the next morning he went to see the United States consul.

He pulled the card out of his pocket and said, "Honorable Sir, I wonder if you would do me a favor. This card was left in my mailbox last night, and when the clerk read it, he made me leave the hotel, and I can't understand it. Will you please read it for me?"

The consul took the card and started to read it, and began to get red in the face, and then he jumped out of his chair and stood up straight and said, "Sir, please to leave this country at once. Go back to the United States where you belong and stay there."

The "rope choker," still further bewildered, set sail for home, and was met at the Galveston dock by his sweetheart, whom he intended to make his bride.

The "rope choker" had not thought of it before, but now he remembered that his sweetheart had studied French, and he said, "I have a card here that has given me a great deal of trouble. It caused me to be thrown out of my hotel, and led to the United States consul ordering me back home. Do you think you know enough college French to read it for me, and explain the whole mystery?"

The sweetheart took the card in her hand, but she had looked at it only once when she cried out to the taxi driver, "Stop," and she climbed out of the car, saying back through the door, "Sir, I do not want ever to speak to you again. Thank God I found out in time what kind of man you are." Then she flounced away.

The "rope choker," growing more hopeless by the minute, headed back at once to the oil town where he formerly worked, and got a room. Then he sat down to think what he should do.

Finally he snapped his fingers with decision, for he had just thought of a friend who knew a little French, and who he knew would not fail him. So he hurried to find the friend and told him his trouble.

His friend said of course he would help him, no matter what was on the card, and that nothing in the world could break their friendship. Absolutely nothing! So then, and only then, the "rope choker" reached into his pocket for the card. It was gone. He had lost it.

Murgatroyd the Kluge* Maker

Murgatroyd enlisted in the Navy, and in some way made practically perfect scores on all the intelligence and other tests given to him. The company chief who interviewed him was much impressed. He asked Murgatroyd what his occupation had been. "Kluge maker," replied Murgatroyd. The chief didn't want to admit, to such an extremely intelligent young man, that he didn't know what a kluge maker was, so he wrote down, in the space labeled "civilian occupation," kluge maker, and Murgatroyd went on to boot training at Sampson. Murgatroyd went through boot camp with flying colors and came to the time when he was interviewed for assignment. This chief, too, was much impressed by Murgatroyd's record and by his superior intelligence. He asked Murgatroyd what his occupation had been, and he, too, didn't want to show his ignorance by asking what a kluge maker was. He said, heartily, "I'll give you the rate of kluge maker, first class." Of course, there is no such rate, but this seemed an exceptional case—an unusually intelligent young man.

* Pronounced "klūj."

Murgatroyd was sent to Boston, where he reported as kluge maker, first, on the *U.S.S. Nymph*, which was going on a shakedown cruise. It was a rugged trip, weather bad, and the crew really batted themselves out. But Murgatroyd just sat by the bulkheads, pitching cigarette butts out in the ocean—he had exerted himself to smoke. When they got back to Boston, the captain was pretty sore at Murgatroyd and accused him of not doing a thing the whole trip.

"Well," said Murgatroyd, "I'm a kluge maker. And I certainly couldn't make kluges without anything to make them with."

"What do you need?" asked the captain.

Murgatroyd was stumped at that, but he sat up all night and made a long list of equipment needed—screws, bolts, hammers, axes, wire, batteries, steel, iron—the longest list you ever saw. They had to send to the Philadelphia Navy Yards and all over to get all the stuff; and when the ship went out, it listed 'way to starboard with the weight of the kluge-making equipment.

The ship was up around the north of Ireland, and Murgatroyd hadn't done much more than on the previous trip, when word came of an inspection by the admiral, who had heard of the kluge maker. The captain told Murgatroyd that he'd better have a kluge made by the time the admiral came aboard; and Murgatroyd thought maybe the captain was right that time.

It was a bleary-eyed Murgatroyd who responded to "Murgatroyd, front and center," when the admiral made his inspection the next morning.

"I understand you have been making kluges."

"That's right, sir."

"Well, let's see one."

Murgatroyd opened his hand, and there was the damnedest-looking little thing you ever saw—wires and springs sticking out in every direction.

Now the admiral had never seen a kluge. It was a tense moment. He did not want to appear ignorant. His honor was at stake. He coughed warily, and said, "It looks like a perfect kluge. If it is a perfect kluge, it should work perfectly; let's see it work."

Now Murgatroyd was on the spot. Nervously, he walked straight ahead to the side of the ship. He was shaking all over. As he

opened up his shaking hand, the kluge slipped out and went overboard, down into the ocean, and went "kkluuge."

The Hero

During its basic training period, a company on our post went on a
routine twenty-five-mile hike with full field packs. The company was
supposed to bivouac overnight and then return to the post the next
day.

When they arrived at the bivouac area, there was a messenger
waiting from regimental headquarters. "All men who are physically
able to make the return march must return to the post immediately," reported the messenger.

The company commander called a formation and made the an-
nouncement. Then he said, "All men who do not feel that they are
physically able to make the return march—take three steps forward."

The whole company stepped forward three paces.

That is, all except one man—a five-foot-three private.

The company commander walked up to the little private, patted
him on the arm and said, "Son, the Army is proud of you."

The little private looked up at the company commander.

"I don't know why," he said. "I can't even walk three more steps."

Laying Off Help

Through the whole depression period everything was secondary to
the business of supplying jobs. Private industry simply couldn't do
it; the government had to. Private employers were forced to slash
their payrolls. John J. Pelley, president of the Central Railroad of
Georgia, . . . had been laying off help with the rest. . . .

Going to his office early one morning, Pelley heard two Pullman
porters talking. One of them told the other he'd had a frightening
dream the night before. He had dreamed that President Pelley was
dead and that he had gone to the funeral. As the casket was being
borne to the grave, Pelley's corpse lifted the lid and asked how many
pallbearers there were. When told that there were six, the corpse ordered, "Let two go."

In the Book

You fellows that always want the law on the book put me in mind of a Swede I worked in the woods with. You know, gotta be in a book—the law is gotta be there in a book before we can do anything. Well, I worked with a fellow and he lost his ax. And it snowed one night and he couldn't find it. And of course in them camps there we were charged up with these tools. If we returned them, well, then, it was all right. And if we couldn't return them or didn't return them, why, we paid for them.

And the Swede knew this. So every holiday and Sundays he's always runnin' around lookin' for the ax. And he couldn't find the ax. So in spring when the camp broke, the foreman informed the Swede—he says, "Well, Ole, I got you charged up here with an ax—in the book."

And Ole says, "Jesus Christ!" He says, "You got me charged up here with an ax in the book?"

"Yeah!"

"Well, here," he says, "I've been lookin' for the ax all winter," he says, "and now you got him in the book."

Notes

Introduction

MOTTO: *The "Man in the Street" Stories from "The New York Times,"* with an Introduction by Chauncey M. Depew, p. 131. New York: J. S. Ogilvie Publishing Company. [N.d.]

ANECDOTE IN INTRODUCTION: Evan Esar, *The Legend of Joe Miller,* p. 18. Copyright, 1957, by Nat Schmulowitz. Anecdota Scowah Number Two. Privately Printed for Members of the Roxburghe Club of San Francisco. April 1, 1957.

1. CRACKER BARREL

MOTTO: Clyde W. Wilkinson, "Backwoods Humor," *Southwest Review,* Vol. 24 (January, 1939), No. 2, p. 164. Copyright, 1939, by the Southwest Review. Dallas, Texas.

ANECDOTE IN INTRODUCTION: Adapted from Earl A. Collins, *Legends and Lore of Missouri,* pp. 97-98. Copyright, 1951, by The Naylor Company. San Antonio, Texas.

IN THE COUNTRY STORE: Marshall P. Wilder, *The Sunny Side of the Street,* pp. 75-76. Copyright, 1905, by Funk & Wagnalls Company. New York and London. As told by Henry Dixey.

"HE DON'T SAY": Keith W. Jennison, "Vermont Wit: Like the State It Typifies, It's Bleak, Tough, and Thoroly Enjoyable, *Chicago Tribune Magazine,* May 20, 1956, p. 25. Copyright, 1956, by the Chicago Tribune.

"HE AIN'T HOME": *Ibid.*

A PAIR OF NEW BOOTS: Rowland E. Robinson, *Uncle Lisha's Outing,* p. 89. Copyright, 1897, by Rowland E. Robinson. Boston and New York: Houghton, Mifflin and Company.

A SHOVEL FOR "UNCLE ED": Robert Davis, "Some Characteristics of Northern

Vermont Wit," *Proceedings of the Vermont Historical Society*, New Series, Vol. V (December, 1937), No. 4, p. 321. Copyright, 1937, by the Vermont Historical Society. Montpelier, Vermont.

WHY HE TALKED TO HIMSELF: As told by Scott Miller and Scott Gay to P. S. Scruton, Hillsboro, New Hampshire. Manuscripts of the Federal Writers' Project of the Works Progress Administration for the State of New Hampshire, 1939. Deposited in the Archive of Folk Song, Library of Congress, Washington, D.C.

ROCK FARM: Arthur Bartlett, "Maine," *Holiday*, Vol. 2 (August, 1947), No. 8, p. 87. Copyright, 1947, by The Curtis Publishing Company. Philadelphia.

BUILDING WALL: Nixon Orwin Rush, editor, *Rufus Jones' Selected Stories of Native Maine Humor*, pp. 13-14. Copyright, 1945, by Clark University Library. Worcester, Massachusetts. 1946.

THE PROPOSAL: *Ibid.*, p. 15.

GRANDMA'S COFFIN: Elizabeth Coatsworth, *Maine Ways*, p. 141. Copyright, 1947, by Elizabeth Coatsworth Beston. New York: The Macmillan Company.

FANNY KEMBLE AND THE YANKEE FARMER: Thomas B. Reed, editor; Justin McCarthy, Rossiter Johnson, Albert Ellery Bergh, associate editors, *Modern Eloquence*, Vol. X, *Anecdotes* . . . , p. 189. Copyright, 1900, by The University Society. Philadelphia: John D. Morris and Company.

A CURE FOR SORE EYES: Truman Abell, *The New-England Farmer's Almanac*, . . . 1843, No. XXIX. Claremont, New Hampshire: Published and Sold at the Claremont Bookstore.

A CURE FOR THE HEAVES: Joseph A. Willard, *Half a Century with Judges and Lawyers*, pp. 339-340. Copyright, 1895, by Joseph A. Willard. Boston and New York: Houghton, Mifflin and Company.

THE GLANDERS: Congressman Martin I. Townsend, of New York, in *The Funny Side of Politics*, by George S. Hilton, p. 13. Copyright, 1899, by G. W. Dillingham Co. New York.

THE FENCE-POST CONTROVERSY: Doret Meeker, "Back to the Blanket: Lore of Steuben County," *New York Folklore Quarterly*, Vol. VIII (Autumn, 1952), No. 3, pp. 171-172. As told by Mr. J. Glenn of Penn Yan.

UNCLE JED: Franklin D. Roosevelt, address at Jackson Day Dinner, January 8, 1940, in *The Public Papers and Addresses of Franklin D. Roosevelt*, The 1940 Volume, edited by Samuel Rosenman, p. 34. Copyright, 1941, by Franklin Delano Roosevelt. New York: The Macmillan Company.

ADVICE TO A YOUNG LAWYER: Senator Samuel J. Ervin, of North Carolina, in "A New Raconteur Rules the Senate," by Russell Baker, *The New York Times*, May 13, 1956, p. 61. Copyright, 1956, by the New York Times Company.

GEORGIA JUSTICE: W. Irwin MacIntyre, "Wiregrass Stories," p. 7. Copyright, 1909, by W. Irwin MacIntyre. Thomasville, Georgia: Times-Enterprise Company Print. Second edition. 1913.

HOW THEY RAISE MEN IN GEORGIA: Thomas B. Reed, editor; Justin McCarthy, Rossiter Johnson, Albert Ellery Bergh, associate editors, *Modern Eloquence*, Vol. X, *Anecdotes* . . . , p. 301. Copyright, 1900, by the University Society. Philadelphia: John D. Morris and Company. As told by General Wheeler.

GUM STARTER: Paul Flowers, *The Greenhouse*, From His Daily Column in *The Commercial Appeal*, Vol. I, November 1, 1944, p. 43. Memphis, Tennessee.

WAR AND PEACE: Contributed by Josiah H. Combs, Fort Worth, Texas, March, 1957.

THE INDISPENSABLE MAN: Alben W. Barkley, *That Reminds Me—*, p. 183.

Copyright, 1954, by Alben W. Barkley; 1954, by The Curtis Publishing Company. Garden City, New York: Doubleday & Company, Inc.

LONGEVITY: *Ibid.*, pp. 16-17.

"MAKE ME TAKE IT": *Ibid.*, pp. 233-234.

THE PATH TO THE GRAVE: Allan M. Trout, *Greetings from Old Kentucky*, p. 114. Copyright, 1947, by Allan M. Trout. Louisville, Kentucky: The Courier-Journal.

TWO CHANCES: Congressman Victor Wickersham, of Oklahoma, in *Laughing with Congress*, by The Honorable Alexander Wiley, p. 187. Copyright, 1947, by Alexander Wiley. New York: Crown Publishers.

BREAKING THE NEWS: Contributed by Josiah H. Combs, Fort Worth, Texas, April, 1957.

2. GOD'S COUNTRY

MOTTO: Cleveland Amory, *The Proper Bostonians*, p. 23. Copyright, 1947, by Cleveland Amory. New York: E. P. Dutton & Co., Inc.

ANECDOTE IN INTRODUCTION: Adapted from Major Alson B. Ostrander, *An Army Boy of the Sixties*, p. 63. Copyright, 1924, by World Book Corporation. Yonkers-on-Hudson, New York.

PASSIONATE PILGRIMS: George H. Chase, *Tales out of School*, pp. 65-66. Copyright, 1947, by the President and Fellows of Harvard College. Cambridge: Harvard University Press.

"PROPER BOSTONIANS": Cleveland Amory, *The Proper Bostonians*, pp. 11, 25, 27, 140-141, 346. Copyright, 1947, by Cleveland Amory. New York: E. P. Dutton & Co., Inc.

THE HALLOWELL BOY'S PRAYER: Cleveland Amory, "High Society, U.S.A.," *Holiday.* Vol. 17 (March, 1955), No. 3, p. 48. Copyright, 1955, by The Curtis Publishing Company. Philadelphia, Pa.

NEW ENGLAND, THERE SHE STANDS!: Daniel C. Roper, in Collaboration with Frank H. Lovette, *Fifty Years of Public Life*, pp. 40-41. Copyright, 1941, by The Duke University Press. Durham, North Carolina.

KANSAS VERSUS MAINE: Thomas B. Reed, editor; Justin McCarthy, Rossiter Johnson, Albert Ellery Bergh, associate editors, *Modern Eloquence*, Vol. X, *Anecdotes . . .*, p. 304. Copyright, 1900, by the University Society. Philadelphia: John D. Morris and Company.

PROSPECTS OF A NORTHERN LAWYER IN THE SOUTH: Martha Lupton, editor, *The Treasury of Modern Humor*, p. 255. Copyright, 1938, by Maxwell Droke. Indianapolis.

SOUTHERN VIRTUES: Daniel C. Roper, in Collaboration with Frank H. Lovette, *Fifty Years of Public Life*, pp. 97-98. Copyright, 1941, by The Duke University Press. Durham, North Carolina.

BLUE BLOOD: As told by Frank H. Wardlaw, University of South Carolina, Columbia, South Carolina, January 25, 1949, who heard it from Pierre F. LaBorde, of Columbia, concerning the Cedar Creek section of Richland County. Recorded and transcribed by B. A. Botkin.

PRIVATE JOHN ALLEN AND THE UNION SOLDIER: Claude Gentry, *Private John Allen*, Gentleman—Statesman—Sage—Prophet, p. 61. Copyright, 1951, by Claude Gentry. Decatur, Ga.: Bowen Press.

ARKANSAS AND THE CIVIL WAR: "Editor's Drawer," *Harper's New Monthly Magazine*, Vol. XXVIII (December, 1863), No. CLXIII, p. 135. New York: Harper & Brothers.

NOTHING WRONG IN HEAVEN: John Wesley Kilgo, *Campaigning in Dixie*, pp. 29-30. Copyright, 1945, by John Wesley Kilgo. New York: The Hobson Book Press.

CANDIDATES FOR HEAVEN—THE TENNESSEAN: Galen Drake, *This Is Galen Drake*, p. 137. Copyright, 1949, by Doubleday & Company, Inc. Garden City, New York.

CANDIDATES FOR HEAVEN—THE HOOSIER: Samuel Ralston, "The Government Back Home," in *After-Dinner Speeches and How to Make Them*, by William Allen Wood, p. 345. Copyright, 1914, by T. H. Flood & Company, Chicago.

CANDIDATES FOR HEAVEN—THE ARKANSAWYER: The Honorable Alexander Wiley, *Laughing with Congress*, p. 144. Copyright, 1947, by Alexander Wiley. New York: Crown Publishers.

THE WISE AND THE FOOLISH VIRGINIANS: Senator A. Willis Robertson, of Virginia, in *Laughing with Congress*, by The Honorable Alexander Wiley, p. 144. Copyright, 1947, by Alexander Wiley. New York: Crown Publishers.

MISSOURIANS VERSUS ARKANSAWYERS: Vance Randolph, *Funny Stories about Hillbillies*, p. 15. Copyright, 1944, by E. Haldeman-Julius. Girard, Kansas: Haldeman-Julius Publications.

NORTH DAKOTA BABY: Meridel Le Sueur, *North Star Country*, p. 263. Copyright, 1945, by Meridel Le Sueur. American Folkways, edited by Erskine Caldwell. New York: Duell, Sloan & Pearce.

BIRD OF PARADISE IN WEST TEXAS: Stanley Walker, "Everything's True about Texas," *Harper's Magazine*, Vol. 200 (March, 1950), No. 1198, p. 36. Copyright, 1950, by Harper & Brothers. New York.

3. NEWCOMERS AND DAMN FOOLS

MOTTO: Clay Fulks, "Arkansas," *The American Mercury*, Vol. 8 (July, 1926), No. 31, p. 291. Copyright, 1926, by The American Mercury, Inc. New York.

ANECDOTE IN INTRODUCTION: Adapted from A. W. Eddins, "Anecdotes from the Brazos Bottoms," in *Straight Texas*, edited by J. Frank Dobie and Mody C. Boatright, pp. 88-89. Publications of The Texas Folk-Lore Society, No. XIII. Copyright, 1937, by The Texas Folk-Lore Society. Austin, Texas.

COUNTRY FOOLS VERSUS TOWN FOOLS: Vance Randolph, *Funny Stories from Arkansas*, p. 11. Copyright, 1943, by E. Haldeman-Julius. Girard, Kansas.

COUNTRY BOY IN CHICAGO: Claude Gentry, *Private John Allen*, Gentleman—Statesman—Sage—Prophet, p. 34. Copyright, 1951, by Claude Gentry. Decatur, Ga.: Bowen Press. As told by John Allen.

UNCLE MONROE'S FIRST VISIT TO THE CITY: E. V. White, *Chocolate Drops from the South*, A Book of Negro Humor and Philosophy, pp. 5-6. Copyright, 1932, by The E. L. Steck Company. Austin, Texas.

THE KENTUCKIAN AND THE CUSPIDOR: *Anecdotes for the Steamboat and Railroad*, Selected from the Best Authors, by an Old Traveller, p. 18. Philadelphia: Lindsay & Blakiston. 1853.

THEIR FIRST AUTOMOBILE: Congressman Brooks Hays, in *Laughing with Congress*, by the Honorable Alexander Wiley, pp. 197-198. Copyright, 1947, by Alexander Wiley. New York: Crown Publishers.

"COME AND EAT": "Editor's Drawer," *Harper's New Monthly Magazine*, Vol. XI (September, 1855), No. LXIV, pp. 567-568. New York: Harper & Brothers.

GOOD ENOUGH: George Franks Ivey, *Humor and Humanity*, p. 72. Hickory, N.C.: The Southern Publishing Co. [1945.]

TOOTHPICK SHORTAGE: Allan M. Trout, "Greetings," Louisville (Kentucky) *Courier Journal*, June 8, 1954.

THE HILLBILLY ENLISTEE: Congressman Charles A. Eaton, in *Laughing with Congress*, by The Honorable Alexander Wiley, pp. 186-187. Copyright, 1947, by Alexander Wiley. New York: Crown Publishers.

WHAT MAINE PEOPLE DO IN THE WINTER: Ellen Talbot, Freeport, Maine. Manuscripts of the Federal Writers' Project of the Works Progress Administration for the State of Maine. 1939. Deposited in the Archive of Folk Song, Library of Congress, Washington, D.C.

VERMONTERS VERSUS SUMMER VISITORS: George H. Chase, *Tales Out of School*, pp. 67-69. Copyright, 1947, by the President and Fellows of Harvard College. Cambridge: Harvard University Press.

THE SILENT VERMONTER: *The Omaha* [Nebraska] *World-Herald*, August 2, 1955, p. 16. Reprinted from *The California Citrograph*.

THE DUDE FROM MEMPHIS: Vance Randolph, *Funny Stories about Hillbillies*, pp. 15-16. Copyright, 1944, by E. Haldeman-Julius. Girard, Kansas: Haldeman-Julius Publications. As told by Mrs. Bernie Babcock, Little Rock, Arkansas.

CROSSED TRACKS: *Ibid.*, p. 21.

DECEIVING DISTANCES: Archer B. Gilfillan, *Sheep*, pp. 17-18. Copyright, 1928, 1929, by Archer B. Gilfillan. Boston: Little, Brown, and Company.

LIVER REGULATOR: Lewis Nordyke, *Cattle Empire*, The Fabulous Story of the 3,000,000 Acre XIT, pp. 140-141. Copyright, 1949, by Lewis Nordyke. New York: William Morrow and Company.

4. MELTING POT AND PRESSURE COOKER

MOTTO: Paul Flowers, *The Greenhouse*, From His Daily Column in *The Commercial Appeal*, Vol. II, November 1, 1945, p. 19. Memphis, Tennessee.

ANECDOTE IN INTRODUCTION: John Crosby, "Radio and Television: Complaints of an Unemployed Comedian," *New York Herald Tribune*, November 11, 1951. Copyright, 1951, by New York Herald Tribune, Inc.

THE RECEIPT: Harold W. Thompson, *Body, Boots & Britches*, p. 307. Copyright, 1939, by Harold W. Thompson. Philadelphia, New York, London, Toronto: J. B. Lippincott Company.

THE CELESTIAL AUTOMOBILES: As told by Henry Berg, Croton-on-Hudson, New York, June 23, 1957. Recorded and transcribed by B. A. Botkin.

AL SMITH'S MORNING AFTER: *Ibid.*

THE PRAYER SHAWL: Sam Levenson, *Meet the Folks*, A Session of American-Jewish Humor, p. 77. Copyright, 1946, 1947, 1948, by The Citadel Press. New York.

JEWISH QUAKERS: Irvin C. Poley and Ruth Verlenden Poley, *Friendly Anecdotes*, p. 79. Copyright, 1946, 1950, by Irvin C. Poley and Ruth Verlenden Poley. New York: Harper & Brothers.

WONDERS OF AMERICA: S. Felix Mendelsohn, *The Merry Heart*, Wit and Wisdom from Jewish Folklore, pp. 185-186. Copyright, 1951, by S. Felix Mendelsohn. New York: Bookman Associates.

THE COMPROMISE: *Ibid.*, p. 183.

THE LAST STRAW: As told by Nathan Frankel to B. A. Botkin, Croton-on-Hudson, New York, June 18, 1957.

WENDELL PHILLIPS AND THE WAITER: *Negro Digest*, Vol. IV (June, 1946), No. 8, p. 72. Copyright, 1946, by Negro Digest Publishing Company. Chicago, Ill. Reprinted from *Washington News-Digest*.

FREDERICK DOUGLASS AND THE SHIP'S OFFICER: Robert Collyer, "Clear Grit," in *Modern Eloquence*, Thomas B. Reed, editor; Justin McCarthy, Rossiter Johnson, Albert Ellery Bergh, associate editors, Vol. IV, Lectures, A-E, p. 263. Lecture copyright, 1901, by A. C. Butters. Book copyright, 1900, by the University Society. Philadelphia: John D. Morris and Company.

HORSE STAY OUT: Melville D. Landon (Eli Perkins), *Kings of the Platform and Pulpit* . . . , pp. 558-559. Copyright, 1890, by Belford-Clarke Co.; 1893, by the Werner Co.; 1906, by the Saalfield Publishing Co. Akron, New York, Chicago.

GIVIN'-AWAY LIQUOR: As told by Raven I. McDavid, Boulder, Colorado, July 18, 1950. Recorded and transcribed by B. A. Botkin.

JACKLEG: *Ibid.*

POINT OF VIEW: Sterling A. Brown, in *A Treasury of Southern Folklore*, edited by B. A. Botkin, p. 59. Copyright, 1949, by B. A. Botkin. New York: Crown Publishers.

BURYING THE GASOLINE: John H. Johnson and Ben Burns, editors, *The Best of Negro Humor*, p. 31. Copyright, 1945, by Negro Digest Publishing Co., Inc. [Chicago, Ill.]

THE TROUBLESOME TENANT FARMER: Harvey M. Williamson, "Smart Steptoe," *Skyline*, Quarterly of Cleveland College, Western Reserve University, Vol. XI (November, 1938), No. 2, p. 15. Copyright, 1938, by Cleveland College of Western Reserve University. Cleveland, Ohio.

SIX-SEEDED COTTON: *Ibid.*

WORKING ON HALVES: Harris Dickson, *The Story of King Cotton*, p. 195. Copyright, 1937, by Funk & Wagnalls Company. New York and London.

TOO MANY "UPS": J. Mason Brewer, editor, *Humorous Folk Tales of the South*, p. 11. Publications of the South Carolina Negro Folklore Guild, No. 1, 1945. Copyright, 1945, by the South Carolina Negro Folklore Guild. Orangeburg, South Carolina: Claflin College.

EFFICIENCY: Sterling A. Brown, *Negro Jokes*, mimeographed. [N.d.]

SEEING THINGS: James D. Corrothers, *In Spite of the Handicap*, An Autobiography, pp. 43-44. Copyright, 1916, by George H. Doran Company. New York.

BLACK, WHITE, AND BLUE: John H. Johnson and Ben Burns, editors, *The Best of Negro Humor*, p. 20. Copyright, 1945, by Negro Digest Publishing Co., Inc. [Chicago, Ill.] As told by Sterling A. Brown.

FARTHEST SOUTH: Harnett T. Kane, *The Bayous of Louisiana*, p. 22. Copyright, 1943, by Harnett T. Kane. New York: The Hampton Publishing Co., distributed by William Morrow & Company.

CHEESE FOR THE SWEDE: Carl Sandburg, *Always the Young Strangers*, p. 84. Copyright, 1952, 1953, by Carl Sandburg. New York: Harcourt, Brace and Company.

THE LETTER: Marshall P. Wilder, *The Sunny Side of the Street*, pp. 207-208. Copyright, 1905, by Funk & Wagnalls Company. New York and London. As told by T. DeWitt Talmage.

THE THREE DREAMS: Lolita Pooler, "Three Spanish Folk Tales," *The New Mexico Folklore Record*, Vol. IV, 1949-50, p. 21. Copyright, 1950, by the New Mexico Folklore Society. Albuquerque, New Mexico: University of New Mexico Press.

THE TOURIST AND THE INDIAN: Erna Fergusson, *Erna Fergusson's Albuquerque*, p. 79. Copyright, 1947, by Erna Fergusson. Albuquerque: Merle Armitage Editions.

FOREIGNERS: S. Felix Mendelsohn, *The Merry Heart*, Wit and Wisdom from

Jewish Folklore, p. 177. Copyright, 1951, by S. Felix Mendelsohn. New York: Bookman Associates.

5. COOL CUSTOMERS

MOTTO: Adapted from Marshall Brown, *Wit and Humor*, A Choice Collection, pp. 287-288. Copyright, 1879, by S. C. Griggs and Company. Chicago.

FIGHTING FARMER: [Freeman Hunt], *American Anecdotes, Original and Select*, by An American, Vol. I, pp. 78-79. Boston: Putnam & Hunt, 1830.

ROTTEN EGGS: R. E. Gould, *Yankee Storekeeper*, p. 73. Copyright, 1946, by Curtis Publishing Co.; 1946, by R. E. Gould. New York and London: Whittlesey House, McGraw-Hill Book Company, Inc.

JUGGLING THE EXPENSE ACCOUNT: R. E. Gould, *Yankee Drummer*, pp. 221-222. Copyright, 1947, by R. E. Gould. New York, London: Whittlesey House, McGraw-Hill Book Company, Inc.

RABBIT SANDWICHES: Seth Parker, of Jonesport, Maine, *Seth Parker's Album*, pp. 33-35. Copyright, 1930, by The Century Co. New York and London.

BRINGING IN THE LOG: William F. Macy, *The Nantucket Scrap Basket*, pp. 27-28. Second Edition. Revised, Expanded and Rearranged. Copyright, 1916, by William F. Macy and Roland B. Hussey; 1930, by William F. Macy. Boston and New York: Houghton Mifflin Company.

DREAMING-MATCH: [Freeman Hunt], *American Anecdotes, Original and Select*, by An American, Vol. I, pp. 262-263. Boston: Putnam and Hunt. 1830.

STOLEN FLOUR: Harold W. Thompson, *Body, Boots & Britches*, p. 165. Copyright, 1939, by Harold W. Thompson. Philadelphia, New York, London, Toronto: J. B. Lippincott Company.

DAVID HANNUM AND THE KICKER: Arthur T. Vance, *The Real David Harum*, The Wise Ways and Droll Sayings of One "Dave" Hannum, of Homer, N.Y., the Original of the Hero of Mr. Westcott's Popular Book . . . , pp. 27-30. Copyright, 1900, by The Baker & Taylor Co. New York.

LES HATHAWAY AND THE GAME WARDEN: William Chapman White, *Adirondack Country*, p. 163. Copyright, 1954, by William Chapman White. American Folkways, edited by Erskine Caldwell. New York: Duell, Sloan & Pearce; Boston: Little, Brown & Company.

THE UMBRELLA DOG: Will M. Clemens, *The Depew Story Book*, pp. 83-84. Copyright, 1898, by Will M. Clemens. London, New York: F. Tennyson Neely, Publisher.

WHY HE WAS A DEMOCRAT: *Ibid.*, pp. 82-83.

JAY GOULD AND THE RECTOR: John Wheeler, "The Old Second Guesser—Some Joe Miller Didn't Transcribe," Omaha (Nebraska) *World-Herald*, February 20, 1955, p. 2. Copyright, 1955, by the North American Newspaper Alliance, Inc. New York. As told by Ernest Cuneo, New York City.

A DEAL IN MANURE: Frank Crowninshield, "The House of Vanderbilt," *Vogue's First Reader*, p. 537. Copyright, 1942, by Condé Nast Publications, Inc. New York: Julian Messner, Inc.

A SWITCH IN TACTICS: "Ed Zern's Page," *Argosy*, Vol. 335 (August, 1952), No. 2, pp. 41, 71. Copyright, 1952, by Popular Publications, Inc. New York.

THE QUAKER AND THE DASHING BUCK: *The Christian Almanac, for New-England*, . . . 1829, Vol. II, No. I. Boston: Published by Lincoln & Edmands, for the American Tract Society.

THE CHALK LINE: [Oliver P. Baldwin], *Southern and South-Western Sketches*,

Fun, Sentiment and Adventure, edited by a Gentleman of Richmond, pp. 24-26. Richmond: J. W. Randolph. [N.d.]

NON-TRANSFERABLE: Daniel C. Roper, in Collaboration with Frank H. Lovette, *Fifty Years of Public Life*, pp. 62-63. Copyright, 1941, by The Duke University Press. Durham, North Carolina.

"OLD BELL-RINGER": "Editor's Drawer," *Harper's New Monthly Magazine*, Vol. XIX (November, 1859), No. CXIV, pp. 857-858. New York: Harper & Brothers.

PUTTING A YANKEE IN HIS PLACE: *Ibid.*, Vol. XVI (February, 1858), No. XCIII, pp. 426-427.

YANKEE PILOT: *Ibid.*, Vol. XXVI (December, 1862), No. CLI, p. 140.

CALLING DALTON'S BLUFF: Martha Lupton, *The Treasury of Modern Humor*, p. 234. Copyright, 1938, by Maxwell Droke. Indianapolis.

HOW ROY BEAN COLLECTED FOR THE BEER: Myron W. Tracy, "Roy Bean: Law West of the Pecos," in *Straight Texas*, edited by J. Frank Dobie; Mody C. Boatright, associate editor, pp. 116-117. Publications of the Texas Folk-Lore Society, No. XIII. Copyright, 1937, by the Texas Folk-Lore Society. Austin, Texas.

THE CORN THIEF: John R. Craddock, *Follow de Drinkin' Gou'd*, edited by J. Frank Dobie, p. 78. Publications of the Texas Folk-Lore Society, No. VII. Copyright, 1928, by the Texas Folk-Lore Society. Austin, Texas. As told by one of our renters in Dickens County.—J.R.C.

6. A PASSEL OF FOOLS

MOTTO: John O. Reid, Canmer, Kentucky, letter to Allan M. Trout, "Greetings," Louisville *Courier-Journal*, June 6, 1949.

ANECDOTES IN INTRODUCTION: Cape Cod Story: Adapted from *Massachusetts, A Guide to Its Places and People*, Written and Compiled by the Federal Writers' Project of the Works Progress Administration for the State of Massachusetts, p. 506. Copyright, 1937, by George M. Nutting, Director of Publicity, Commonwealth of Massachusetts. Boston: Houghton Mifflin Company. The Tough Kid from Brooklyn: Cheyenne (Wyoming) *State Tribune*, July 15, 1950. Grand Canyon Story: Hoffman Birney, *Roads to Roam*, p. 73. Copyright, 1930, by the Penn Publishing Company. Philadelphia.

BLUNDERING UPON WEALTH: [Freeman Hunt], *American Anecdotes, Original and Select*, by An American, Vol. I, pp. 60-61. Boston: Putnam & Hunt. 1830.

GREAT-COATS AND CHILDREN: James Croake [James Paterson], *Curiosities of Law and Lawyers*, p. 592. New York: Funk & Wagnalls Company. 1899.

THE LIMITS OF TELEGRAPHY: *The Jolly Joker*, or A Laugh All Round! . . . , [no page numbers]. New York: Dick & Fitzgerald, Publishers. [N.d.]

STRAINING THE MILK: Warren H. Wilson, *The Evolution of the Country Community*, A Study in Religious Sociology, p. 175. Copyright, 1912, by Luther H. Cary. Boston, New York, Chicago: The Pilgrim Press.

THE RESCUE: Jacob Richman, *Jewish Wit and Wisdom*, pp. 389-390. Copyright, 1952, by Pardes Publishing House, Inc. New York.

OB HOAG: Carl Carmer, *Dark Trees to the Wind*, p. 355. Copyright, 1949, by Carl Carmer. New York: William Sloane Associates.

"T.M.": Henry Martyn Kieffer, *The Funny Bone*, p. 176. Copyright, 1910, by Dodge Publishing Company. New York.

THE FERTILE GONDOLAS: W. W. Rostow, "The Fallacy of the Fertile Gondolas,"

Harvard Alumni Bulletin, Vol. 59 (May 25, 1957), No. 15, p. 633. Copyright, 1957, by the Harvard Bulletin, Inc. Cambridge, Mass. As told by Alvin Johnson.

OLD JAKE AND PRESIDENT CLEVELAND: Daniel C. Roper, in Collaboration with Frank H. Lovette, *Fifty Years of Public Life,* pp. 73-74. Copyright, 1941, by The Duke University Press. Durham, North Carolina.

CALLAHAN MAKES UP HIS MIND: Jack Kofoed, *Moon over Miami,* p. 161. Copyright, 1955, by Jack Kofoed. New York: Random House.

THE LAWYER AND THE POODLE: Contributed by Josiah H. Combs, Fort Worth, Texas, March, 1957.

BARNSTORMING: Alben W. Barkley, *That Reminds Me—,* p. 108. Copyright, 1954, by Alben W. Barkley; 1954, by The Curtis Publishing Company. Garden City, New York: Doubleday & Company, Inc.

THE HELPFUL WOODPECKERS: Allan M. Trout, "Greetings," Louisville (Kentucky) *Courier-Journal,* May 21, 1949.

THE TRAVELING MAN'S ACQUAINTANCE: Claude Gentry, *Private John Allen, Gentleman—Statesman—Sage—Prophet,* pp. 82-83. Copyright, 1951, by Claude Gentry. Decatur, Ga.: Bowen Press.

THE JUDGE AND THE HOG: Annabel Lee, *Little Stories by Big Men,* pp. 111, 112-113. Copyright, 1913, by Annabel Lee. New York and London: G. P. Putnam's Sons. The Knickerbocker Press. As told by Hon. B. P. Harrison of Mississippi.

BIG FLOOD: Vance Randolph, *Funny Stories from Arkansas,* p. 11. Copyright, 1943, by E. Haldeman-Julius. Girard, Kansas. Haldeman-Julius Publications.

WISHES AND HORSES: Contributed by George Milburn, New York City, 1954.

MULE EGG: *Ibid.*

THE BET: Joe M. Evans, *A Corral Full of Stories,* p. 29. Copyright, 1939, by Joe M. Evans. El Paso, Texas.

SOBERING UP: *Ibid.,* p. 28.

HOW TWO SANTA FE BROTHERS SOLD A KEG OF WHISKY: Santa Fe *New Mexican,* Fiesta Edition, August 27, 1950, Section C, p. 2.

THE PROMOTER AND THE BANKER: Frank C. Mortimer, *Put That Dust Back! and Other Stories,* p. 1. Copyright, 1946, by Frank C. Mortimer. San Francisco: John Howell.

7. WHOPPER WIT

MOTTO: Benjamin Franklin, *Works,* edited by Jared Sparks, Vol. VII, pp. 289-290. Boston. 1847.

ANECDOTES IN INTRODUCTION: Kansas Wind Story: Contributed by S. J. Sackett, Fort Hays Kansas State College, Hays, Kansas, March 2, 1957. Johnny Darling: Henry Roser, Sand Pond, New York, cited by M. Jagendorf, *The Marvelous Adventures of Johnny Darling,* p. 237. Copyright, 1949, by M. Jagendorf. New York: The Vanguard Press, Inc.

JOE MA FRAU, STRONG MAN: Chas. A. Gardner ("Karl"), *Forty-Five Years on the Stage,* Funny Stories and Experiences of the Sweet Singer, written "Yust for Fun," pp. 105-106. Copyright, 1912, by Chas. A. Gardner and J. Regan. Chicago: J. Regan & Co., Publishers. From a vaudeville monologue. "Joe Ma Frau" is also known as Joe Mufraw, the French-Canadian logger and boaster associated with Paul Bunyan.

THE LAZIEST MAN IN VERMONT: Robert Davis, "Some Characteristics of Northern

Vermont Wit," *Proceedings of the Vermont Historical Society*, New Series, Vol. V (December, 1937), No. 4, pp. 330-331. Copyright, 1937, by the Vermont Historical Society. Montpelier, Vermont.

WOLF DOG: Henry Hupfeld, *Encyclopaedia of Wit and Wisdom*, p. 880. Copyright, 1877, by Henry Hupfeld; 1897, by David McKay. Philadelphia.

THE BENT GUN AND THE THIEVING FOX: Joseph C. Allen, *Tales and Trails of Martha's Vineyard*, pp. 202-203. Copyright, 1938, by Joseph C. Allen. Boston: Little, Brown and Company.

LES HATHAWAY AND THE BUCK: William Chapman White, *Adirondack Country*, p. 164. Copyright, 1954, by William Chapman White. American Folkways, edited by Erskine Caldwell. New York: Duell, Sloan & Pearce; Boston: Little, Brown & Company.

F-ANT-ASTIC: As told by Richard Del Bourgo, age sixteen, Croton-on-Hudson, New York, May 25, 1957. Recorded and transcribed by B. A. Botkin.

THE SAFEST SAFE: Thomas B. Reed, editor; Justin McCarthy, Rossiter Johnson, Albert Ellery Bergh, associate editors, *Modern Eloquence*, Vol. X, Anecdotes . . . , p. 296. Copyright, 1900, by the University Society. Philadelphia: John B. Morris and Company.

THE BIGGEST TOBACCO CHEWER ON OCRACOKE ISLAND: Ben Lucien Burman, *It's a Big Country*, pp. 265-266. Copyright, 1956, by Ben Lucien Burman; 1954, 1955, 1956, by The Reader's Digest Association; 1953, 1954, 1955, by the Crowell-Collier Publishing Company. New York: Reynal & Company.

THE QUAIL BOY: Joe H. Palmer, *This Was Racing*, edited by Red Smith, pp. 137-138. Copyright, 1953, by A. S. Barnes and Company, Inc. New York.

THE KNITTINGEST WOMAN: William Aspenwall Bradley, "In Shakespeare's America," *Harper's Magazine*, Vol. CXXXI (August, 1915), No. DCCLXXXIII, p. 438. Copyright, 1915, by Harper and Brothers. New York.

ROAST DUCK: Clyde W. Wilkinson, "Backwoods Humor," *Southwest Review*, Vol. 24 (January, 1939), No. 2, pp. 180-181. Copyright, 1939, by the *Southwest Review*. Dallas, Texas. Cited from R. Brown, "Now You Tell One," *Ozark Magazine*, May, 1936.

LUTE GOINS' SAWMILL: Adapted from Jack Conroy, 100, A Magazine without Illusions or Delusions, Vol. I (June, 1952), No. 12, pp. 24-25. Copyright, 1952, by Ben Krit. Chicago, Illinois.

THE BIGGEST LIAR IN MCDONALD COUNTY: Contributed by George Milburn, New York City, 1954.

HOGS AND HIGH WATER: Vance Randolph, *Funny Stories about Hillbillies*, pp. 3-4. Copyright, 1944, by E. Haldeman-Julius. Girard, Kansas: Haldeman-Julius Publications. As told by Nancy Clemens.

HOG-WILD I: Stetson Kennedy, *Palmetto Country*, p. 235. Copyright, 1942, by Stetson Kennedy. American Folkways, edited by Erskine Caldwell. New York: Duell, Sloan & Pearce.

HOG-WILD II: Vance Randolph, *We Always Lie to Strangers*, pp. 34-38. Copyright, 1951, by Columbia University Press. New York.

TIN LIZZIE: Contributed by Samuel J. Sackett, Fort Hays Kansas State College, Fort Hays, Kansas, 1957.

THE LAZIEST MAN IN OKLAHOMA: Jim Thompson, Manuscripts of the Federal Writers' Project of the Works Progress Administration for the State of Oklahoma. 1939. Deposited in the Archive of Folk Song, Library of Congress, Washington, D. C.

THE STINGIEST MAN: *The Annals of Elder Horn*, Early Life in the Southwest, arranged by John Wilson Bowyer and Claude Harrison Thurman, pp. 166-167. Copyright, 1930, by Richard R. Smith, Inc. New York.

HOGS AND WOODPECKERS: *Ibid.*, pp.198-199.

THE GROWING SALVE: Will H. Robinson, *Yarns of the Desert*, p. 14. Copyright, 1921, by William Henry Robinson. Phoenix, Arizona: The Berryhill Company.

HOTTER 'N HELL: James F. Meline, *Two Thousand Miles on Horseback: Santa Fé and Back . . . in 1866*, pp. 53-54. New York: Hurd & Houghton. 1867.

JOHN HANCE'S FOG YARN: Edwin Corle, *Listen, Bright Angel*, pp. 211-212. Copyright, 1946, by Edwin Corle. New York: Duell, Sloan and Pearce.

THE BELLED BURRO: Harry Oliver, *Desert Rat Harry Oliver's Joke Book*, Special Fourth Anniversary Edition, Packet 4 of Pouch 4, *Desert Rat Scrap Book*, p. 6. Old Fort Oliver, Thousand Palms, California.

DEATH VALLEY SCOTTY'S HEROISM: George Palmer Putnam, *Death Valley and Its Country*, pp. 4-5. Copyright, 1946, by George Palmer Putnam. American Folkways, edited by Erskine Caldwell. New York: Duell, Sloan & Pearce, Inc.

"WHISPERING" THOMPSON AND HIS PET TROUT: Verne Bright, "Tall Tales from the Oregon Country," *The Northwest's Own Magazine, The Sunday Oregonian*, Portland, Oregon, December 9, 1951, pp. 12-13. Copyright, 1951, by The Oregonian. Portland, Oregon.

8. "THE GOSPEL ACCORDING TO JOE MILLER"

MOTTO: Alben W. Barkley, cited by M. B. Schnapper, "Tall-Tale Teller from Paducah, The Vice-President Spins His Fabulous Yarns in the Old-Style Pattern of Political Humor," *The New York Times Magazine*, November 18, 1951, p. 22. Copyright, 1951, by the New York Times Company.

ANECDOTES IN INTRODUCTION: Beecher Story: Joseph Bucklin Bishop, *Notes and Anecdotes of Many Years*, p. 39. Copyright, 1925, by Charles Scribner's Sons. New York. Prodigal Son Story: As told by Cliff Frank to B. A. Botkin, "Back Home in Indiana," *Folk-Say: A Regional Miscellany, 1930*, edited by B. A. Botkin, pp. 72-73. Copyright, 1930, by B. A. Botkin. Norman: University of Oklahoma Press. Negro Minister Story: J. Mason Brewer, *The Word on the Brazos*, p. 85. Copyright, 1953, by the University of Texas Press. Austin.

"P.C.": Robert B. Thomas, *The (Old) Farmer's Almanack, . . . 1895*, p. 39. Boston: William Ware & Company.

HORSE-TRADING PREACHER: Henry Hupfeld, *Encyclopaedia of Wit and Wisdom*, p. 531. Copyright, 1877, by Henry Hupfeld; 1897, by David McKay. Philadelphia.

RAISING THE MINISTER'S SALARY: William Tegg, *The Cruet Stand; or Sauce Piquante to Suit All Tastes*, pp. 88-89. London: William Tegg. [N.d.]

THE SKINFLINT: Nixon Orwin Rush, editor, *Rufus Jones' Selected Stories of Native Maine Humor*, pp. 21-22. Copyright, 1945, by Clark University Library. Worcester, Massachusetts. 1946.

SOAPING THE PREACHER'S HORN: Joseph C. Allen, *Tales and Trails of Martha's Vineyard*, pp. 226-228. Copyright, 1938, by Joseph C. Allen. Boston: Little, Brown and Company.

"SCHOONER ASHORE!": Irving Browne, *Humorous Phases of the Law*, pp. 19, 21, 22-23. Copyright, 1876, by Irving Browne. San Francisco: Summer Whitney & Co.

THE MILLERITE: Will M. Clemens, *The Depew Story Book*, pp. 66-67. Copyright, 1898, by Will M. Clemens. London and New York: F. Tennyson Neely.

WATCH AND PRAY: Henry Hupfeld, *Encyclopaedia of Wit and Wisdom*, pp. 802-803. Copyright, 1877, by Henry Hupfeld; 1897, by David McKay. Philadelphia.

THE QUAKER'S VERACITY: Irvin C. Poley and Ruth Verlenden Poley, *Friendly Anecdotes*, pp. 58-59. Copyright, 1946, 1950, by Irvin C. Poley and Ruth Verlenden Poley. New York: Harper & Brothers.

A LETTER TO THE LORD: *Talk-Tactics*, pp. 51-52. Copyright, 1936, by Leewin B. Williams. Washington, D. C.: Leewin B. Williams & Son, Publishers.

GOING TO HEAVEN BY LAND: Guy B. Johnson, *Folk Culture on St. Helena Island, South Carolina*, p. 153. Copyright, 1930, by The University of North Carolina Press. Chapel Hill. As written by Nathan J. Smalls, student at Penn School.

THE HOLY GHOST: As told by Charles King to Mary A. Hicks, Raleigh, North Carolina, 1936. Manuscripts of the Federal Writers' Project of the Works Progress Administration for the State of North Carolina. 1939. Deposited in the Archive of Folk Song, Library of Congress, Washington, D. C.

PRAYING TO THE LORD: Daniel C. Roper, in Collaboration with Frank H. Lovette, *Fifty Years of Public Life*, p. 12. Copyright, 1941, by The Duke University Press. Durham, North Carolina.

THE PREACHER AND THE BEAR: *Wit and Humor of the American Pulpit*, pp. 94-96. Copyright, 1904, by George W. Jacobs & Company. Philadelphia.

THE HARD-SHELL KERNEL: Melville D. Landon (Eli Perkins), *Wit and Humor of the Age . . .* , p. 326. Copyright, 1883, by L. W. Yaggy; 1901, by R. W. Patton. Chicago: Star Publishing Company.

IN PARTNERSHIP WITH THE LORD: Alben W. Barkley, *That Reminds Me—*, p. 39. Copyright, 1954, by Alben W. Barkley; 1954, by The Curtis Publishing Company. Garden City, New York: Doubleday & Company, Inc.

THE LANGUAGE OF APPRECIATION: *Ibid.*, p. 30.

THE PREACHER AND THE CAT: Julian Lee Rayford, *Whistlin' Woman and Crowin' Hen*, The True Legend of Dauphin Island and the Alabama Coast, p. 17. Copyright, 1956, by Julian Lee Rayford. Mobile: The Rankin Press.

A RELIGIOUS CAPTAIN: Meridel Le Sueur, *North Star Country*, p. 138. Copyright, 1945, by Meridel Le Sueur. American Folkways, edited by Erskine Caldwell. New York: Duell, Sloan & Pearce.

DENOMINATIONAL DIFFERENCES: Earnest Elmo Calkins, *They Broke the Prairie*, p. 176. Copyright, 1937, by Earnest Elmo Calkins. New York: Charles Scribner's Sons.

THE SAME THREE FELLOWS: John W. Gunn, *The Humor and Wisdom of Abraham Lincoln*, pp. 32-33. Pocket Series, No. 382, edited by E. Haldeman-Julius. Copyright, 1923, by Haldeman-Julius Company. Girard, Kansas.

NEARLY OUT OF BIBLE: Edgar DeWitt Jones, *Lincoln and the Preachers*, p. 146. Copyright, 1948, by Harper & Brothers. New York. As told by John G. Nicolay, who heard it from Abraham Lincoln.

"DONE WITH THE BIBLE": R. D. Wordsworth, *"Abe" Lincoln's Anecdotes and Stories*, pp. 91-92. Boston, Mass: The Mutual Book Company. 1908.

ON THE LORD'S SIDE: The Honorable Alexander Wiley, *Laughing with Congress*, p. 216. Copyright, 1947, by Alexander Wiley. New York: Crown Publishers.

PADRE MARTINEZ AND THE STOREKEEPER: The Santa Fe *New Mexican*, August 27, 1950, Fiesta Edition, Section B, p. 9.

LORENZO DOW AND GABRIEL: *Tit-Bits of American Humor*, pp. 3-4. New York and London: White & Allen. [N.d.]

LORENZO DOW RAISES THE DEVIL: *History of Cosmopolite;* or The Writings of Lorenzo Dow: Containing His Experience and Travels . . . , p. 203. Sixth edition. Cincinnati. 1856.

ON WINGS OF SONG: Edwin Hamlin Carr, *Putnam's Ready Speech-Maker,* p. 94. Copyright, 1922, by Edwin Hamlin Carr. New York and London: G. P. Putnam's Sons. The Knickerbocker Press.

HOLDING THE GUN ALL OVER THE TREE: *The Life and Sayings of Sam P. Jones,* A Minister of the Gospel, by his Wife, assisted by Rev. Walt Holcomb, A Co-worker of Mr. Jones, p. 87. Copyright, 1907, by Mrs. Sam P. Jones. Atlanta, Ga.: A. N. Jenkins & Scott Co.

FROM A PREACHER'S JOE MILLER: George B. Gilbert, *Forty Years a Country Preacher,* pp. 266-270. Copyright, 1939, 1940, by Harper & Brothers. New York and London.

OIL STRIKE IN HELL: Charles F. Arrowood, "There's a Geography of Humorous Anecdotes," in *In the Shadow of History,* edited by J. Frank Dobie, Mody C. Boatright, Harry H. Ransom, pp. 79-80. Publications of the Texas Folk-Lore Society, No. XV. Copyright, 1939, by The Texas Folk-Lore Society. Austin, Texas.

BIBLICAL WILDCATTING: From *The Open Road,* reprinted in *The Postage Stamp.* Lincoln, Nebraska: Lincoln Letter Service, Henry Westfall, Manager. Clipping collection of Mamie Meredith, Lincoln, Nebraska.

9. HEROES WITHOUT HALOES

MOTTO: *The Complete Works of Artemus Ward (Charles Farrar Browne),* with a biographical sketch by Melville D. Landon, "Eli Perkins," p. 19. Copyright, 1862, by Charles F. Browne; 1898, by G. W. Dillingham Co. New York.

ANECDOTES IN INTRODUCTION: Ethan Allen Stories: Adapted from Stewart H. Holbrook, *Ethan Allen,* pp. 12, 251. Copyright, 1940, by The Macmillan Company. New York. Abraham Lincoln Story: Adapted from Arthur D. Graeff, "Anecdotes Related in Pennsylvania-German Almanacs," *The American German Review,* Vol. VI (April, 1940), No. IV, pp. 13, 37. Copyright, 1940, by the Carl Schurz Memorial Foundation, Inc. Philadelphia.

"OLD WOLF" TESTS THE BRITISH MAJOR'S COURAGE: *The Rip-Rap Joker,* The Funniest and Spiciest Joker of the Times, p. 4. New York: Benedict Publishing Company. [1860?]

FRANKLIN AND THE STAMP ACT: Henry Hupfeld, *Encyclopaedia of Wit and Wisdom,* pp. 917-918. Copyright, 1877, by Henry Hupfeld; 1897, by David McKay. Philadelphia.

REVISING THE SIGN: [Freeman Hunt], *American Anecdotes, Original and Select,* by An American, Vol. I, pp. 11-13. Boston: Putman & Hunt. 1830.

ASTRONOMICAL TOASTS: Arthur D. Graeff, "Anecdotes Related in Pennsylvania-German Almanacs," Part II, *The American-German Review,* Vol. VI (June, 1940), No. V, p. 9. Copyright, 1940, by the Carl Schurz Memorial Foundation, Inc. Philadelphia.

FRANKLIN'S ADVICE: Reuben and Sholto Percy, *The Percy Anecdotes,* p. 951. London: Frederick Warne and Co. New York: Scribner, Welford and Co. [1868.]

FARMER-GOVERNOR CHITTENDEN: Dorothy Canfield Fisher, *Vermont Tradition,* p. 329. Copyright, 1953, by Dorothy Canfield Fisher. Boston: Little, Brown and Company.

ETHAN ALLEN'S WIFE: *Ibid.*, p. 142.

WASHINGTON'S GUARD: William Fields, *The Scrap-Book*, p. 207. Philadelphia: Claxton, Remsen & Haffelfinger. 1875.

JEFFERSON AND THE LANDLORD: Arthur D. Graeff, "Anecdotes Related in Pennsylvania-German Almanacs," *The American-German Review*, Vol. VI (April, 1940), No. IV, pp. 11-12. Copyright, 1940, by the Carl Schurz Memorial Foundation, Inc. Philadelphia. From *New Reading Kalender*, 1840.

RUM AND RAIN: Albert J. Beveridge, "Maryland, Marshall, and the Constitution," Proceedings of the Maryland State Bar Association for 1920, p. 174. As told by Senator McDonald.

JOHN MARSHALL, ERRAND BOY: Paul Wilstach, *Patriots off Their Pedestals*, p. 202. Copyright, 1927, by the Bobbs-Merrill Company. Indianapolis.

JOHN RANDOLPH AND THE LANDLORD: "Editor's Drawer," *Harper's New Monthly Magazine*, Vol. VI (May, 1853), No. XXXVI, p. 853. New York: Harper & Brothers.

DANIEL WEBSTER'S FIRST DEFENSE PLEA: Arthur D. Graeff, "Anecdotes Related in Pennsylvania-German Almanacs, Part II," *The American-German Review*, Vol. VI (June, 1940), No. V, p. 12. Copyright, 1940, by the Carl Schurz Memorial Foundation, Inc., Philadelphia. From *Pennsylvanischer Kalender*, 1874.

DANIEL WEBSTER AT SCHOOL: F. B. Carpenter, *Six Months at the White House with Lincoln*, pp. 131-132. Entered . . . , 1866, by Hurd and Houghton. New York. As told by Mrs. Ann S. Stephens to Abraham Lincoln.

WEBSTER AND THE STAGE DRIVER: Alfred H. Miles, *One Thousand & One Anecdotes*, p. 312. New York: Thomas Whittaker. 1895.

WHY JOHNNY APPLESEED PUNISHED HIS FEET: Robert Price, *Johnny Appleseed, Man and Myth*, p. 166. Copyright, 1954, by Robert Price. Bloomington: Indiana University Press. Reprinted from Mansfield *Ohio Liberal*.

CROCKETT AND THE FUR HAT: "Editor's Drawer," *Harper's New Monthly Magazine*, Vol. XIX (October, 1859), No. CXIII, pp. 712-713. New York: Harper & Brothers.

CROCKETT ON WASHINGTON: Daniel C. Roper, in Collaboration with Frank H. Lovette. *Fifty Years of Public Life*, p. 20. Copyright, 1941, by The Duke University Press. Durham, North Carolina.

POLITE PHILLIPS: John H. Johnson, Ben Burns, editors, *The Best of Negro Humor*, pp. 2-3. Copyright, 1945, by Negro Digest Publishing Co., Inc. [Chicago, Ill.]

GREELEY'S HANDWRITING: Junius Henri Browne, "Horace Greeley," *Harper's New Monthly Magazine*, Vol. XLVI (April, 1873), No. CCLXXV, p. 741. New York: Harper & Brothers.

STONEWALL JACKSON IN HEAVEN: Isaac Erwin Avery, *Idle Comments*, in *Library of Southern Literature*, Edwin Anderson Alderman, Joel Chandler Harris, editors in chief; Charles William Kent, literary editor, Vol. I, pp. 139-140. Copyright, 1907, 1909, by The Martin and Hoyt Company. Atlanta, New Orleans, Dallas. As told by Col. Peter Akers.

SHORT RATIONS: George W. Bagby, *The Old Virginia Gentleman and Other Sketches*, p. 62. Copyright, 1884, 1885, by Mrs. George W. Bagby; 1910, by Charles Scribner's Sons. New York.

LINCOLN AND THE WHETSTONE: Edna M. Colman, *Seventy-Five Years of White House Gossip*, From Washington to Lincoln, pp. 290-291. Copyright, 1925, by Doubleday, Page & Company. Garden City, New York. As told by Judge Landis.

THE UGLIER MAN: R. D. Wordsworth, *"Abe" Lincoln's Anecdotes and Stories*, p. 37. Boston: The Mutual Book Company, Publishers. 1908.

LINCOLN ON BAGGING PRAIRIE CHICKENS: *Ibid.*, p. 14.

LINCOLN SHORTS: George S. Hilton, *The Funny Side of Politics*, pp. 235-236. Copyright, 1899, by G. W. Dillingham Co. New York.

GROVER CLEVELAND'S ADVICE: Carl Sandburg, *Always the Young Strangers*, p. 33. Copyright, 1952, 1953, by Carl Sandburg. New York: Harcourt, Brace and Company.

TEDDY ROOSEVELT AND MOSES: As told by J. C. Meekins to John G. Bragaw, in "Random Shots," by John G. Bragaw, the Raleigh (North Carolina) *State*, June 27, 1936, p. 11. Manuscripts of the Federal Writers' Project of the Works Progress Administration for the State of North Carolina. 1939. Deposited in the Archive of Folk Song, Library of Congress, Washington, D.C.

HOW TAFT STOPPED A THROUGH TRAIN: Archie Robertson, *Slow Train to Yesterday*, A Last Glance at the Local, p. 105. Copyright, 1945, by Archie Robertson. Boston: Houghton Mifflin Company.

SILENT CAL: Cameron Rogers, *The Legend of Calvin Coolidge*, pp. 169, 171-172. Copyright, 1928, by Doubleday, Doran & Company, Inc. Garden City, New York.

THE ART OF MAKING ENEMIES: As told by Nathan Frankel, Croton-on-Hudson, New York, June 23, 1957. Recorded and transcribed by B. A. Botkin.

MESSAGE TO MOSCOW: As told by Henry Berg, Croton-on-Hudson, New York, June 23, 1957. Recorded and transcribed by B. A. Botkin.

ROOSEVELT'S GREATNESS: Anthony Gish [Nancy Clemens], "Yes, I'm a Hillbilly," *Esquire*, Vol. VII (April, 1937), No. 4, p. 95. Copyright, 1937, by Esquire, Inc. Chicago.

POLITICS IN WESTCHESTER COUNTY: George E. Allen, *Presidents Who Have Known Me*, pp. 238-239. Copyright, 1950, by George E. Allen. New York: Simon and Schuster.

10. SPELLBINDERS AND BUREAUCRATS

MOTTO: *San Francisco Call*, December 3, 1856, cited by Richard H. Thornton, *An American Glossary*, Vol. II, p. 970. Philadelphia: J. B. Lippincott Company. 1912.

ANECDOTE IN INTRODUCTION: E. M. Berry, "The Same Old Delmar," in "Sawmill Divertissements," *Folk-Say, A Regional Miscellany: 1931*, edited by B. A. Botkin, pp. 215, 216-217. Copyright, 1931, by B. A. Botkin. Norman: University of Oklahoma Press.

BOUNDING THE UNITED STATES: John Fiske, cited in *Talk-Tactics*, pp. 68-69. Copyright, 1936, by Leewin B. Williams. Washington, D.C.

LINCOLN'S JACKASS STORY: The Honorable Alexander Wiley, *Laughing with Congress*, pp. 170-171. Copyright, 1947, by Alexander Wiley. New York: Crown Publishers. Attributed to Abraham Lincoln.

BURYING THE JACKASS: Congressman Hadwen C. Fuller, of New York, in *Laughing with Congress*, by The Honorable Alexander Wiley, pp. 223-224. Copyright, 1947, by Alexander Wiley. New York: Crown Publishers.

THE GREAT MAN: Henry Watterson, *"Marse Henry,"* An Autobiography, Vol. I, pp. 45-46. Copyright, 1919, by George H. Doran Company. New York.

WASHINGTON "NUT" STORY: Congressman Joe Hendricks, of Florida, in *Laughing with Congress*, by The Honorable Alexander Wiley, pp. 224-225. Copyright, 1947, by Alexander Wiley. New York: Crown Publishers.

"ARSENAL OF BUREAUCRACY": Mercedes Rosebery, *This Day's Madness*, A Story of the American People Against the Background of the War Effort, p. 124. Copyright, 1944, by Mercedes Rosebery. New York: The Macmillan Company. From *Newsweek*, reprinted in *Reader's Digest*.

THE DEAF ANTI-NEW DEALER: As told by Henry Berg, Croton-on-Hudson, New York, June 23, 1957. Recorded and transcribed by B. A. Botkin.

PROGRESS: Earl Conrad, *Jim Crow America*, p. 173. Copyright, 1947, by Earl Conrad. New York: Duell, Sloan & Pearce.

TOP KNOT COME DOWN: Senator Samuel J. Ervin, North Carolina, in "A New Raconteur Rules the Senate," by Russell Baker, *The New York Times*, May 13, 1956, p. 61. Copyright, 1956, by the New York Times Company.

THE SUCCESSFUL CANDIDATE: North Callahan, *Smoky Mountain Country*, p. 235. Copyright, 1952, by North Callahan. American Folkways, edited by Erskine Caldwell. New York: Duell, Sloan & Pearce; Boston: Little, Brown & Co.

THE ELOQUENT CANDIDATE: *Ibid.*, pp. 234-235.

"PITCHFORK" BEN TILLMAN: Daniel C. Roper, in Collaboration with Frank H. Lovette, *Fifty Years of Public Life*, p. 81. Copyright, 1941, by The Duke University Press. Durham, North Carolina.

A BORN ORATOR: Eugene Field in the *Chicago News*, in *The Peerless Speaker* . . . , p. 191. Copyright, 1900, by Thomas and Thomas. Chicago.

THE COUNTY ATTORNEY DEFENDS THE JUDGE: Contributed by Josiah H. Combs, Fort Worth, Texas, March, 1957.

TESTING THE WHISKY: *Stories and Speeches of William O. Bradley*, with Biographical Sketch by M. H. Thatcher, pp. 76-77. Copyright, 1916, by The Transylvania Printing Company. Lexington, Kentucky.

THE CANDIDATE'S QUALIFICATION: Beverly Smith, "Washington's Greatest Storyteller," *The Saturday Evening Post*, Vol. 222 (July 2, 1949), No. 1, p. 68. Copyright, 1949, by the Curtis Publishing Company. Philadelphia. As told by Alben W. Barkley.

RIDING SLOW: Alben W. Barkley, *That Reminds Me—*, pp. 195-196. Copyright, 1954, by Alben W. Barkley; 1954, by The Curtis Publishing Company. Garden City, New York: Doubleday & Company, Inc.

PRIVATE JOHN ALLEN IN NEW YORK: Claude Gentry, *Private John Allen*, Gentleman—Statesman—Sage—Prophet, p. 24. Copyright, 1951, by Claude Gentry. Decatur, Ga.: Printed by Bowen Press.

PRIVATE JOHN ALLEN AND BILBO: George E. Allen, *Presidents Who Have Known Me*, p. 29. Copyright, 1950, by George E. Allen. New York: Simon and Schuster.

ALFALFA BILL IN HEAVEN: Josh Lee, *How to Hold an Audience without a Rope*, p. 180. Copyright, 1947, by Ziff-Davis Publishing Company. Chicago and New York.

QUANAH'S TWO WIVES: W. M. Kiplinger, *Washington Is Like That*, p. 430. Copyright, 1942, by W. M. Kiplinger. New York and London: Harper & Brothers.

"LOUDER!": Alex E. Sweet and J. Armoy Knox, *On a Mexican Mustang through Texas*, from the Gulf to the Rio Grande, p. 74. Copyright, 1883, by Sweet & Knox. Hartford: S. S. Scranton & Co. Marshalltown, Iowa: The Barnes & Ballou Publishing Co. 1884.

COEDUCATION IN TEXAS: Contributed by Josiah H. Combs, Fort Worth, Texas, April, 1957.

THE MOST ORDERLY LYNCHING IN YEARS: As told by Raven I. McDavid, Boulder, Colorado, July 18, 1950. Recorded and transcribed by B. A. Botkin.

JIM FERGUSON'S DEFENSE: George Sessions Perry, *Texas: A World in Itself*, p. 149. Copyright, 1942, by the McGraw-Hill Book Company, Inc. New York and London: Whittlesey House.

POLITICS IN WYOMING: Robert E. Coontz, *True Anecdotes of an Admiral*, pp. 14-15. Copyright, 1935, by Dorrance & Company, Inc. Philadelphia.

THE FARMER IS THE GOAT: Meridel Le Sueur, *North Star Country*, p. 271. Copyright, 1945, by Meridel Le Sueur. American Folkways, edited by Erskine Caldwell. New York: Duell, Sloan & Pearce. As told by a Farm Holiday Member.

WINNING STATEHOOD FOR NEW MEXICO: Erna Fergusson, *Erna Fergusson's Albuquerque*, pp. 71-72. Copyright, 1947, by Erna Fergusson. Albuquerque: Merle Armitage Editions.

MAN-EATING PACKER: George E. Allen, *Presidents Who Have Known Me*, pp. 232-234. Copyright, 1950, by George E. Allen. New York: Simon and Schuster. As told by Palmer Hoyt, Denver, Colorado.

"MELANCHOLY" MCCULLON: *Wit and Humor of American Statesmen*, pp. 14-15. Copyright, 1902, by George W. Jacobs & Company. Philadelphia.

11. FABLE AND FOIBLE

MOTTO: F. B. Carpenter, *Six Months at the White House with Abraham Lincoln*, pp. 260-261. New York: Hurd and Houghton. 1866. By A. Lincoln.

ANECDOTES IN INTRODUCTION: The Sardine Story: Adapted from Evan Esar, *The Animal Joker*, p. 252. Copyright, 1946, by Evan Esar. New York: Harvest House, Publishers. Three Idle Sons Story: A. Craig, *Room at the Top: or, How to Reach Success, Happiness, Fame and Fortune*, p. 162. Augusta, Maine: True & Co. [N.d.]

THE TWO TRAVELERS AND THE OYSTER: Robert B. Thomas, *The (Old) Farmer's Almanack . . . 1901*, No. 109, p. 48. Boston: William Ware & Company. [1900.]

FRANKLIN'S FABLE OF THE SPECKLED AX: *The Autobiography of Benjamin Franklin*, pp. 151-152. Copyright, 1901, by the Century Company. The Century Classics. New York. 1920.

THE CAPTAIN'S RULE: *Ibid.*, p. 258.

THE YANKEE AND THE QUAKER: S. G. Goodrich, *Recollections of a Lifetime*, Vol. I, pp. 96-97. New York and Auburn: Miller, Orton & Co. 1857.

THE QUAKER'S COAT: William F. Macy, *The Nantucket Scrap Basket . . .*, p. 33. Second Edition. Revised, Expanded and Rearranged. Copyright, 1916, by William F. Macy and Roland B. Hussey; 1930, by William F. Macy. Boston and New York: Houghton Mifflin Company.

AN INDIAN'S PARABLE: Rev. Henry White, *The Early History of New England, Illustrated by Numerous Interesting Incidents*, pp. 238-239. Entered . . . 1841, by Rev. Henry White. . . . Boston: Sanborn, Carter, Bazin & Co.

"DON'T SWAP HORSES IN MIDSTREAM": Henry L. Williams, *The Lincoln Story Book*, pp. 246-247. Copyright, 1907, by G. W. Dillingham Co. New York. Heard by Superintendent Tinker, war telegrapher.

THE EAGLE AND THE OWL: Thomas B. Reed, editor; Justin McCarthy, Rossiter Johnson, Albert Ellery Bergh, associate editors, *Modern Eloquence*, Vol. X, *Anecdotes . . .*, p. 191. Copyright, 1900, by The University Society. Philadelphia: John D. Morris and Company.

THE OX AND THE MULE: Homer Croy, *What Grandpa Laughed At*, pp. 58-59. Copyright, 1948, by Homer Croy. New York: Duell, Sloan and Pearce.

"SNAIL, SNAIL."—: Zora Neale Hurston, *Mules and Men*, p. 165. Copyright, 1935, by Zora Neale Hurston. Philadelphia and London: J. B. Lippincott.

THE ANIMALS' CONVENTION: Claude Gentry, *Private John Allen*, Gentleman—Statesman—Sage—Prophet, p. 37. Copyright, 1951, by Claude Gentry. Decatur, Ga.: Bowen Press.

EINSTEIN EXPLAINS THE THEORY OF RELATIVITY: "Scientist Explained His Theory with Wit and Homey Parables," *New York Times*, April 19, 1955, p. 26.

WHAT SWEETENS THE TEA: Jacob Richman, *Jewish Wit and Wisdom*, p. 389. Copyright, 1952, by Pardes Publishing House, Inc. New York.

JUSTICE: Mark Feder, *It's A Living*, p. 12. Copyright, 1948, by Mark Feder. New York: Bloch Publishing Company.

CHINESE PHILOSOPHER IN THE SUBWAY: Berenice Abbott (photographs) and Henry Wysham Lewis (text), *Greenwich Village, Today & Yesterday*, pp. 25-26. Copyright, 1949, by Harper & Brothers. New York.

THE HONEST LAWYER: James J. MacDonald, *Life in Old Virginia*, pp. 198-199. Copyright, 1907, by The Old Virginia Publishing Company, Inc. Norfolk, Va.

LAWYERS IN HELL: Emelyn Elizabeth Gardner, *Folklore from the Schoharie Hills, New York*, p. 38. Copyright, 1937, by the University of Michigan. Ann Arbor: University of Michigan Press.

THE FOX HUNTER IN HEAVEN: Lealon N. Jones, "Symphony of the Ozarks," in *Eve's Stepchildren*, selected and edited by Lealon N. Jones, pp. 62-63. Copyright, 1942, by the Caxton Printers, Ltd. Caldwell, Idaho.

THE ADMIRAL IN HEAVEN: Senator (former Admiral) Thomas C. Hart, in *Laughing with Congress*, by The Honorable Alexander Wiley, pp. 187-188. Copyright, 1947, by Alexander Wiley. New York: Crown Publishers.

THE ARCHANGEL MICHAEL VISITS NEW MEXICO: Mary Austin, *One-Smoke Stories*, pp. 149-150. Copyright, 1934, by Mary Austin. Boston and New York: Houghton Mifflin Co.

THE GLOBE: Contributed by Carl Withers, New York City, May, 1957. As heard in Missouri.

GOD AND THE DEVIL: Robert Davis, "Some Characteristics of Northern Vermont Wit," *Proceedings of the Vermont Historical Society*, New Series, Vol. V (December, 1937), No. 4, p. 331. Copyright, 1937, by the Vermont Historical Society. Montpelier, Vermont.

WHY FOLKS AIN'T GOT TAILS: Stetson Kennedy, *Palmetto Country*, pp. 157-158. Copyright, 1942, by Stetson Kennedy. American Folkways, edited by Erskine Caldwell. Duell, Sloan & Pearce, Inc. New York.

WHY WOMEN TALK SO MUCH: *Ibid.*, pp. 160-161.

WHY WE SAY "UNH-HUNH": Zora Neale Hurston, *Mules and Men*, pp. 204-205. Copyright, 1935, by Zora Neale Hurston. Philadelphia and London: J. B. Lippincott Company.

BIBLE AND SWIMMING: From "Negro Folk Tales from the South (Alabama, Mississippi, Louisiana)," by Arthur Huff Fauset, *Journal of American Folklore*, Vol. 40 (July-September, 1927), No. 157, p. 273. From Kowaliga, Ala.

ORGANIZED: J. Mason Brewer, "Juneteenth," *Tone the Bell Easy*, edited by J. Frank Dobie, pp. 23-24. Publications of the Texas Folk-Lore Society, No. X, 1932. Copyright, 1932, by the Texas Folk-Lore Society. Austin, Texas.

TEN-CENT COTTON: John A. Lomax, "Adventures of a Ballad Hunter," in *From Hell to Breakfast*, edited by Mody C. Boatright and Donald Day, pp. 19-20. Texas Folk-Lore Society Publications, No. XIX, J. Frank Dobie, General Editor. Copyright, 1944, by the Texas Folk-Lore Society. Texas Folk-Lore Society, Austin, and University Press in Dallas, Texas. Contributed by J. L. Goree, Houston, Texas.

A STILL TONGUE MAKES A WISE HEAD: A. W. Eddins, "Brazos Bottom Philosophy," *Southwestern Lore,* edited by J. Frank Dobie, pp. 159-160. Publications of the Texas Folk-Lore Society, No. IX, 1931. Copyright, 1931, by the Texas Folk-Lore Society. Dallas: The Southwest Press.

THE GREATEST PLEASURES: Joe H. Palmer, *This Was Racing,* edited by Red Smith, pp. 177-178. Copyright, 1953, by A. S. Barnes and Company, Inc. New York.

THE HOG DEALER'S CONSOLATION: Marshall P. Wilder, *The Sunny Side of the Street,* pp. 51-52. Copyright, 1905, by Funk & Wagnalls Company. New York and London. As told by President Benjamin Harrison.

SECRET OF A HAPPY LIFE: Stanley Walker, *Home to Texas,* pp. 53-54. Copyright, 1956, by Stanley Walker; 1941, 1943, 1952, 1953, 1954, by Stanley Walker. New York: Harper & Brothers. As told by John Messenger.

THE WISDOM OF A LIFETIME: Allan M. Trout, *Greetings from Old Kentucky,* p. 113. Copyright, 1947, by Allan M. Trout. Louisville, Kentucky: Published by The Courier-Journal.

"HELP YOURSELF TO THE MUSTARD": Mary Jourdan Atkinson and J. Frank Dobie, "Pioneer Folk Tales, in *Follow de Drinkin' Gou'd,* edited by J. Frank Dobie, p. 72. Publications of the Texas Folk-Lore Society, No. VII. Copyright, 1928, by the Texas Folk-Lore Society. Austin, Texas.

A MORTGAGE ON HELL: *The Annals of Elder Horn,* Early Life in the Southwest, Arranged by John Wilson Bowyer and Claude Harrison Thurman, p. 207. Copyright, 1930, by Richard R. Smith. Inc. New York.

"KEEP YOUR SEAT, MR. GREELEY": Jack M. Dodson, "Notes and Queries," *Western Folklore,* Vol. VI (July, 1947), No. 3, pp. 276-277. Copyright, 1947, by The California Folklore Society. Berkeley and Los Angeles: University of California Press. The story is commonly told by Hank Monk.

A LITTLE LEATHER: A. J. Rojas, *California Vaquero,* pp. 97-98. Copyright, 1953, by Academy Library Guild. Fresno, California.

THE NON-UNION CALF'S HEAD: As told by Arthur Boose, Portland, Oregon, August 31, 1950. Recorded and transcribed by B. A. Botkin. From an I. W. W. street-corner spiel by Arthur Boose, the "last of the Wobblies."

12. SPUN YARN

MOTTO: [Freeman Hunt], *American Anecdotes, Original and Select,* by an American, Vol. I, p. 294. Boston: Published by Putnam & Hunt. 1830.

SETTLING A VILLAGE QUARREL: [Freeman Hunt], *American Anecdotes, Original and Select,* by An American, Vol. II, pp. 178-180. Boston: Putnam & Hunt. 1830.

SALMON OR COD?: Joseph A. Willard, *Half a Century with Judges and Lawyers,* pp. 302-303. Copyright, 1895, by Joseph A. Willard. Boston and New York: Houghton, Mifflin and Company.

THE WOMAN WHO SOLD WINDS: Elizabeth Coatsworth, *Country Neighborhood,* pp. 61-62. Copyright, 1944, by Elizabeth Coatsworth Beston. New York: The Macmillan Company.

THAR SHE BLOWS!: Paul Johnston, *Thar She Blows, An Early New Bedford Whaling Yarn.* Copyright, 1931, by Random House, Inc. New York.

THE MUSIC-CHAIR: Joseph C. Lincoln, *Cape Cod Yesterdays*, pp. 279-280, 281-283. Copyright, 1935, by Joseph C. Lincoln and Harold Brett. Boston: Little, Brown & Company.

A SIMPLE FAMILY: Emelyn Elizabeth Gardner, *Folklore from the Schoharie Hills, New York*, pp. 182-184. Copyright, 1937, by The University of Michigan. Ann Arbor. As told in January, 1897, by George Harder, who had heard the tale related by the hill folk as an actual occurrence.

"HORSE-CAR POETRY": Joseph Bucklin Bishop, *Notes and Anecdotes of Many Years*, pp. 77-81. Copyright, 1925, by Charles Scribner's Sons. New York.

ON THE CITY DESK: Levi Hubert, "Living Lore of New York City," Manuscripts of the Federal Writers' Project of the Works Progress Administration in New York City, 1939. Deposited in the Archive of Folk Song, Library of Congress.

THE MATTRESS: Mark Hellinger, *The Ten Million*, p. 302. Copyright, 1934, by Mark Hellinger. New York: Farrar & Rinehart, Inc.

THE GHOST RIDER: *Ibid.*, pp. 302-303.

THE MINK COAT: Robert J. Casey, *More Interesting People*, pp. 93-95. Copyright, 1947, by the Bobbs-Merrill Company. Indianapolis and New York. As told by Robert M. Yoder.

THE GUILTY HOTEL GUEST: William Oliver Stevens, *Washington the Cinderella City*, p. 289. Copyright, 1943, by Dodd, Mead and Company, Inc. New York.

THE BLANKET: Hy Gardner, *Champagne before Breakfast*, pp. 142-143. Copyright, 1954, by Hy Gardner. New York: Henry Holt and Company.

MOUNTAIN HOSPITALITY: [Freeman Hunt], *American Anecdotes, Original and Select*, by An American, Vol. I, pp. 151-153. Boston: Putnam & Hunt. 1830.

THE SETTIN' UP: Edward C. L. Adams, *Congaree Sketches*, pp. 29-30. Copyright, 1927, by the University of North Carolina Press. Chapel Hill. By permission of George C. S. Adams and Stephen B. Adams.

WAITING FOR HENRY: Alben W. Barkley, *That Reminds Me—*, p. 37. Copyright, 1954, by Alben W. Barkley; 1954, by The Curtis Publishing Company. Garden City, New York: Doubleday & Company, Inc.

HOOSIER HOT BED: Millard Fillmore Kennedy, in Collaboration with Alvin F. Harlow, *Schoolmaster of Yesterday*, A Three-Generation Story, pp. 42-44. Copyright, 1940, by Millard Fillmore Kennedy and Alvin F. Harlow. New York: Whittlesey House, McGraw-Hill Book Company, Inc.

THE BRIDGE THAT WASN'T THERE: W. H. Milburn, *The Lance, Cross and Canoe . . .*, p. 363. Entered . . . , 1892, by William Henry Milburn. New York and St. Louis: N. D. Thompson Publishing Co.

THE ROSE AND THE BALDWIN: Henry L. Williams, *The Lincoln Story Book*, pp. 127-129. Copyright, 1907, by G. W. Dillingham Co. New York.

THE RATTLESNAKE-BIT BOOT: James R. Masterson, *Tall Tales of Arkansaw*, pp. 390-391. Copyright, 1942, by Chapman & Grimes. Boston. As told by Velton B. McKinley, Polk County, Arkansas.

AN EAR FOR MUSIC: Virginia Madison, *The Big Bend Country of Texas*, pp. 33-35. Copyright, 1955, by The University of New Mexico Press. Albuquerque.

THE PIE-BITER: John Gould, "Pie-Biter," *Coyote Wisdom*, edited by J. Frank Dobie, Mody C. Boatright, Harry H. Ransom, pp. 189-191. Texas Folk-Lore Society Publications, No. XIV. Copyright, 1938, by The Texas Folk-Lore Society. Austin.

OIL VERSUS WATER: Stanley Walker, *Home to Texas*, p. 225. Copyright, 1956, by Stanley Walker; 1941, 1943, 1952, 1953, 1954, by Stanley Walker. New York: Harper & Brothers.

MOLASSES: Forest Crossen, *Anthony Arnett Empire Builder* (1933), cited by

Levette J. Davidson, "Western Campfire Tales," *California Folklore Quarterly*, Vol. II (July, 1943), No. 3, pp. 184-185. Copyright, 1943, by the California Folklore Society.

A RUN ON CASTOR OIL: *A Ton of Jokes from the Wisest Men* [no page numbers]. Copyright, 1904, by Arkell Company. New York: J. S. Ogilvie, Publisher.

THE "JERKY" TRIAL: Contributed by Verne Bright, Tolovana Park, Oregon, April, 1957. As told by Rolly Canfield of Gold Beach, Curry County, Oregon (who was present at the trial), to Verne Bright.

13. BARNYARD AND BARROOM

MOTTO: Vance Randolph, *Funny Stories from Arkansas*, pp. 23-24. Copyright, 1943, by E. Haldeman-Julius. Girard, Kansas.

ANECDOTES IN INTRODUCTION: Davy Crockett Story: James B. Davis, *Early History of Memphis* (1873), cited in *A Treasury of Southern Folklore*, edited by B. A. Botkin, p. 261. Copyright, 1949, by B. A. Botkin. New York: Crown Publishers. Mae West Story: "Go West, Young Man, Mae Is Sure She'll Like You," *The Sunday Oklahoman*, May 19, 1935. By Associated Press. Oklahoma City, Oklahoma.

A GOOD SHORT STORY: *"That Reminds Me,"* Jokes and Stories for Use by Union Organizers and Papers, p. 11. New York: Educational Department, International Ladies' Garment Workers' Union. [1940.]

THE BITER BIT: Isaiah Thomas, Junior, Massachusetts, Connecticut, Rhode Island, New Hampshire and Vermont *Almanack*, with an Ephemeris, for the Year of Our Lord, 1810 . . . , [no page numbers]. Worcester, Mass.

A CARELESS CUSS: Joseph C. Allen, *Tales and Trails of Martha's Vineyard*, pp. 92-93. Copyright, 1938, by Joseph C. Allen. Boston: Little, Brown and Company.

PLOWING WITH THE BULLS: As told by Moritz Jagendorf to B. A. Botkin, Carmel, New York, July 6, 1957. As told to him by Bill Harkins, Carmel.

"BONEY" QUILLAN GETS EVEN: Leslie C. Wood, *Rafting on the Delaware River*, pp. 209-210. Livingston Manor, New York: Livingston Manor Times. 1934.

WHY THE OLD FARMER WOULDN'T TELL THE DRUMMER THE TIME OF DAY: Joseph Mitchell, *Old Mr. Flood*, pp. 63-65. Copyright, 1943, 1944, 1945, 1948, by Joseph Mitchell. New York: Duell, Sloan and Pearce.

HOW DID HE FIND OUT?: *The Hobo News*, Vol. II (December, 1953), No. 84. Copyright, 1953, by The Hobo News. Newark, New Jersey.

BALM IN GIDEON: George E. Allen, *Presidents Who Have Known Me*, p. 40. Copyright, 1950, by George E. Allen. New York: Simon and Schuster.

IT COULD HAVE BEEN WORSE: As told by Charles Aguado, Croton-on-Hudson, New York, May 13, 1957. Recorded and transcribed by B. A. Botkin.

THE EXURBANITE'S STORY: A. C. Spectorsky, *The Exurbanites*, p. 127. Copyright, 1955, by A. C. Spectorsky; 1955, by Street & Smith Publications, Inc. Philadelphia and New York: J. B. Lippincott Company.

MAKING FRIENDS: As told by Lawrence Kalik, New York City, May 16, 1957. Recorded and transcribed by B. A. Botkin.

"THE FROG PRINCE" UP-TO-DATE: Evan Esar, *The Animal Joker*, p. 130. Copyright, 1946, by Evan Esar. New York: Harvest House.

BEULAH'S BABIES: George E. Allen, *Presidents Who Have Known Me*, pp. 28-29. Copyright, 1950, by George E. Allen. New York: Simon and Schuster.

EVEN STEPHEN: Ben Lucien Burman, *It's a Big Country*, p. 257. Copyright, 1956, by Ben Lucien Burman; 1954, 1955, 1956, by The Reader's Digest

Association; 1953, 1954, 1955, by the Crowell-Collier Publishing Company. New York: Reynal & Company.

THE PARROT AND THE PRIEST: As told by Fant Thornley, Columbia, South Carolina, January 25, 1949. Recorded and transcribed by B. A. Botkin.

THE STUD: Carl Carmer, *Stars Fell on Alabama*, p. 120-121. Copyright, 1934, by Carl Carmer. New York: Farrar & Rinehart, Inc.

HONEST, IMPULSIVE HARRY: Herbert Halpert, "George Washington's Father Wasn't There," *Western Folklore*, Vol. XV (April, 1956), No. 2, pp. 124-125. Copyright, 1956, by The California Folklore Society. Berkeley, California: University of California Press. Contributed by Edith Vickers, as told by "some man from Wingo, Kentucky."

"BLACK" SHADE AND THE CHIPPY: Contributed by Josiah H. Combs, Fort Worth, Texas, March, 1957.

SETTLING PATERNITY: *Ibid.*

SAVED: Charles Hurd, *Washington Cavalcade*, pp. 301-302. Copyright, 1948, by Charles Hurd. New York: E. P. Dutton & Co., Inc. As told by Senator Tom Connally of Texas.

VERBAL TABOO: Allan M. Trout, *Greetings from Old Kentucky*, p. 109. Copyright, 1947, by Allan M. Trout. Louisville, Kentucky: The Courier-Journal.

THE SMART SOW: Contributed by George Milburn, New York City, 1954.

THE TALKING HEIFER: *Ibid.*

GRANDPA AND THE BENZINE: *Ibid.*

A MORALS CASE: *Ibid.*

FIGURING RELATIONSHIP: *Ibid.*

THE BOLSTER TEST: Vance Randolph, *Funny Stories about Hillbillies*, p. 20. Copyright, 1944, by E. Haldeman-Julius. Girard, Kansas: Haldeman-Julius Publications.

THE HAYLOFT: As told by Lawrence Treat, Yorktown Heights, New York, to B. A. Botkin, May 20, 1957, and as told to him by Ryerson Johnson, Lubec, Maine, who heard it from Winfred Van Atta, Pomona, N. Y.

UPBRUSH WEDDING: Charles Morrow Wilson, "Backwoods Behavior," *The Nation*, Vol. 131 (November 12, 1930), No. 3410, p. 524. Copyright, 1930, by The Nation, Inc. New York.

THE SHIVAREE: Thomas B. Reed, editor; Justin McCarthy, Rossiter Johnson, Albert Ellery Bergh, associate editors, *Modern Eloquence*, Vol. X, *Anecdotes* . . . , p. 171. Copyright, 1900, by The University Society. Philadelphia: John D. Morris and Company.

HOWARD MACE: Stanley Walker, *Home to Texas*, p. 102. Copyright, 1956, by Stanley Walker; 1941, 1943, 1952, 1954, by Stanley Walker. New York: Harper & Brothers.

INDIAN SIGN: As told by Arthur L. Campa, Denver, Colorado, July 23, 1950. Recorded and transcribed by B. A. Botkin.

14. WIT'S END

MOTTO: *Illinois Central Magazine*, Vol. II (October, 1913), No. 4, pp. 80-81.

ANECDOTE IN INTRODUCTION: As told by Oscar Brand to B. A. Botkin, New York City, May 16, 1957.

MEYER: Mark Feder, *It's a Living*, A Personalized Collection of Jewish Humor, pp. 39-40. Copyright, 1948, by Mark Feder. New York: Bloch Publishing Company.

A CRITIC: Contributed by Ruth Rubin, New York City, December, 1956.

THE LOST THEATER TICKETS: Hy Gardner, *Champagne before Breakfast*, pp. 145-147. Copyright, 1954, by Hy Gardner. New York: Henry Holt and Company.

THE CAKE: *The Hobo News*, A Little Fun to Match the Sorrow, Vol. 2 (May, 1953), No. 78, p. 8. Copyright, 1952, by The Hobo News. Newark, New Jersey.

THE ACCOMMODATING MORTICIAN: *Quote, the Weekly Digest*, Vol. 33 (Feb. 24, 1957), No. 8, p. 12. Indianapolis: Droke House, A *Quote* original.

MORRIS: As told by Charles Aguado, Croton-on-Hudson, New York, May 13, 1957. Recorded and transcribed by B. A. Botkin.

ASKING QUESTIONS: As told by Eli Krotman, Croton-on-Hudson, New York, May 13, 1957. Recorded and transcribed by B. A. Botkin.

THE BOY ON THE BUS: As told by Nathan Frankel, Croton-on-Hudson, New York, May 18, 1957. Recorded and transcribed by B. A. Botkin.

THE CAB DRIVER'S STORY: Recorded by Tony Schwartz, New York City, 1955. Transcribed by B. A. Botkin.

SHAGGY SCALE TALE: As told by Arthur Beane, *The Commuter*, Vol. I (November, 1955), No. 1, p. 12. Copyright, 1955, by Commuters, Inc. New Canaan, Connecticut.

RELIGION IN SUBURBIA: As told by Oscar Brand to B. A. Botkin, New York City, May 16, 1957.

PINOCHLE IN THE CATSKILLS: Contributed by Ruth Rubin, New York City, December, 1956.

WHAT HE FOUND IN THE FISH: Jacob Richman, *Jewish Wit and Wisdom*, p. 316. Copyright, 1952, by Pardes Publishing House, Inc. New York.

BETTING ON THE FISH: Joe H. Palmer, *This Was Racing*, edited by Red Smith, p. 60. Copyright, 1953, by A. S. Barnes and Company, Inc. New York.

THE SMART UMPIRE: Ira L. Smith and H. Allen Smith, *Three Men on Third*, A Second Book of Baseball Anecdotes, Oddities, and Curiosities, p. 151. Copyright, 1951, by Ira L. Smith and H. Allen Smith. Garden City, New York: Doubleday & Company, Inc.

OLD CHRIS AND THE THIRD BASEMAN: Ira L. Smith and H. Allen Smith, *Low and Inside*, A Book of Baseball Anecdotes, Oddities, and Curiosities, p. 88. Copyright, 1949, by Ira L. Smith and H. Allen Smith. Garden City, New York: Doubleday & Company, Inc.

THE MUSICAL MICE: As told by Robert Strand, Croton-on-Hudson, New York, December 30, 1950. Recorded and transcribed by B. A. Botkin.

SO WHAT!: As told by Nathan Frankel, Croton-on-Hudson, New York, May 18, 1957. Recorded and transcribed by B. A. Botkin.

KING OF THE JUNGLE: As told by Sterling A. Brown, Washington, D.C., January 13, 1949. Recorded and transcribed by B. A. Botkin.

THE EDUCATED BULLDOG: Carl Carmer, *The Hurricane's Children*, Tales from Your Neck o' the Woods, pp. 22-26. Copyright, 1937, by Carl Carmer. Farrar & Rinehart, Inc. New York. Toronto.

GRANDPA SNAZZY'S FROG: James Thurber, in *While You Were Gone*, edited by Jack Goodman, p. 312. Copyright, 1946, by Simon and Schuster, Inc. New York.

THE NEAR-SIGHTED TEXAN: Laura Z. Hobson, "To the Ladies: Code to Tone Down High-Livin' Texans," *New York Journal-American*, June 9, 1954, p. 29.

THE TALKING HORSE IN THE OIL FIELDS: C. K. Stillwagon, *Rope Chokers*, pp. 116-118. Copyright, 1945, by C. K. Stillwagon. Houston, Texas. 1955.

WHAT WAS ON THE CARD?: *Ibid.*, pp. 122-125.

MURGATROYD THE KLUGE MAKER: Agnes Nolan Underwood, "Folklore from

G.I. Joe," *New York Folklore Quarterly*, Vol. III (Winter, 1947), No. 4, pp. 295-297. Copyright, 1947, by New York Folklore Society. Cooperstown, N.Y. As told by an Infantryman who got it from a Marine who told it about the Navy.

THE HERO: Sgt. Bill Davidson, *Tall Tales They Tell in the Services*, p. 41. Copyright, 1943, by Thomas Y. Crowell Company. New York.

LAYING OFF HELP: George E. Allen, *Presidents Who Have Known Me*, p. 72. Copyright, 1950, by George E. Allen. New York: Simon and Schuster.

IN THE BOOK: As told by Arthur Boose, Portland, Oregon, August 31, 1950. Recorded and transcribed by B. A. Botkin. From an I. W. W. street-corner spiel by Arthur Boose, the "last of the Wobblies."

Index

CAPS AND SMALL CAPS indicate authors, contributors, informants, and editors represented and authorities quoted. Titles of selections and sections of this book are set in *italics*. Page numbers in parentheses refer to *Notes*.